W9-AXY-656

02628

745.5   Stribling, Mary Lou
Str

Crafts from North
American Indian

DATE DUE		

CRAFTS FROM

NORTH AMERICAN INDIAN ARTS

GEORGE WALTON COMPREHENSIVE HIGH SCHOOL
1590 BILL MURDOCK ROAD
MARIETTA, GEORGIA 30060

02628

Also by Mary Lou Stribling

ART FROM FOUND MATERIALS: DISCARDED AND NATURAL
MOSAIC TECHNIQUES

CRAFTS FROM

NORTH AMERICAN INDIAN ARTS

Techniques, Designs, and Contemporary Applications

Mary Lou Stribling

CROWN PUBLISHERS, INC., NEW YORK

To Jeffrey

© 1975 by Mary Lou Stribling

All rights reserved. No part of this book may be reproduced or utilized in any form or by any means, electronic or mechanical, including photocopying, recording, or by any information storage or retrieval system, without permission in writing from the Publisher.

Inquiries should be addressed to Crown Publishers, Inc., 419 Park Avenue South, New York, N.Y. 10016.

Printed in the United States of America
Published simultaneously in Canada by
General Publishing Company Limited

Designed by Ruth Smerechniak
and M. C. Lewis

Library of Congress Cataloging in Publication Data

Stribling, Mary Lou.
  Crafts from North American Indian arts.

  Bibliography: p.
    1. Indian craft.   2.   Indians of North America—
Industries.   I.   Title.
TT22.S84   1975   745.5   75-12842
ISBN 0-517-51612-8

CONTENTS

ACKNOWLEDGMENTS

Assembling the materials for this book has been like taking a short journey back into the early history of America. The route was not always clearly marked, and I am grateful to the many persons who pointed out directions or opened gates that appeared to be closed forever.

I am especially indebted to Pomo basket weaver Mabel McKay, who taught me techniques for Pomo basketmaking and some of the traditions of her culture. I am equally indebted to Hopi potter Daisy Nampeyo Hooie for generously sharing with me some of the legends and pottery methods of the pueblo peoples, including the ancient process of making ceramic paint from beeweed. Special thanks, also, to Lee De Kokker for introducing me to Seminole pine needle basketry.

Examples of Indian arts from the large collections in major museums have already been well publicized, and I have turned to other sources for fresh material. I greatly appreciate the cooperation of historical societies, museums, the Bureau of Indian Affairs, and private collectors who enabled me to present a wide variety of art forms, most of which have not been shown in other books. They are credited beside their contributions, as are artists and photographers whose help was invaluable. Appreciative credit also goes to Bessie Long, Katimae Barnette, and Lu Lundstrum for working up some of my designs.

It would have been impossible to reconstruct many special Indian techniques without the opportunity to study actual samples. Thanks to Deborah Harding for providing me with Seminole patchwork, and to Rolfe Ockenden, Helen Irish, and Elizabeth Craster for allowing me to examine and photograph at leisure pieces from their collections. Thanks to Jackie Curry and Helen Heit-kamp for scouting help, and to Rich Rains for adding the chore of printing my negatives to his already full schedule.

And warmest thanks, as always, to my husband, who was a fellow traveler on this fascinating trip and helped with whatever needed doing. His cheerful support made the rough spots bearable, and the smooth spots even more enjoyable.

Mary Lou Stribling

(All photos, crafts, and drawings are by the author unless otherwise credited.)

FOREWORD

The story of Indian arts can never be told in one book, nor by one narrator. It is not just a story of creative "things," but of the peoples who made them, and of cultures that are thousands of years older than the colonization of America.

For many generations after Indian lands were discovered and claimed by foreigners, their arts reflected ancient traditions, far removed from the imitation tomahawks, feathered headdresses, and other souvenir trinkets they made purely for sale. But from increasing economic pressures, they were forced to pawn or trade treasured family and tribal possessions. As more and more beautiful old baskets, jewelry, textiles, pottery, and carvings were acquired by museums and private collectors, public interest was gradually aroused. It gained momentum when a great wave of nostalgia for all things relating to ethnic origins swept across the country in the 1960s.

Within a short period of time real treasures were scarce, and it was ironically apparent that our only indigenous arts had become aesthetically "in," just as they were physically fading out.

Indian arts are not really dying—they are simply changing. But the Indian has always been inventive, adapting to his needs whatever he found useful, and it is unrealistic to expect him to remain picturesquely suspended in time, like the face on an old nickel, while the world around him moves on.

The older reservation craftsmen are fearful that increasing non-Indian influences will eventually dilute their arts until they lose racial identity. Their fears are well founded. The concept of mass production is alien to Indian nature, and although prices for good traditional work have zoomed to astronomical figures, the work is tedious, and it may take months to make a single basket or small rug. Pay often amounts to just a few cents an hour, which is hardly attractive to the most dedicated craftsman. The young artists no longer feel bound to the old ways and beliefs, and they are more concerned with creating a better future than with preserving sentimental elements of the hard, bitter past.

Happily, there are some encouraging signs of renewed craft vitality. A number of guilds and tribal craft centers have been formed all over the country to provide Indian artists with competent instruction and sales outlets. Seminole patchwork and dollmaking have been revived in Florida. Plains seamstresses are relearning the beautiful arts of ribbon appliqué and braided textiles that were almost extinct a few decades ago. Fine wood carving is once again being produced on the Northwest Coast, and in California several basket weavers have been persuaded to share their ancient secrets with both Indian and non-Indian students.

The scene is liveliest in the Southwest, where there is a curious mixture of philosophies. On one side are traditionalists who are devoted to preserving the old methods and designs; on the other, a new school of artists who are equally devoted to establishing their own traditions.

This book is a similar mixture of the old and new. Much can be learned from the past, but we can extract from it what is useful for the present, and discard what is not, without being disrespectful. Many "authentic" materials for Indian arts are now almost impossible to obtain, and there is no need to apologize for modern substitutes that are often actually better.

Substitutes do not always produce exactly the same effects, but then it is not my purpose to encourage duplication of Indian arts, nor to routinely copy their designs. This privilege should be left to the Indians. These are mutual heritages, however, that we can share together, and as such they are invaluable sources for contemporary craft inspiration.

Drums were made from wood, gourds, skins, or pottery in every region of the continent. The deep resonant tones of large drums could be heard for many miles, but there were also small drums for subtle accents to songs, rituals, and dances.
Fig. 1. Alaskan drum. *Courtesy, The Oregon Historical Society.*

1

THE
PEOPLE

THE EARLY PEOPLE

They came from Asia twenty thousand or more years ago across a narrow, frozen land bridge between Siberia and Alaska. They traveled in small groups over a long period of time, advancing perhaps only a few miles in a single generation.

They were not Indians then. They were simply People—nomadic hunters who followed game and camped wherever conditions made survival possible. They brought little with them but a few primitive weapons, some rudimentary knowledge of stone carving, and an inherent capacity for adapting themselves to their surroundings.

As the Ice Age declined, the great glaciers shrunk toward the north, leaving long streaks of green foliage across the white slopes and valleys of the continent. Some of the People settled permanently in the Arctic and pitted their resourcefulness against its harsh climate. But many others continued to move, drifting farther and farther southward through the newly warmed corridors.

At first they shared the land with woolly mammoths, mastodons, tigers, long-horned bisons, and bearlike sloths. The ancient animals gradually disappeared and were replaced by thousands of new creatures, but the People lived on, changing as the earth changed.

Large numbers wandered across the central grassy plains to the humid rim of the Gulf of Mexico. Others spread north through the forests to the Great Lakes, and still farther north to lands where winters were ten months long. And some moved south through the Isthmus of Panama, until finally there was practically no habitable region on the two continents that had not known the print of a moccasin, the whine of a snapped bow, or the throb of a ceremonial drum.

By then, many years had passed. The sea had nibbled away the fragile span between the old and new worlds and the migrants were isolated on the side that was to become America. There were no written records of their ancestry in Asia, and the story of the ancient trail had disappeared from the memories of even the oldest tribal historian.

Fig. 2. Moosehide drum, Ksan Village, British Columbia.

Fig. 3. Cottonwood and rawhide drum, Taos, New Mexico.

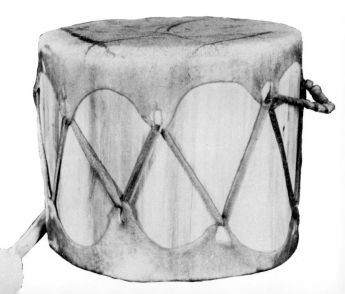

The early People were no more alike than are their descendants today. Their bodies and faces had different shapes and proportions. Their skins were different colors. They had different religious beliefs and tribal customs, and they preferred different kinds of food. They spoke more than two hundred languages north of Latin America alone, and each language was divided into many dialects. But they did have certain physical things in common—long eyes, high cheekbones, and thick, straight, black hair. Philosophically, they also had in common a deep respect for the land they lived on.

They respected the rain, wind, stars, moon, sun, and the powerful forces that controlled their cycles. They gave names and symbolic shapes to these forces and paid them tribute through prayers and devout ceremonies. They respected the animals they killed for food and performed rituals to ensure their reincarnation so that the species would be perpetuated. They honored the earth as the mother of all living things, and centered their creative activities on their responsibilities as her appointed stewards.

As the years went by, the People moved less, though they continued to change. They invented new shelters and perfected more efficient weapons and tools. They learned to shape clay into cooking pots, skin and fibers into warm fabrics, and pliant twigs into nets, snares, huts, clothing, bedding, and baskets. And then, mysteriously, they learned to grow corn.

No one can say for certain how or where it began. It probably originated in South America and came into North America through the Southwestern tribes, but the mystery is deeper than that. Cultivated plants start from wild seeds and wild corn is unknown in the world today. Perhaps it existed in those early times, or perhaps it was accidentally created by cross-pollination and eventually became a separate species. To the People, however, corn was simply a gift from the gods—a gift that might be withdrawn if they became ungrateful, or disobedient to the laws that kept all things in nature balanced and harmonious.

They began to farm. The crops had to be tended, harvested, and stored, so they established camps near their fields, and the camps grew into villages. Laws and religious rituals were formalized and leaders were selected to see that they were properly observed. There was need for protection, too, for not all the People became farmers. Among many tribes, war was a way of life and the farmers were as fair game as the animals they hunted in the forests.

Haphazard communities were rebuilt on less vulnerable sites, and were fortified with barriers of stones, woven branches, poles, packed mud, or whatever materials were available. In the Southwest, some tribes carved rooms along the ledges in sheer cliff walls. Others used sunbaked clay to build terraced, thick-walled houses that had no openings at ground level.

Although contacts between tribes were not always peaceful, they promoted the spread of new ideas—ideas for irrigating crops or for making a better basket, arrow, or pot. Decorative ideas were exchanged, too, and often alien influences became so thoroughly blended with traditional concepts that in time they could no longer be separated.

A faint, tangled network of trade routes became more clearly defined throughout both Americas. Ideas and goods found their way across thousands of miles of desert and mountain ranges. Sometimes exotic materials became parts of a necklace, headdress, or dance apron—a continent and several generations away from their points of origin.

Nothing the People used in their daily lives was too humble to be decorated. They became builders, weavers, potters, embroiderers, carvers, and basket-makers, and perhaps the glow of their emerging civilization might have flamed into one of the most brilliant cultures of all times. But we will never know, for suddenly the light was extinguished. The white man came.

Fig. 4. Digging stick from the Nestucca River area. The large antler handle is 28½″ long and is decorated with carved designs, including a human figure. Women of the Oregon Plateau tribes dug edible roots and materials for making woven bags with tools of this kind. *Courtesy, The Oregon Historical Society.*

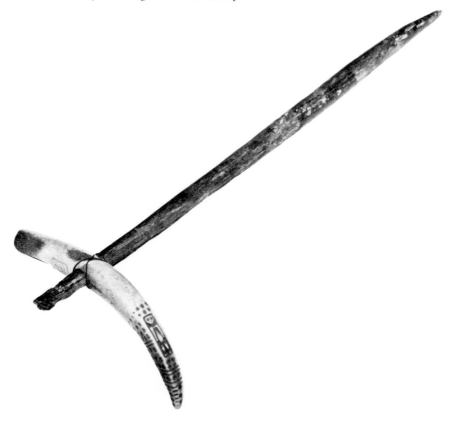

Fig. 5. Haida (Northwest Coast) carved-bone needle case. *Courtesy, The M. H. De Young Memorial Museum.*

Fig. 6. Kwakiutl (Northwest Coast) carved wooden bowl. *Courtesy, The M. H. De Young Memorial Museum.*

Fig. 7. Owl paint mortar from the Columbia River (Oregon) region. *Collection, Favell's Museum.*

THE INDIANS

In the Old World, civilizations had been extinguished many times, perhaps many more times than will ever be known. Europe remained in the Stone Age for centuries after Egypt's pyramids had been built, and its Pharaohs had lived and died. But by the time Columbus made his way to the New World, it had moved through the dimness of medievalism and had entered the blazing era of the Renaissance.

Spain was then a melting pot of many different peoples. They were fiercely nationalistic and anxious to expand their economic power, and had a fanatic determination to purge the world of paganism, by whatever means were necessary. It was these elements of "Spanishness" that eventually brought the evolving American civilizations to a standstill.

Columbus sailed from Spain in 1492, hoping to find a new trade route to India, thereby winning for himself titles, honor, and great riches. He found the Bahama Islands instead, but unconvinced that his geographical theories were faulty, he named the inhabitants "Indians." The error was never to be corrected.

Other voyages and explorers soon followed. In 1497, Vespucci planted the Spanish flag on Venezuela, and John Cabot established England's claim to the northeastern regions of North America. About fifteen years later Ponce de León claimed the Florida regions for Spain, and in a few more years Jacques Cartier acquired territories around the Great Lakes and Mississippi River for France.

Hunger for conquest grew increasingly intense from rumors of a golden kingdom on the shores of a great ocean to the west. Balboa found the Pacific Ocean in 1513, but before he could find the gold, he was betrayed by one of his lieutenants, Francisco Pizarro, and was executed for treason.

Pizarro reached the realm of the Incas in 1527, and the gold was there—more than he had ever imagined. It took five years to complete his plan for total conquest, and then, with a single cannon, a hundred and fifty foot soldiers, and forty cavalry, he subdued fifty thousand warriors, captured their Lord-Inca, and looted the land of its treasures.[1]

Word of the rich New World spread quickly, and within a short span of time, its cultural destruction was well under way.

The People, who had owned these lands for countless centuries, were bewildered at first, for they had thought surely the pale, strange beings who had such deadly weapons and powerful magic must be gods. It quickly became clear, however, that they had the appetites of men, and they would not be satisfied until they had devoured everything the People held sacred.

They fought back angrily, then bitterly, then desperately, but tribe by tribe they were overcome. The story of the end of the fighting and the relocation of the natives on Indian reservations has been written many times, often in official documents that cloak the human elements in statistics. But perhaps no one has

---

[1] Victor W. Von Hagen, *Realm of the Incas* (New York: Mentor Books, 1957), pp. 204–8.

recorded more poignantly the end of a civilization than Nez Percé Chief Joseph at his surrender in the Bear Paw Mountains, Montana, in 1877:

"I am tired of fighting. Our chiefs are killed. . . . It is cold and we have no blankets. The little children are freezing to death . . . my heart is sick and sad. From where the sun now stands I will fight no more forever."

Fig. 8. These petroglyphs were carved into steep cliff walls by a Stone Age people. They did not represent a written language, though it is possible that they were records of some kind pertaining to tribal history or memorable events. Occasionally they appear to symbolize plant forms or animals.

Fig. 9. Certain abstract graphics, such as rows of dots and short lines, suggest a form of tabulation—perhaps a method of keeping track of the passage of time, or of population. But this is pure conjecture. (Tule Lake, California, area.)

Fig. 10. Prehistoric rock carvings and paintings have fascinated and mystified scientists for many years, but as yet they have reached no positive conclusions about their purpose. These examples are unusually refined and representational, but in view of the effort required to incise them with primitive tools it hardly seems likely that they were idle doodles. Petroglyphs from Jack Point, British Columbia. *Collection, The Centennial Museum, Nanaimo.*

Fig. 11. Vandals threaten to destroy the few aboriginal engravings that remain in their original sites. This is a replica of petroglyphs from a remote California desert canyon, estimated at being more than 1,500 years old, yet it clearly shows on the left an attack by a souvenir hunter. *Replica, Pacific Western Traders.*

Fig. 12. Indians first showed these carvings to white men in 1860, but even they were unable to interpret the designs, or explain why they might have been left in this place.

Fig. 13. Man's urgency to leave some record of his passing is universal, however, and by no means restricted to primitive cultures. Although they are regrettably as permanent, the contemporary etchings at the lower right demonstrate considerably less sensitivity than those of the ancient past. *Petroglyphs near Nanaimo, Vancouver Island, B.C.*

Fig. 14. Designs from North American Indian petroglyphs.

NATIVE AMERICAN ARTS

Most existing examples of early Indian arts are made from stone, clay, ivory, shells, and bones, but excavated tools indicate that they also worked with various perishable materials that have long since disintegrated.

It is safe to assume that all groups used hides and other animal by-products in their arts, and that all made nets, mats, and containers of some kind from twigs, plant fronds, grasses, or roots. But as they adapted to special environmental

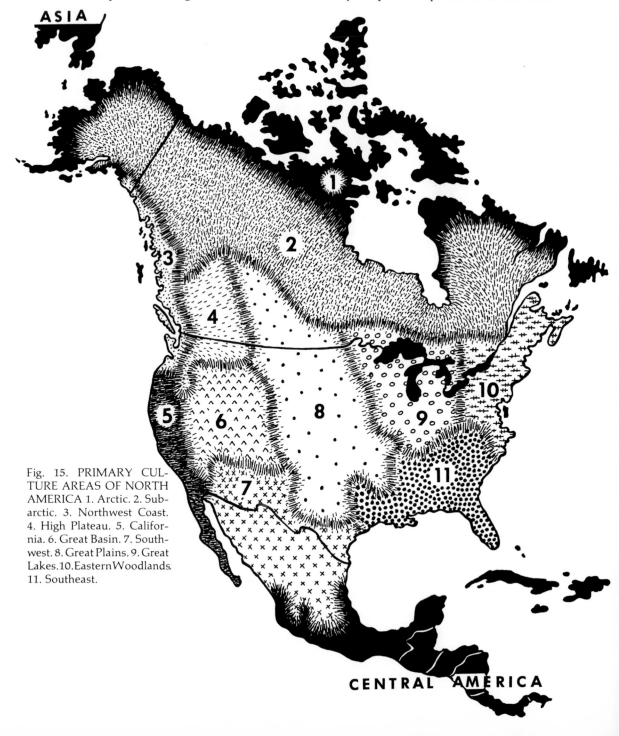

Fig. 15. PRIMARY CUL-TURE AREAS OF NORTH AMERICA 1. Arctic. 2. Sub-arctic. 3. Northwest Coast. 4. High Plateau. 5. California. 6. Great Basin. 7. Southwest. 8. Great Plains. 9. Great Lakes. 10. Eastern Woodlands. 11. Southeast.

situations, distinct cultures emerged in different geographical locations, and each had arts that in style, purpose, or construction were unique to them alone.

The geographical division of North America into separate culture areas has been accepted for so long that it seems almost irreverent to suggest that it can be somewhat misleading. However, it does imply that the Indian peoples permanently segregated themselves within certain territories. It may also give the impression that all work within a prescribed area was alike.

The Indian artist then, as now, was an individual. Although he had a tendency to follow established decorative styles because they were familiar, and therefore appealing to him, he never felt obliged to routinely duplicate forms and designs unless they were intended to be used in religious ceremonies. In this case, his arts served to preserve sacred traditions, and consistency was important.

There were no rigid boundaries where one culture abruptly stopped and another began. Instead, there were broad margins around the hearts of each area where neighboring cultures often became so intermingled that they almost deserved a separate label of their own.

Tribes often migrated in search of better land for farming or more ample game. Sometimes they were forced to move because of prolonged droughts, plagues, or invasions by enemies.

However, certain arts did grow out of cultural and geographical conditions, and the following map and brief notes are included to supplement more detailed descriptions in later chapters. Some of the best known tribes are listed in each area. Their identification with specific cultures is primarily based on historical relationships without regard for the location of modern reservations.

Art Specialties of Major North American Culture Areas

---

1. ARCTIC: *Aleut and Eskimo*

Recent studies indicate that all the native American peoples had common origins in Asia, though the Eskimos and Aleutians came much later than other groups, probably by boat two or three thousand years ago.

The men had a gift for mechanics. Tribes that lived around the sea produced superb carvings and engravings in bone and ivory, and many works demonstrate a keen sense of humor. Eskimo women were expert hideworkers, and even made fine garments and appliqués from fishskins, birdskins, and seal intestines.

Aleutian women wove grasses and silk threads into the most delicate baskets that were produced in North America.

Tribes that lived farther inland carved wood, stone, and horn, and the Copper Eskimos, who lived around the Coronation Gulf, made metal tools.

---

2. SUBARCTIC: *Cree, Ojibwa, Chipewyan, Beaver, Koyukon, Montagnais-Naskapi, Ingalik, Eskimo, Carrier, Sekani, Tutchone*

The Subarctic tribes were skilled wood-carvers of imaginative sculptures, as well as functional objects. They fashioned excellent canoes, utensils, and containers from bark. After the introduction of French techniques and commercial thread, embroidery became a specialty in some southern tribes.

Eskimos are famous for their stone carving. White markets have helped keep this art alive, but have also contributed to a weakening of quality.

3. NORTHWEST COAST: *Bellacoola, Chinook, Haida, Kwakiutl, Nootka, Cowichan, Tlingit, Chilkat, Tsimshian, Tillamook, Coos*

This was a highly materialistic culture, and since art objects represented wealth and prestige, artists were not only respected, but subsidized. They produced very sophisticated shellwork, hidework, bone and ivory carvings, and wove beautiful baskets from colored grasses and spruce roots. Their textiles from animal hair and shredded bark compare favorably with loomed products of the Southwestern tribes. Chilkat blankets are the best nonloom textiles of North America.

Their most impressive accomplishments are wood carvings, and their totem poles are the world's largest wood sculptures. Like their masks, they were usually painted and sometimes inlaid with shells.

Fig. 16. Not many totem poles remain in old Northwest Coast villages. These are at Kitmankool, British Columbia.

Fig. 17. For a time the art of carving the huge sculptures was nearly extinct, but through the encouragement of individuals, museums, and government agencies, it is being revived in some areas. Carvers at Ksan Village, B.C., are producing fine traditional work.

Fig. 18. "Raven," by Ray Wesley, Tsimshian, is an example of contemporary work that is based on but not routinely copied from old symbolic designs. *Collection, Mary Lou Stribling.*

Fig. 19. The mysticism of Northwestern poles inspired "White Bird Totem," by Lucile Brokaw. *Courtesy, artist.*

4. HIGH PLATEAU: *Umatilla, Yakima, Shuswap, Klikitat, Nez Percé, Flathead (Salish), Columbia, Klamath, Okanagon, Modoc*

The western Plateau region has many different kinds of terrain from forests and mountains to desolate, weed-strewn wildernesses, and foraging for food kept its inhabitants constantly on the move. Greatly influenced by their Plains neighbors, their arts were centered primarily on plant fibers and skins, though fine carvings of an unusual style were specialties of the Columbia River region. Basketry was well developed, as were some nonloom textiles. Decorative bags from cornhusks and rushes were made throughout the area.

5. CALIFORNIA: *Hupa (Hoopa), Karok, Maidu, Mission, Pomo, Yurok, Miwok, Yokuts, Chumash, Cahuilla, Serrano, Wintu*

The California peoples were largely fishers, hunters, and gatherers. They worked with hides and bones, carved shells into beads and pendants, and their featherwork equaled products from Polynesia and Peru. They produced practically no pottery since their beautifully constructed and patterned baskets filled their needs for every kind of container, including cooking pots. Pomo basketmakers are rated as masters of the art.

6. GREAT BASIN: *Paiute, Ute, Shoshone-Bannock, Washo, Mono, Panamint*

The Great Basin area east of the Rockies includes some of the harshest lands in the United States. The tribes who lived there were forced to convert into food everything that could possibly sustain life—acorns, insects, grubs, small animals, roots, nuts, and seeds. They were cyclic nomads, and their most significant art was basketry.

Fig. 20. California/Nevada baskets. *Collection, The Nevada State Historical Society.*

7. SOUTHWEST: *Jicarilla, Apache, Hopi, Navajo, Papago, Pima, Yuma, Zuñi, Havasupai, Eastern Keres (Cochita, San Felipe, Santa Ana, Santa Domingo, Zia), Western Keres (Acoma, Laguna), Tewa (Tesque, San Ildefonso, San Juan, Santa Clara)*

The dry climate in this area has preserved many old artifacts, and more is known of its early history than any other region. Nearly all major art forms were explored to some extent. Their fetishes, effigies, masks, and carved ceremonial dolls are of high quality, as are their woven and coiled baskets. They produced the only loomed textiles in North America and their pottery is outstanding. Zuñi, Navajo, and Hopi silverwork dates from Spanish contacts and is highly prized by collectors.

This is one of the few areas where traditional arts are still significantly active today.

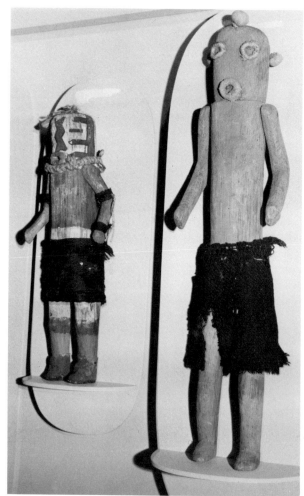

Fig. 21. Southwestern Kachina dolls were used for the religious education of children. Hopis are best known for this work today, and their figures are often elaborately dressed in symbolic costumes. These old examples are Zuñi. A clown Kachina is on the right. The left figure is unidentified, though it resembles the Earth and Sky Being. *Collection, The Nevada State Historical Society.*

Fig. 22. Navajo rug. *Photo, Jim Toms, courtesy, Nevada State Museum.*

8. GREAT PLAINS (HIGH PLATEAU): *Arapaho, Assiniboin, Blackfoot, Cheyenne, Teton, Comanche, Cree, Crow, Dakota (Sioux), Iowa, Kiowa, Yanktonai, Mandan, Omaha, Pawnee, Santee, Osage, Wichita, Ojibwa, Missouri*

After the Spaniards brought horses, the Plains peoples became great hunters and their arts were largely centered on hides and furs. Even their conical shelters (tipis) were made from skins, as were their furnishings, storage bags and containers, and clothing. These were often decorated with paint, quills, or beads. Some finger-woven textiles were produced and feathers were worked into ornaments and ceremonial costumes. In later years, women appliquéd cut ribbons into distinctive designs.

9. GREAT LAKES: *Chippewa, Fox, Kickapoo, Menomini, Ottawa, Potawatomi, Winnebago, Illinois, Shawnee, Miami, Huron, Algonquian*

The tribes around the Great Lakes and east to the Atlantic had a wide variety of art materials. They wove textiles from plant fibers and animal hair. Their pottery was of high quality, though not as colorful as that made in the Southwest. The men were skillful workers of wood and bark, and in later periods, made fine jewelry from both copper and silver. Moose-hair embroidery, quillwork, and beadwork were notable specialties.

10.   EASTERN WOODLANDS: *Delaware, Mohawk, Sokoki, Powhatan, Micmac, Conestoga, Abenaki, Iroquois*

The arts of this area were essentially the same as those around the Great Lakes, though the ocean provided them with a source of shells, which they used in many ways. Their famous cylindrical white and purple clamshell beads, called "wampum," were used as currency. Woven wampum belts had great value, and figured prominently in peace treaties and tribal ceremonies.

Fig. 23. Iroquois mask. The False Face Society used grotesque carved masks in healing ceremonies. They were designed to frighten away the malignant spirits that had caused the patient to become ill. *Courtesy, Bureau of Indian Affairs.*

11.   SOUTHEAST: *Cherokee, Chickasaw, Choctaw, Biloxi, Pensacola, Creek, Seminole, Catawba, Caddo, Calusa, Natchez, Apalachee, Chitimacha*

Southeastern arts are distinctive for their relationship to a cultural preoccupation with death and funeral practices. They carved, modeled, worked with feathers and shells, and wove textiles, including a particularly delicate cloth from milkweed. Their fine pottery reinforced with crushed shells and dried plant fibers was unique in North America, and it hints at the possibility that at some time they had made contact with potters in South America who produced similar ware. Design similarities between the two cultures are equally fascinating, and are most clearly evident in stone and wood carvings.

Many Cherokee arts have been revived, and the unusual Seminole patchwork from Florida is receiving national attention.

2

ORNAMENTS AND FINERY

The American Indians had few inhibitions when it came to decorating themselves, and they did not overlook any spot where art could improve on nature, including the partings in their hair. A few lines of red clay or berry juice on their faces might suffice for everyday wear, but for important occasions, whatever was exposed received meticulous attention. In milder climates this could include most, or all, of the body, and preparations for a party could take a great deal of time.

Some groups invented methods that were faster than hand-painting. Tlingits carved symbols on wooden paddles, coated them with animal fat and pulverized charcoal, and used them to "block print" their faces. Scarification created permanent designs, but tattooing was more colorful and represented the ultimate in indelible body decoration.

There was no shortage of display space for jewelry, though if personal collections were extensive, it could become, quite literally, a very weighty matter. Ears, nostrils, lips, ankles, toes, arms, wrists, and fingers carried their share of the burden, but the bulk of the exhibition was reserved for necks. The choice has been consistent throughout history.

STONE AND CLAY BEADS

Glass was not produced in prehistorical America, but there was an abundance of other materials for ornaments and beads. Wood, seeds, grains, cones, teeth, bones, talons, beaks, hooves, horns, minerals, and stones were almost universally available, and everything that could be perforated was put to use.

20

Stone beads were often left as they had been carved by nature, and were simply drilled for suspension on a sinew cord. Sometimes they were refined on a sandstone block, or were incised with simple lines and dots. They were probably also painted with colored earths, vegetable juices, and other perishable materials.

Slate and sandstone beads were made by the Eastern Woodland tribes. Californians carved soapstone (steatite) [1] into polished beads of many different shapes and sizes—some quite large, and their tubular magnesite beads were as precious as rare gems. The beads were baked in open fires to change the greyish color to warm salmon pinks. Early explorers were unfamiliar with the mineral and mistook it for coral.

Tribes that made pottery rolled clay into beads, ear spools, and lip plugs, and clay probably remains the most versatile material for contemporary beadmaking. In Chapter 9, open firing is described as an alternative to hardening clay without a kiln. However, kiln fired beads are certainly more durable, and since ceramic shops that charge only a small fee for firing are now so widespread, this should not really be a problem.

A few substitutes deserve consideration, even though they may be more fragile. Commercial clay compounds that are formulated for air drying are quite hard, especially when they are coated with nonfired finishes. They will not withstand a fall to a cement floor, but then, neither will glass.

Most of these products have a tendency to dry fairly fast, so take out only small amounts at a time, and periodically moisten your fingers on a damp cloth. Many ideas for bead shapes can be obtained from old Indian jewelry.

You can also use the following old recipe to make a surprisingly durable, plastic dough from salt and cornstarch. It requires no baking.

Unbaked Modeling Dough:

In a large saucepan, mix 2 cups salt with ⅔ cup water. Stir over medium heat until it is hot. In a separate pan, moisten 1¼ cups cornstarch with ½ cup plus 1 tablespoon cold water. Remove salt mixture from heat, and add about a quarter of the damp cornstarch at a time, beating well in between each. Return dough to heat and stir vigorously for 3 or 4 minutes. (Extra help with stirring is handy at this point).

Spread a generous layer of dry cornstarch on a sheet of waxed paper. Place warm dough on top of it, and knead thoroughly until the starch is worked in. Work in more starch if the dough is still tacky.

Wrap dough tightly in an unperforated plastic bag, and it will keep indefinitely without refrigeration.

---

[1] Soapstone is a soft, greyish black talc in rock form.

Whether you use clay or other modeling products, allow beads to dry slightly before making the holes or you may push them out of shape. A small drill bit, round toothpick, or tapestry needle can be used as perforating tools, but do not punch them straight through the bead. Instead, twirl the points gently into each end until the opening meets in the middle.

Clay substitutes are somewhat porous, and should be sealed with several coats of varnish or acrylic medium. Use toothpicks to suspend them on a Styrofoam block until the coatings are dry.

Keep painted designs simple, and limit the number of colors on a single necklace. Seal the beads first with one coat of acrylic medium, then apply a second coat after they are painted.

Fig. 24. Many prehistoric tribes made drilled stone beads before the introduction of glass trade beads. This necklace was made in the Southwest. *Photo, Cloyd Sorensen, Jr.*

Fig. 25. Air-dried clay compounds are useful for persons without kilns. The undecorated string in the foreground was threaded on a soft cotton cord before beads were completely hard so that they could be pressed to fit closely together. The chunky irregular beads at the top are kiln-fired stoneware.

SHELLS

Shells were traded across the continent long before the arrival of Europeans, and shell embroidery on clothing was used to some extent in nearly all tribes. However, shell arts reached their greatest heights in the coastal areas where materials were plentiful. California dance costumes were heavily encrusted with cowrie and conus dangles. Necklaces were made from olivella shells by grinding off the ends to expose the central openings through which a cord could be passed. Abalone pendants were carved by the thousands, and were attached to almost everything, including baskets.

Great quantities of abalone shells were imported on the Northwest Coast from the south, and were cut into nose pendants and other ornaments, as well as insets for carved wooden rattles, masks, bowls, and totemic figures. High-fashion wooden lip plugs, or labrets, were also occasionally inlaid with abalone shells.

Fig. 26. Detail, Plateau costume. Plateau dresses were often ornately decorated with shells, beads, carved bones, and metal thimbles. This example is made from green wool blanket material, embroidered with small trade beads and cowrie shells. The pendants on the necklace are bear teeth. *Collection, Glenbow–Alberta Institute.*

Fig. 27. Sarah Winnemucca, the daughter of a Paiute chief, made a lifelong crusade against the injustices of Indian agents. A colorful, articulate, and controversial figure, she was often referred to as "Princess Sarah" by reporters and promoters of her lectures. In many respects, the costume in this photograph taken in the 1880s is closely related to the Plateau costume in Figure 26. *Courtesy, The Nevada Historical Society.*

Slender, tusk-shaped dentalium shells were abundant along Vancouver Island. The Nootkas strung them into crowns, hair ornaments, necklaces, and earrings, and traded them to the California tribes, where they were used as money. Their value was determined by a standardized ten-shell string of perfect specimens. Men measured the string for accuracy by holding one end between thumb and forefinger, and the other end at a special tattoo mark on the upper arm.

Dentalium shells were also traded up the Northwest Coast, though they were not a basic medium of exchange in that area. They did not reach the Plains peoples in significant quantities until the mid 1880s. By that time, glass trade beads had become available, but shells were still highly regarded. Dentalium embroidery on women's dresses was sometimes so elaborate that the foundation fabric was completely covered from the neck to the elbows, creating the effect of a shell cape.

Clamshell beadmaking was a very early art in California. The shells were first chipped into rough disks, and holes were drilled through the centers.[2] They were then strung on taut fiber cords and rubbed on a sandstone block until the edges were rounded and smooth.

The word "wampum" has been greatly abused, and is often misapplied to all forms of Indian beads. It correctly refers only to distinctive Northeastern cylindrical beads made from white and purple quahog clam shells. The purple area on these shells is large enough for only one or two beads, so they were more valuable.

The Northeastern Algonquians are usually credited with first developing wampum, but they were also made by the Iroquois, and possibly other tribes of that area.

The California method for making disk beads was slow, but comparatively simple. Wampum was made the hard way. A thick strip of shell was cut out and laboriously ground into a smooth cylinder, then a hole was drilled through the ends to make a tiny tube. Many beads must have shattered or split during that last tedious step, canceling the hard work involved in bringing them to that stage.

When English and Dutch settlers found supplies of their own currency running short, they substituted wampum and established rules to fix its value. Eventually, it was mass-produced in a New Jersey factory. It ceased to be a stable medium of exchange, however, when a few shrewd profiteers flooded the market with European porcelain counterfeits.

Pueblo tribes made shell beads that were very similar to California products, though they improved the basic technique and applied it to chips of turquoise as well. The finest and most valuable shell necklaces were (and are) made with beads so small and perfectly polished that they appear to be cast in glass. Since

[2] The Indians invented a number of hand drills, but the "pump" drill brought by the Spaniards was so much more efficient that it is still used in some tribes today.

GEORGE WALTON COMPREHENSIVE HIGH SCHOOL
1590 BILL MURDOCK ROAD
MARIETTA, GEORGIA 30060

02628

these beads were strung before they were ground into shape, they fit perfectly against each other and the joints in between are scarcely discernible. It is almost impossible to reassemble the elements of a broken strand in exactly the same way. Necklaces of graded shell beads were often combined with turquoise, coral, or carved shell figures, and are still produced today.

Pendants with overlaid designs of turquoise and jet chips were very old pueblo specialties. The mosaic was set in pitch on the backs of flattish shells, such as cockles, small scallops, and clams.[3] And as far back as 900 years, the Hohokams of southern Arizona developed a technique for etching designs on shells with cactus acid. It was unknown in any other part of North America.

Turquoise mosaics are too exotic for the craftsman without lapidary equipment, but the idea can be borrowed for jewelry mosaicked with ordinary eggshells. Remove the inner membrane from the shells, and paint them in several shades of turquoise. Apply two or three coats of clear gloss varnish. After they are thoroughly dry, break them into small chips and attach them to the basic form with white glue.

To make a grouting mixture to fill the crevices, combine ten parts of tile grout with three parts of black cement color. (Use teaspoon measurements for small amounts.) Mix one part white glue with three parts water. Stir enough of the liquid into the dry grout to make a smooth paste the consistency of pancake batter, then brush it into the cracks. Rub with your fingers to remove air bubbles. When the paste is firm, but not dry, remove excess with slightly dampened paper towels. Let harden overnight before polishing with a damp cloth. Inspect the grout for any unfilled air pockets, and correct them with a second, thinner application if necessary. Allow the mosaic to dry for several days, then seal it with a coat of clear varnish.

Black cement color can usually be obtained where masonry supplies are sold, but if it is unavailable, add black acrylic paint to the moistened grout mixture until the desired depth of color is obtained.

The cross pendant at the top of Fig. 28 is a Southwestern motif of Spanish origin. The basic form was cut from thin pressed board and painted black. Narrow strips of lead were glued around the edges and the enclosed sections were mosaicked as just described.

The form for the lower pendant is a limpet shell with the convex side painted black. The white border was attached first and allowed to dry before filling in the central area.

Some of the finest ornaments of the prehistorical period were made by the Southeastern Mound Builders. The line designs on their engraved shell gorgets have provided a great deal of information about their cultures, since along with crosses, birds, and faces they often realistically portrayed dancers in ceremonial costumes, or warriors equipped with weapons and trophies.[4]

---

[3] Modern interpretations of this ancient art are made today by the Zuñi.

[4] A few painted designs have been found, and since most pigments deteriorate rapidly, the practice might have been more common than the rarity of existing examples indicates.

Fig. 28. Eggshell jewelry inspired by old pueblo shell pendants that were mosaicked with turquoise chips.

Fig. 30. Modern interpretations of Indian shell jewelry. The central necklace is made from large and small dentalium shells, buttons, black wooden beads, and a black wooden curtain ring. In the lower necklace, stacked pearl buttons are linked together with silver beads.

Fig. 29. The old Indian necklaces on the left and right have dentalium shells strung with glass trade beads and abalone pendants. The lower necklace has cobalt trade beads strung with prehistoric Mimbres shell beads. *Photo, Cloyd Sorensen, Jr.*

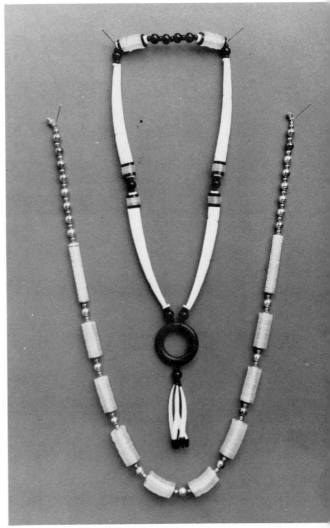

These expertly carved medallions have aroused considerable curiosity among historians, who suspect that their stylistic similarity to the designs of Central America is more than coincidental. Since the relationship also exists in other arts, notably pottery and carving, proof of some connecting link may eventually be discovered.

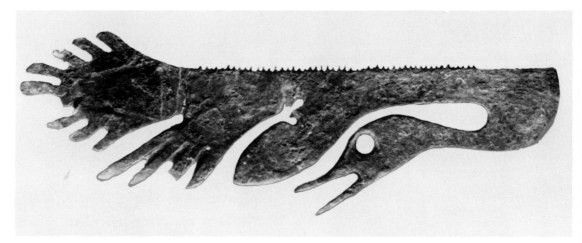

Fig. 31. Hopewell shell comb, made from the carapace of a turtle. *Courtesy, The Ohio Historical Society.*

If you lack patience or equipment for carving shells, much can be done with small whole shells and broken fragments picked up on the beach. The grinding action of sand and water often takes care of sharp edges, and sometimes provides convenient suspension holes. But holes in most shells can be quickly made with the tip of a very sharp craft knife. This is easier, in fact, than using a power drill, which has a tendency to skid on the smooth surface.

As an alternative, attach an eyelet bell cap to the top with epoxy glue. Shape the prongs against the shell before gluing down the cap, and just before the adhesive hardens, gently seat them more securely with sharp-nosed pliers.

Inexpensive jewelry findings of this kind can be obtained from hobby stores and craft shops, but for the most part, they are too aggressively shiny to be compatible with shells and other found objects. A propane torch will most effectively antique them, but even a candle flame can make them less obtrusive.

If shells are badly worn from sand abrasion, colors can be restored with several coats of clear gloss or satin finish varnish. This will also help reinforce delicate shells, such as starfish and sand dollars.

The most valuable dentalium ornaments had shells that were engraved, painted, or wound with strips of leather. (Shells that were wrapped with snakeskin were "unclean" and used only for blood money.)

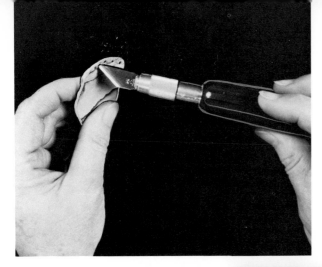

Fig. 32. To make suspension holes in shells, twirl the tip of a sharp craft knife against the surface until a slight indentation is formed, then twirl the blade rapidly back and forth with increasing pressure. When the shell is penetrated about halfway, complete the opening from the other side.

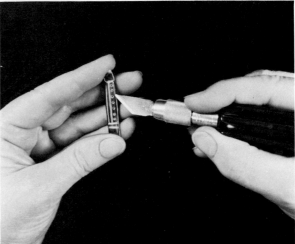

Fig. 33. Simple designs on certain kinds of shells, such as sea urchin spines, can be engraved with a knife. Once the polished outer skin is scratched through, the lines can easily be incised deeper.

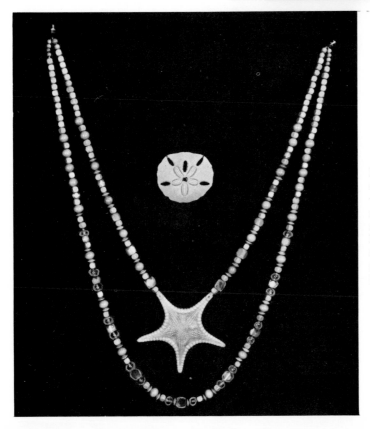

Fig. 34. Several coats of satin finish varnish will reinforce the walls and seal the porous surfaces of sand dollars (top) and starfish. The starfish pendant here is combined with a double string of wooden beads and old faceted honey-colored glass beads.

Engraving effects can be obtained with paints or waterproof inks. The large dentalium shells and the cone shell pendant in Fig. 35 were decorated with a pen and ink, then sprayed with six light coats of clear plastic for protection. Border lines require a steady hand and are easier to make with black printed circuit tape that comes as narrow as 1/32″. Press the tape in place first, to serve as guidelines for the rest of the design.

Baby crab shells, ranging in size from 1″ to 2½″, can be collected from the Atlantic, Pacific, and Gulf coasts. Their honey and coral tints are good backgrounds for designs from Indian engravings. To make them durable enough for pendants, pack the inside cavities with water putty, and sand it smooth after it has hardened.

Fig. 35. The cone shell pendant and large dentalium shells in this necklace were decorated with a pen and waterproof ink, then were coated with clear plastic. The pendant design was adapted from Eskimo engravings. Symbols on the dentalium shells are from the Carrier phonetic alphabet in Figure 36. Buttons, bone beads, silver beads, and glass beads are other materials in the necklace.

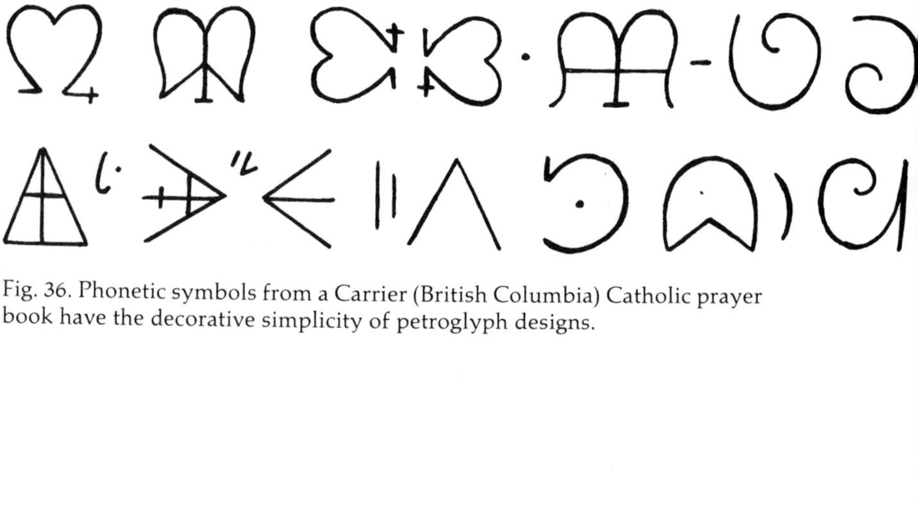

Fig. 36. Phonetic symbols from a Carrier (British Columbia) Catholic prayer book have the decorative simplicity of petroglyph designs.

BONES

Wild game was an important part of Indian diets, and the leftovers were not wasted. Horns and bones were especially useful for tools and ornaments, and were easier to carve than shells.

The basic equipment for horn and bone working consists of a sharp knife and several grades of sandpaper. To make holes through long pieces, you will also need a drill (hand or electric) and a fine bit. A hacksaw or hand-scroll saw can be used for slicing.

Cow and steer horns are hollow and can be sliced into rings for belt fastenings, earrings, and pendants. Thick sections of deer antlers may have hollow parts, but the tips are usually solid and make beautiful beads and buttons when they are drilled and polished.[5]

[5] Indians softened horns in water to make them easier to carve. Ready-made bone and antler beads and buttons can be purchased from shops carrying Indian supplies, and from many general craft shops.

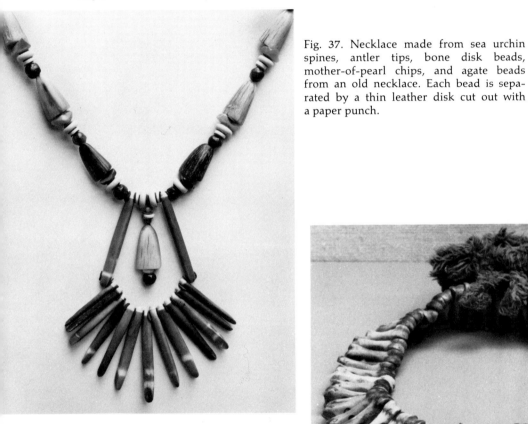

Fig. 37. Necklace made from sea urchin spines, antler tips, bone disk beads, mother-of-pearl chips, and agate beads from an old necklace. Each bead is separated by a thin leather disk cut out with a paper punch.

Fig. 38. Bone necklace, Blackfoot. A nicely organized ornament from animal foot bones, feathers, fur, and the skull of a hawk. *Collection, Glenbow–Alberta Institute.*

Old sun-cured bones often have interesting shapes that need no further carving to be turned into ornaments, though several coats of low-sheen varnish will improve the surface quality. Clean new bones by boiling them in soapy water until all traces of tissue can be scrubbed away. Dry them thoroughly in a barely warm oven for several hours, then place them on a sunny windowsill for a few weeks.

Pare away the sharp points on chicken and turkey vertebrae and you will have a collection of unusual beads of graduated sizes, complete with stringing holes. Like other bones, they can be tinted with fabric dyes, and they take paints well.

Fig. 39. The distinctive hair pipe breastplates of the Plains peoples date from the late 1800s, and were made from long, tubular cow bone beads that were commercially manufactured. They were styled after earlier, less elaborate versions made from dentalium shells. Men's breastplates usually came to the waist, or just below it. Women's sometimes touched the ground, and were very heavy.

Fig. 40. The hair pipes were often combined with glass beads, and were strung with leather separators that kept the strands together. The bottom fringe was trimmed with bells or other dangles that clacked musically with the slightest movement. These photos were taken in 1910, and were researched by Louis Garcia. *Courtesy, Indian America.*

Fig. 41. Bone hair pipes can still be purchased from Indian shops, but this adaptation was made with wooden beads, small glass beads, and thin bamboo tubes from a beaded curtain. Separators are segments of Popsicle sticks with eight holes drilled in the lower strip; four holes in the side pieces. The bottom dangles are coral branches.

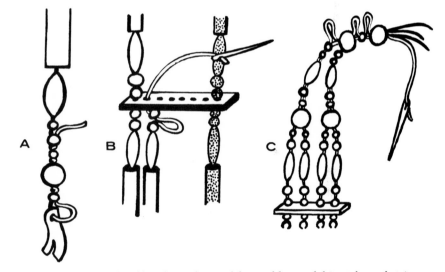

Fig. 42. Other kinds of beads can be used for necklaces of this style, and strips of leather can be substituted for wooden separators. A. Start at the bottom of the outside strand and string the tassel. Knot and reweave the loose end back through several beads and clip. B. Continue the strand around the neck and down the other side, then string the adjacent inside strand. C. At the shoulder, go back through several beads of the previous strand to reduce down to two strings, then reduce down to one string at the back of the neck.

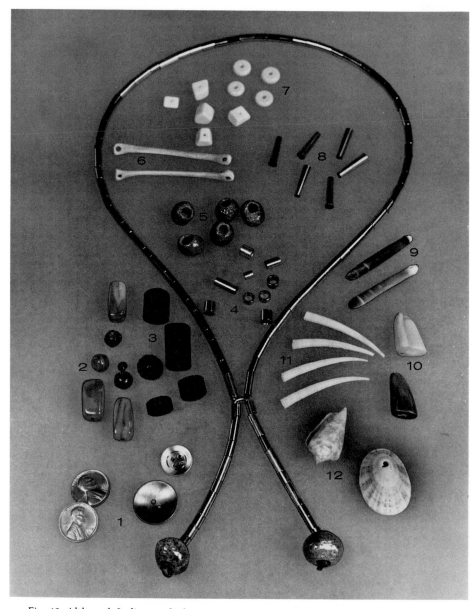

Fig. 43. Although Indian craft shops carry a variety of authentic materials for jewelry making, you can collect or make many yourself, or substitute objects that are similar in feeling. If the simple necklace in the center had been made from silver tube beads and chunks of turquoise, it would be very expensive. It cost very little to make it from chrome spacers (4) and large Egyptian paste "donkey" beads (5). Other possibilities are (1) pennies and old metal buttons, (2) Oriental agate beads, (3) driftwood twigs, sliced, drilled, and engraved with a wood burning tool, (6) fowl leg bones, (7) commercial cow bone beads, (8) Indian tin cones, (9) sea urchin spines, (10) antler tips, (11) dentalium shells, (12) cone and limpet shells.

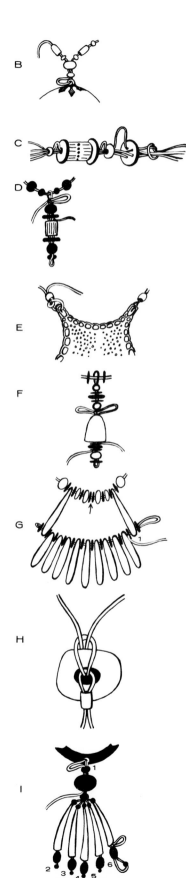

Fig. 44. ASSEMBLING NECKLACES

These general instructions for assembling necklaces shown in this chapter will also apply to different materials.

A. To attach a clasp, carry thread through the eye, tie a tight square knot, then go back through several beads, knotting in between each before clipping the thread short. Draw beads close together and attach the other side of the clasp.

B. If shells, coins, or rocks do not have holes, use pliers to shape a bell cap to fit the top, and secure it with epoxy glue. String half the necklace, then go through a large bead, a small bead, and the eye of the pendant. Go back through the small and large beads and continue the necklace.

C. String buttons and other objects with more than one hole on multiple threads—one for each hole. Reinforce heavy necklaces by periodically tying the bundle together with the last thread.

D. String finials separately, then attach them to the necklace thread. Tie on the finial tightly, then carry the loose ends back through several beads. Knot threads, and clip short.

E. Suspend delicate pendants from two points to distribute the strain. Where possible, reinforce the holes with bits of matching leather. Attach as described for clasps A.

F. To follow the basic design in Figure 37, string finial elements with leather disk separators and attach to the necklace thread as described in D.

G. String the fringe next, and knot tightly at 1. Go through several adjacent beads and knot again. Assemble the necklace by stringing beads and fringe suspensions on each side of the finial (indicated by the arrow). Long bones or driftwood twigs can be substituted for sea urchin spines.

H. When there is an existing hole in shells or rocks, a Lark's Head knot in the suspension cord can also carry dangling elements. Bring the center of the suspension cord through the hole and over the cord for dangles. Draw the ends through the loop and pull tight. (See color pages.)

I. String tassels on a single thread to eliminate extra knots. Tie a thread to a pendant, or the center of the necklace (1), go through a medium bead, large bead, medium bead, then through the elements of one strand of the tassel (2). Go back to the beginning again and repeat for each strand (3, 4, 5, 6). Knot securely at the top, then weave loose ends back through several beads.

FEATHERS

The popular image of the North American Indian is almost inseparably connected with feathers, largely because the flamboyant war bonnets of the Plains peoples have received more than their share of attention from movie producers, artists, and Scout leaders. But this was by no means a typical accessory, and it represents only a small part of the broad field of Indian featherwork.

No examples of early featherwork have been preserved, but pictorial carvings in wood, stone, and shells document their existence. From descriptions of early explorers, we also get tantalizing glimpses of forms that have become extinct. These records indicate that some work produced in the Southeast must have come close in quality to the magnificent feather mosaics of the Mayas and Aztecs. Elaborate cloaks and headdresses that sometimes incorporated whole stuffed birds were reserved for ranking officials, but since brilliant plumage was abundant in that region, undoubtedly even the ordinary citizen could indulge in a colorful dance bustle and ornaments for his hair and ears. Feathers also figured prominently in burial ceremonies and adornment of the dead.

The flowing style of the Plains war bonnets originated with Eastern tribes. They were made of eagle feathers, and were worn only by tribal warriors. The

Fig. 45. Alaskan mask. Many masks of this kind were too fragile to wear, and were simply carried in front of the face as symbolic ornaments. *Collection, Phoebe F. McCoy; courtesy, The M. H. De Young Memorial Museum.*

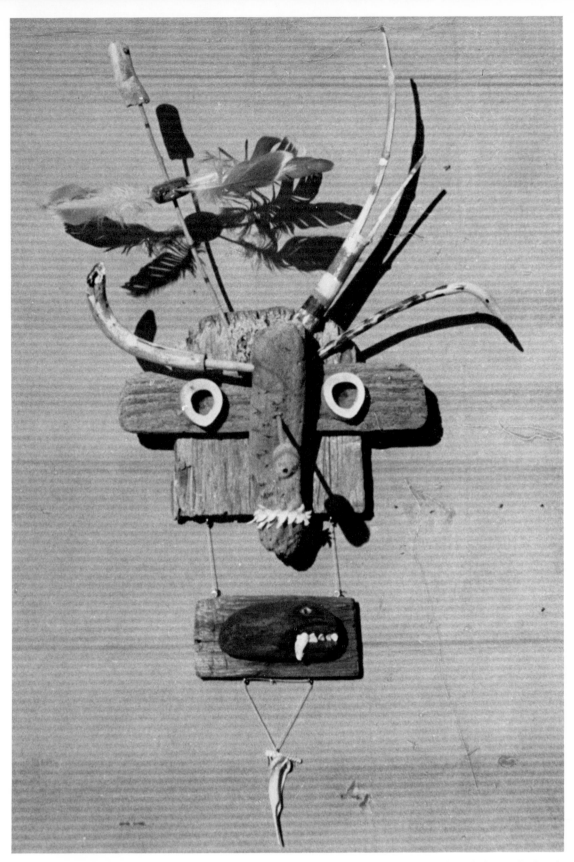

Fig. 46. "Killer Whale," an ornamental wall mask of wood, bones, feathers, and other found objects, by Lucile Brokaw. *Courtesy, artist.*

number and coloring of the feathers denoted achievements earned in contests with enemies. They were trimmed with borders and rosettes of beads, fur, or ribbons, or preferably all three. Large dance bustles, shaped like rosettes, were other Plains specialties, as were fans, war shield covers, and decorations for their horses' heads. Pipes, men's most sacred personal possessions, were often profusely embellished with snakeskin, feathers, and birds' heads.

California featherwork was more delicate and refined, and excited the admiration of early Spanish explorers and missionaries. Father Vicente Santa Maria describes in his diary how Indians they first saw from a distance left a rod decorated with feathers stuck in the sand as a symbol of peace. Later, he observed shafts with circular ornaments at their tips made from black and red feathers, arranged like symbols of the sun. On one occasion, the Indians wore garlands of black and red feathers and chest-length feather jackets. The rest of their bodies, though bare, were "all worked over with various designs in charcoal and red ochre. . . ." [6]

Belts with mosaic designs made by overlapping multicolored feathers like shingles were Pomo specialties that were kept alive for a long time. They were worn by men across one shoulder, and served as a protective charm.

The association of feathers with magic was not unique with the Pomos. They had a religious significance to all Indian peoples, probably because of their link with the mysterious act of flying.

In the Southwest, birds were thought to be messengers of the gods, and feathers symbolized man's spiritual connection with supernatural powers. Murals found in the ruins of Arizona pueblos show feathered prayer wands and other ritualistic objects, and figures wearing feathered headdresses. The practice of decorating Kachina masks and dolls with feather ruffs, tassels, and halos continues to this day.

FEATHERED JEWELRY

Use heavy felt and kidskin or other soft leathers as foundations for feathered collars, chokers, headbands, and abbreviated breastplates. For allover mosaic designs, separate your feathers by colors and clip off the tips. Draw a pattern for the basic shape and try it on for size before cutting the permanent material.

[6] John Galvin, ed., *The First Spanish Entry into San Francisco Bay, 1775* (San Francisco: John Howell-Books, 1971), p. 63.

Fig. 47. FEATHERED GORGET
Start at the bottom edge of the foundation and glue down a row of feathers, keeping their quill ends pointing toward the center. Continue until you reach the center where the quill ends of three or four feathers come together.

Fig. 48. Select a single attractive feather with a bit of fluff to cover this spot, and use a very thin film of glue to invisibly attach it. An abalone shell disk or cluster of beads can also be used in the center. Sew a twisted cord around the inside edge, or string beads from each tip to go around the neck.

Fasten ends of collars and neckpieces with snaps, hooks-and-eyes, or thong ties. Sew a strip of elastic at the back of headbands, and suspend gorgets and pendants from cords, chains, or beads.

A gorget fitted to the base of the neck can be made quickly and is a good practice project. The same technique can be applied to all feather mosaics, regardless of size. The feathers are attached in overlapping rows, the way they grow on the bird, and they must be overlapped far enough to cover the glued-down area on the previous row. For neat work, keep glue to a minimum, and apply it to one spot at a time with a toothpick. A heavy bodied glue works best, or you can pour a small amount of ordinary white glue in a foil-lined jar lid and allow some of the solvent to evaporate.

Fig. 49. "Squash blossom" necklace in tawny colors made with bundles of rooster feathers and wooden beads.

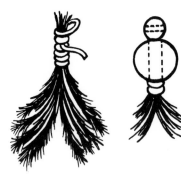

Fig. 50. To make feather squash blossoms, wrap bundles of feathers with yarn until they fit snugly inside the holes of large wooden beads. Set aside. Glue small wooden beads on top of large beads with epoxy, keeping holes perpendicular to each other. Let dry overnight, then put a drop of white glue in holes of the large beads, and carefully twist in the feather bundles.

Fig. 51. Feathered macramé necklaces, by Joan Sestak. Lady Amherst pheasant feathers are in the necklace on the left. The necklace on the right is made with alternating square knots, but the cords are manipulated freely to add interest to the linear pattern. Parakeet, duck, and pigeon feathers are glued in the beads.

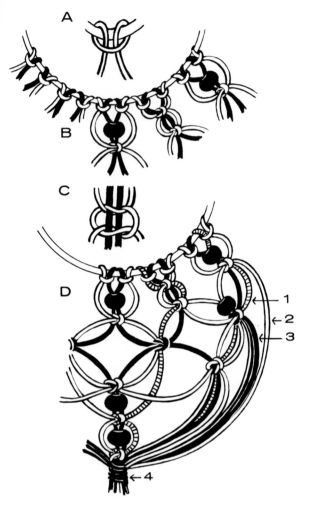

Fig. 52. MACRAMÉ FRAMEWORK FOR FEATH-
ERED NECKLACES

A. Cut ten strands of waxed linen warp about three times
the lengths desired for the finished necklace. Bring ends
together and attach centers to a leather thong with Lark's
Head knots.

B. Slip the two center strands through a bead, and tie
adjacent cords around it in a square knot.

C. Tie square knots alone in the four cords on each side,
and repeat the center knot in the remaining cords.

D. Tie alternate square knots for two or three rows,
adding beads where they seem appropriate. To vary the
linear pattern, occasionally carry a single cord through
an adjacent knot as shown by the shaded line in the
middle group of cords. Dangling cords on the edges can
also be brought through knots to the center (1). For a
pleasing frame to the knotted design, sweep outside
threads at 2 and 3 into a gentle curve, and combine them
with remaining cords. Tie together with a separate length
of cord at 4. Clip about 2″ below 4. Use white glue to
fasten feathers in beads and knots, and to conceal ends at
the bottom.

WOOD AND GOURDS

A jigsaw is one of the most useful tools that have ever been invented, and it can
open up a whole new world to persons who find handsaws too heavy and difficult
to control. Small table models are quite inexpensive, and are as easy to operate as
sewing machines. In fact, the two tools have much in common, which may
account for the growing number of women woodworkers.

Pendants of almost any shape can be cut from pressed board with a jigsaw.
The oak separators used in office desk drawers are tougher and thinner than
pressed board, and will take all kinds of finishes beautifully. With luck, you may
be able to find used pieces in secondhand furniture stores or junk shops.

Acrylics are ideal for painted designs, but if you are more comfortable with
scissors than a brush, try cutting out the larger areas from colored paper or
self-adhering plastic, and use a waterproof felt-tipped pen for lines and fine

Fig. 53. Well-dried gourd shards are very durable, yet are easy to carve with a knife, and the curved surface adds interest to the simplest shape. Rough out the basic form with a hand-scroll saw, then gradually pare it down a sliver at a time. Direct cuts away from the tips of sharp points to keep from breaking them off.

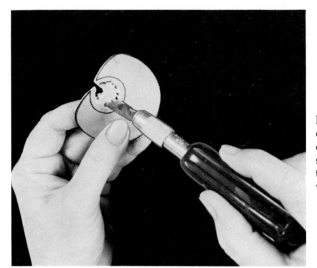

Fig. 54. Drill a row of adjacent holes to remove excess material in inside curves. Carve to the outline with a knife, then bevel all edges sharply to the back to eliminate bulk. Refine top, back, and edges with emery boards, and with fine sandpaper wrapped around a pencil.

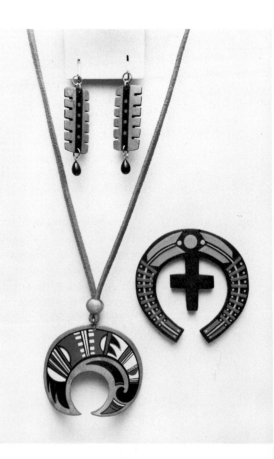

Fig. 55. The edges of the gourd earrings at the top were slashed with a fine saw blade, then the cuts were widened and polished with an emery board. They were painted with acrylics. The left gourd pendant was also painted with acrylics. The design was inspired by a Zuñi mosaic of turquoise, jet, and shell. The pendant on the right was cut with a jigsaw from pressed board. The design was made with self-adhering plastic and 1/16'' tape.

details. Apply five or six coats of clear acrylic medium or decoupage varnish to the finished design.

The pendant at the right in Fig. 55 was cut from pressed board, then was sanded smooth and painted flat black. The solid areas of the feather design are turquoise self-adhering plastic, and the lines were made with cobalt blue 1/16" drafting tape.[7] It was sealed with four coats of decoupage varnish, and a final coat of satin-finish varnish.

METALS

Copper was the only metal worked to any significant degree in prehistoric North America. There were large surface deposits around the Great Lakes, and local tribes hammered it into crude tools for several thousand years before the European invasion.

It reached Southeastern tribes through trade and was used for making ceremonial plaques, pendants, and other ornaments. Processes of melting and casting were unknown. It was worked only by cutting, hammering, and indenting, but they created remarkably fine designs of costumed figures, birds, fish, snakes, and animals.

In historic periods, copper bracelets, necklaces, and masks were made on the Northwest Coast, as well as strange, shield-shaped plaques that represented wealth and prestige. These "coppers" were often engraved or painted with totemic designs and were displayed at potlatch festivities, where tribal leaders made a great show of their possessions to belittle competitive chieftains.

Beads made from hammered and rolled copper tubes have been found in the Columbia River area, as well as around the Great Lakes. The Plains tribes made

[7] These tapes are available where art materials and drafting supplies are sold. See "Supply Sources" in the Appendix.

Fig. 56. Hammered copper plates were included in the treasuries of Northwest Coast chieftains. This copper was paid by the Nass River people to the Gilidzar Tribe of Port Simpson in retribution for the killing of one of their chiefs and his brother. The painted design symbolizes a bear, the crest of the Gilidzar. *Collection, The Museum of Northern British Columbia.*

tubular ornaments for their hair from pieces of brass pots, and the Apaches rolled strips of scrap tin into cones for decorating the fringes of baskets, bags, and clothing. But the metal most favored for jewelry by both Indians and their non-Indian clients has continued to be silver.

Indian silversmithing has a short but important history. The treasuries of the Aztecs and Incas had yielded rich plunder of gold and silver to the raiding parties led by Cortez and Pizarro, and it was assumed that similar riches existed in the North. It is not surprising, then, that other Spanish adventurers eagerly accepted as fact the myth of Cibola, a fabulous territory somewhere in the Southwestern desert that was reported to contain seven heathen cities made of silver and gold.

The search for Cibola began in 1539 with an exploration party led by Fray Marcos de Niza, and was soon followed by Coronado and teams of Catholic missionaries. They found no gold, only the heathens—outlandish people who lived in houses of sunbaked mud, and worshiped an array of pagan gods.

Although the discovery was disappointing, it was not entirely worthless, for the people also raised crops and made fine textiles, baskets, and pottery. They clearly deserved the spiritual benefits of Christian conversion, and it was only fair that the conquistadores were entitled to material benefits in return. Whatever sacrifice this might require from the natives was undoubtedly justified on the grounds that it was good for their souls.

Dreams of Cibola gradually faded, but as more and more settlers continued to arrive, a curious paradox occurred. Instead of taking precious metals from the savages, as they had originally intended, the settlers brought in the only examples the Indians had ever seen. The Indians had always been fond of bright, shiny materials, and quickly acquired a taste for foreign coins, buttons, tools, and other attractive metallic objects.

Eastern colonists also brought metals with them, and the Iroquois were working silver by 1800. Their jewelry became so popular that it was soon copied by neighboring tribes and, eventually, by the Plains peoples. Each group added decorative elements of their own, but a certain stylistic similarity remained since the work was mostly limited to hammered or cut forms from sheet silver, with stamped or engraved designs.

The Navajos received their first silver jewelry from the Spaniards—sometimes legally, sometimes not. Later, they learned the principles of silversmithing from itinerant Mexican peddlers who wandered through the Southwest making ornaments for trade. They did not, however, take up the art themselves until after their confinement at Bosque Redondo in 1865. At first, they made only rough copies of Mexican and Spanish trinkets, and most were hammered from coins. After U.S. law prohibited this practice, they learned to work ingots and sheets obtained from traders.

Good Navajo jewelry is distinguished by its massive simplicity and restrained use of turquoise or other stones. Their famous "squash blossom" beads are not symbols of fertility, a romantic notion that has been perpetuated by traders, but are adaptations of Spanish ornaments that were shaped like pomegranates.

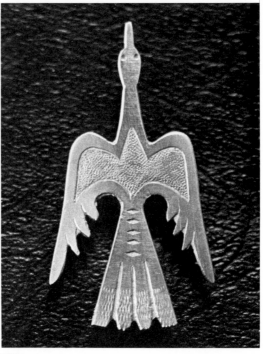

Figs. 57–59. PLAINS SILVER JEWELRY
Man's earrings, 3″ long; Aquatic Bird stickpin, 4¼″; pendant, 2½″ × 2″. These pieces of cut and engraved German silver jewelry by Julius Ceasar, Pawnee, were made in 1970. They reflect the traditions of early Plains designs. *Courtesy, U.S. Dept. of Interior, Museum Arts and Crafts Board, Southern Plains Indian Museum and Crafts Center.*

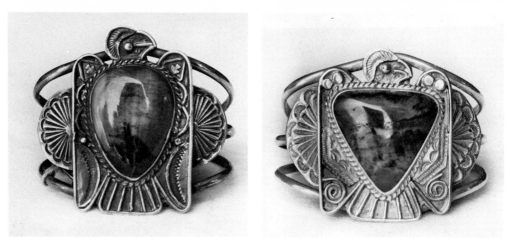

Figs. 60, 61. Silver rings, made around the turn of the century in the Grand Canyon area. The stones are polished petrified wood with subtle markings that resemble desert landscapes. *Collection, Christina Bee Bug.*

Their crescent pendants, called "najas," also came from the Spaniards, who borrowed the shape earlier from an African charm used as protection against the "evil eye."

The Zuñis learned silversmithing from the Navajos, but their decorative styles are entirely different. In Zuñi designs, the metal serves primarily as a vehicle to support colored stones, and they are often so ornate that little silver is visible. They are also well known for their mosaic inlays of silver and chips of turquoise, which are meticulously ground and polished until the surface is completely flat.

Fig. 62. Some Navajos began making jewelry from copper and brass while they were interned at Bosque Redondo. They switched to silver shortly after being returned to their reservation. The style of this heavy old piece is much simpler than modern silver versions, and the naja has domed pennies on its horns. *Collection, Mary Lou Stribling.*

46

Fig. 63. Navajo silver bracelet and squash blossom necklace. Credit for setting the first piece of turquoise in silver has been given to "Ugly Smith," who made a turquoise ring in 1880. *Courtesy, The M. H. De Young Memorial Museum.*

Hopi smiths use turquoise sparingly, and their most popular style was developed after 1930. This is an overlay technique in which two sheets of silver are laminated by solder. The upper sheet is perforated with cutout designs that are brought into prominence by chemically blackening the exposed areas of the foundation sheet.

Fig. 64. Navajo necklace with sand-cast cross. Navajo molds for casting silver were carved in pumice, or other soft stone, and bound against a flat capstone. The mold was filled with molten silver, and the cast form was refined and polished with abrasives. Rings and bracelets were cast flat and bent into shape after they were finished.

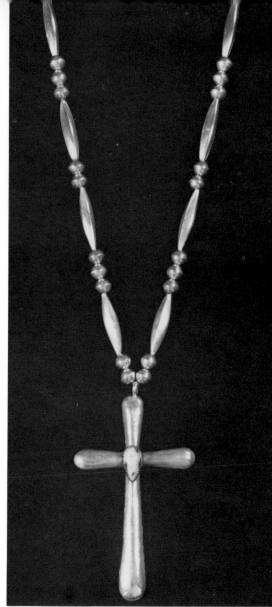

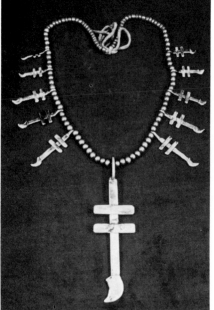

Fig. 65. Old pueblo necklace. A beautiful combination of brass trade beads and silver double-barred crosses. Brick red "Cornaline d' Aleppo" glass beads, also known as "Early Hudson's Bay" trade beads, are added at the back of the necklace. *Photo, Cloyd Sorensen, Jr.*

Silversmithing is a complex art that is obviously beyond the scope of this book, but Indian silver designs lend themselves to other materials.[8] Indians also used many found metal objects as ornaments, such as small bells, buttons, thimbles, and coins, and often combined them with assorted trade beads.

[8] The mosaicked cross in Fig. 28 was inspired by the necklace in Fig. 65. The necklaces in Figs. 49 and 66 borrowed certain elements of silver squash blossoms.

This same concept of using ordinary materials in unordinary ways distinguishes some of the best contemporary jewelry, and we have many choices that were not available to the Indians—brass and steel washers, metal friction rings, gears, clock parts, and other attractive hardware. They can add the element of surprise to what might otherwise be a stereotyped product, and they can seldom be planned on paper. It is better to freely shift them about on a table until a combination looks promising, then make several experimental strings before attempting a permanent piece. It is easier to adjust the lengths of necklaces if they are worked from the centers out.

Coins are soft enough to perforate with a drill—hand or electric. Make a slight indentation first with a nail or impact punch to keep the drill from slipping. Buff away burrs that could cut the suspension threads.

Old metal buttons can often be found in Salvation Army and Goodwill outlets. Buttons that are slightly cupped, such as those in the necklace in Fig. 66, are especially interesting to work with, and add a certain fluidity to designs.

Fig. 66. The lower necklace combines pennies, cupped brass buttons, small bronze beads, agate beads, and beads made from driftwood twigs about 5/8″ thick. The engraved designs were made with a wood-burning tool. For stringing the eucalyptus seeds in the upper necklace, tiny screw eyes were twisted through drops of epoxy into the tops of the seeds and allowed to dry. The seeds were then rubbed with wood stain, and the insides of the cups were painted turquoise. They were strung on a leather bootlace with white and turquoise beads, chrome spacers, and Indian tin cones.

Fig. 67. Unusual necklace from coins, tusks, and glass trade beads, excavated in northern Arizona. Most of the coins are large copper cents, the earliest legible date being 1825. Holes are crudely punched, and the edges are scalloped. The tusks have recently been identified as alligator teeth from Florida, further proof of the distance trade materials often traveled. *Photo, Cloyd Sorensen, Jr.*

Fig. 68. Pendant designs adapted from Indian ornaments. A. Southwestern shell beads. B and C. Southeastern copper ornaments. D. Zuñi mosaic inlays. E. Eskimo ivory engravings. F. California "banjo" abalone pendants. G. Plains silverwork. H. Navajo najas.

3

NETS AND BASKETS

In 1579 a small party of English explorers led by Francis Drake sailed cautiously through the fog along northern California, searching for a break in the rocky coast that might be a passage to the Atlantic. They were forced ashore to repair the ship, and with considerable apprehension, fortified themselves against a hostile reception by the natives of the land.

For a time the natives watched with equal apprehension, wondering if the aliens were gods, or ghosts. But like other forest creatures that are as curious as they are timid, they gradually came out of their hiding places, bringing exquisite nets, baskets, and feathers as signs of friendliness.

Fletcher, Drake's lieutenant, recorded that the baskets were shaped like deep bowls with decorations of shell disk beads and abalone shell pendants. Designs of colored feathers were worked into the fibers, and they were woven so tightly that they would hold water. Even the crown of their leader was a netted construction, perfectly interwoven with feather designs that appeared to have some special significance.

These were the Miwoks, whom Fletcher describes as "people of a tractable, free, and loving nature, without guile or treachery." Basketry and netmaking were their greatest arts, and the gifts they gave the men who claimed their lands for Queen Elizabeth were their most treasured possessions.

Evidently the Miwoks had little, if any, further foreign contact until the Spaniards explored San Francisco Bay in 1775. The diary of Father Vicente Santa Maria documents nets and baskets that were like, or very similar to, those mentioned by Fletcher. Some hairnets were "made of their hair, in design and shape best described as like a horse's girth, though neater and decorated at intervals with very small white snail shells." Others were made of hemplike cord and very small feathers dyed a deep red.[1]

Over the next hundred years, the west was overrun by settlers and gold-hungry adventurers. The Miwoks were moved from their hills and forests into presidios and missions, where they worked and gradually died. Finally, nothing remained of the people or their fine nets and baskets except accounts in dusty journals, and scattered bones and ornaments in ancient burial grounds.

Fortunately the cultures of other netters and basketmakers were less fragile. Although products that have survived undoubtedly represent only a small fraction of what once existed, our craft heritage would be immeasurably poorer without them.

NETS

Netting is a form of utilitarian lacemaking that has been widely distributed throughout the world since ancient times. The netting strands may be arranged vertically, or horizontally, or they may radiate out from the center. Various techniques of knotting, tying, or wrapping may be used to interlace them into a weblike structure.

The fundamentals of many modern methods of netting, such as tatting, crocheting, knitting, and macramé, were known and practiced by American Indians years before machine-made bobbins, shuttles, and hooks were invented. They made simple, very elastic nets by looping strands together. A two-strand knot was used in a number of regions for forming the meshes of large animal snares and fish traps, carrying bags and slings, delicate crowns, and hairnets.

A net is easier to make than a basket, since it does not have to be self-supporting. The Indians used many of the same materials for both, but anything that is cordlike, or can be cut into strong pliant strips, can be turned into a net. String, soft rope, yarn, raffia, and plastic thongs are among popular modern materials.

Although the projects described here are easy and quick to make, the techniques can be applied to other materials for larger, more complex structures. For example, by using rope or strong nylon cord, the net in Fig. 73 could be adapted for a hammock.

LOOPED NETS
The style of the net in Fig. 70 dates back to the Basketmaker Culture in the

---

[1] John Galvin, ed., *The First Spanish Entry into San Francisco Bay, 1775* (San Francisco: John Howell-Books, 1971), pp. 25 and 31.

It is likely that the feathers Father Santa Maria identified as *dyed* red were actually scarlet woodpecker scalps. They were highly valued by California tribes, especially the Pomos. At night, nets were placed over nesting holes. Just before daybreak, the men set up a loud racket with clackers and other noisemakers, causing the startled birds to fly out blindly into the traps.

Southwest, about A.D. 400. Similar supports for delicate, low-fired clay pots were made from twisted plant fibers, often yucca.

Select a container with an indented rim or shoulder. Draw around the bottom to make a paper pattern. Cut out the pattern, fold it in half, then in quarters, then in eighths. Unfold, and tape it to a scrap of leather and trace around the outline. With a nail or large needle, perforate a hole on each fold line, ⅜" in from the edge.

Remove pattern and enlarge the holes with a nail or awl. Cut out the disk and use glue or double-stick carpet tape to attach it to the bottom of the container. Twist a strong rubber band tightly above the shoulder, or in the rim indentation. Cut a strand of artificial raffia about 4½ yards long, dampen it slightly, and string it between the rubber band and holes in the leather disk as described in Fig. 69.

Figs. 69–70. SIMPLE LOOPED NET

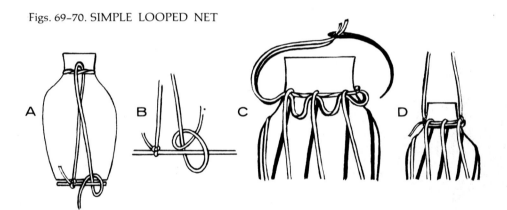

Fig. 69A. Cut a leather disk to fit the bottom of a container, and perforate the edge with 8 equally spaced holes. Fasten it to the container. Thread raffia in a curved upholstery needle, bring through a hole in the leather, and tie. Carry raffia up under the rubber band at the top, then down through the next hole in the leather. Pull taut, without stretching the rubber band. The raffia will shrink slightly as it dries.
B. Tie a firm knot, then carry raffia back under the rubber band. Continue until you return to the starting point. Tie ends together; brush white glue on the knot. Trim ends to 1", and push out of sight under the container.
C. Cut a strand of raffia about 3 yards long and tie the center to a top loop. Thread both ends in the needle and go through other loops around the container. Tie tightly. Clip and remove rubber band. Adjust loops until they are evenly spaced, then carry raffia through them again, and tie.
D. Knot end of raffia through the opposite loop to make a hanger. Brush knots with white glue and allow to dry before clipping ends short.

Fig. 70. The style of simple nets like this goes back nearly 2,000 years, but it is still useful for making hanging containers from bottles, jars, and pottery.

NET SLINGS

Along with nets that were strictly utilitarian, California tribes made feathered dance aprons with net foundations very similar to Figure 73. The strands were tied to a strip that fastened around the waist. Large turkey feathers were attached in each knot by shaving the quills to sharp points, then folding the ends over the cords and down into the hollow shafts, like safety pins. The feathers were arranged to overlap so that the net was completely covered.

You may have little need for a turkey feather apron. The basic sling, however, makes an unusual suspension for pots and bowls.

The meshes are formed by alternating square knots, so an even number of strands are required. Sixteen to eighteen are enough for medium-sized bowls. The instructions here are for a large bowl 10″ in diameter.

Tape two or three sheets of graph paper to a celotex board. At the top of the paper, set a row of 10 T pins, 1″ apart. Cut 20 strands of jute, or heavy twine, 40″

long. Tie one end of the bundle in an overhand knot and pin it to the board about 3″ above the middle pins on the graph paper. Separate strands into pairs, and tie each in a square knot under a pin.

Set a second row of pins 1″ below the first and halfway in between so that the knots will alternate. Tie together one strand from each of the previous knots, leaving the outer strands dangling. Space and tie the third row like the first. This will bring the outer strands back into the mesh.

Continue until the net is 20″ to 22″ long, then remove it from the board and untie the supporting knot. The net will be springy, and an extra pair of hands will be useful for making it into a sling. Finish as shown in Figures 71–73.

Figs. 71–73. NET SLING

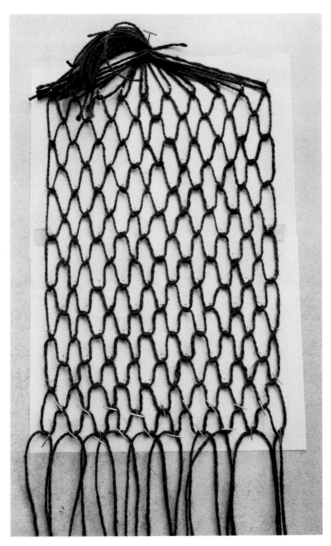

Fig. 71. Many tribes made nets with simple alternating knots. Functional snares and carrying slings were left plain. Hairnets and ceremonial accessories were lavishly decorated with shells, beads, and feathers. Tape graph paper to a Celotex board as a guide for spacing the knots. Tie knots under T pins to keep the tension of individual meshes consistent.

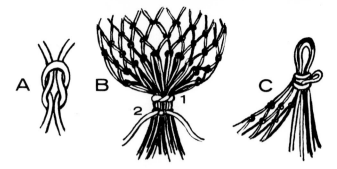

Fig. 72A. Use square knots for forming the meshes.

B. When the net is long enough, remove it from the board, gather the strands of each end into flat bundles, and twist rubber bands around them close to the knots (1). Dampen the jute slightly and stretch it over the back of the bowl. Pull the end of each strand in turn until the net is shaped to the bowl. The knots on the outer edges will be drawn closer to the rubber bands than those in the center. Tie lengths of jute tightly around the bundles just beneath the rubber bands (2).

C. Clip and remove rubber bands. Bring net ends over the ties to form a loop. Wrap ties around each bundle several times, and carry ends into the loose strands. Trim tassels evenly.

Fig. 73. To add feathers in the tassels, strip off the down, dip quill ends in white glue, and push them up between the jute strands. Rooster feathers are used in this example.

BRAIDED NETS

Nets can be made from braided strands by dividing and subdividing them at intervals to alternate the braided segments.

To make the net in Figure 75, cut 6 strands of white, yellow ochre, and black acrylic or cotton rug yarn, 3 yards long. Separate them into two equal bundles. Attach the center of each strand to a small café curtain ring with a Lark's Head knot.[2] You will then have six working strands of each color on each ring.

[2] A Lark's Head knot is shown in Chapter 2.

Hang the ring on a nail or hook, preferably in a doorway or similar spot where all sides will be accessible. Separate the colors of one bundle and braid them for 18″. Twist a plant tie or soft wire around the bottom of the braid to hold the strands together, then braid the other bundle to match.

Continue as shown in Figures 74 and 75.

Figs. 74, 75. BRAIDED NET

Fig. 74A. Braid 2 bundles of rug yarn for 18″, and secure with a plant tie.
B. Twist a second set of plant ties 2″ down from the first.
C. Separate strands into colors, braid each for 3″, and tie. You will then have 3 small braids of 6 strands on each side.
D. Drop down 2″, take 3 strands from each braid, bring them together with 3 strands from the adjacent braid, and tie.
E. Braid 3″ and tie.
F. Drop down 2″ again, subdivide, and tie.
G. Braid 3″ and tie. The net is now completed except for joining all the strands at the bottom.

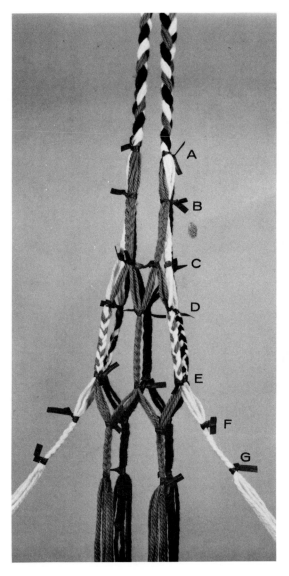

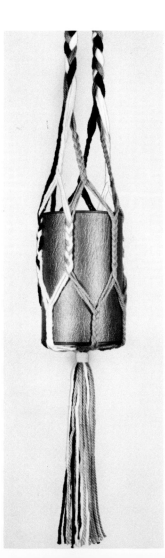

Fig. 75. Bind ends together with a length of yarn, and set a container in the net to adjust the meshes evenly. Wrap the yarn tie several times around the bundle, and trim strands into a long tassel. The container shown here is a coffee can covered with Naugahyde.

BEADED NETS

The netting strands in Figure 76 radiate from a center point, and they are joined together by wooden beads. Since no knots are used, the netting material must be fairly thick and resilient so that it can be firmly compacted in the bead holes. Otherwise, the beads would slide out of position. Cotton, wool, or acrylic rug yarns are better choices than twine or other tightly twisted cords.

Cut 8 strands of yarn about 2 yards long. Fold each in half, and use a Lark's Head knot to fasten the centers around a small café curtain ring. Bend a 4″ length of fine jeweler's wire in half to make a needle. (A in Figure 76.) String 8 pairs of strands through wooden beads and draw them close to the ring. String the next row of beads about ½″ from the first, using 1 strand from each of 2 adjacent beads. Continue alternating the strands in this way to form diamond-shaped meshes. Gradually increase spaces between rows ½″ to 1″ at the time.

The pattern can be changed at intervals by stringing several beads on the strands instead of one. When the body of the net is large enough, reduce the working strands down to a bundle on each side as described in Figure 77.

Figs. 76, 77. SIMPLE BEADED NET

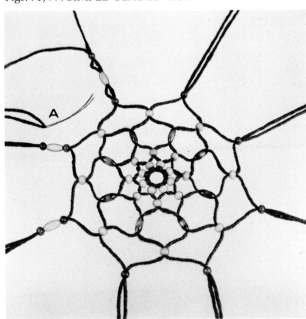

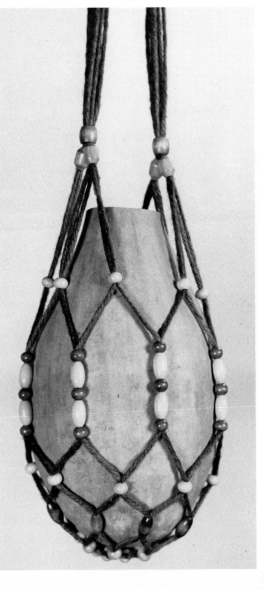

Fig. 76. Tie the centers of 8 strands of cotton rug yarn around a small café curtain ring, and string pairs through wooden beads. Separate strands so that the beads on the next row will fall in between those on the first. Work 5 or 6 rows, then change the pattern by stringing 3 to 6 beads on the same pair of threads.

Fig. 77. Draw a strand from adjacent beads for forming the meshes of the next row, then bring bundles of 4 strands each through larger beads. You will then have 4 bundles of yarn. Bring them together in pairs, and draw each pair through a single large bead. At the top, tie all strands together into a soft tassel, and trim ends.

BEADED MACRAMÉ NETS

Some Indian baskets had spokes of grasses or other soft fibers. Since these would not stand upright, as would rigid materials, the baskets were woven upside down, often by hanging them from a low tree branch, or by supporting them on a post.

The same problem exists with certain kinds of nets, and the support shown in Figure 78 was used for several projects in this chapter.

Use a thick coil of floral clay to fasten a 22" length of ⅝" wood doweling in the center of a large can. Mix plaster of Paris with water to form a thick batter, and pour it around the post until the can is about two-thirds full. When it is hard, slip a long-necked bottle over the post.

Large bottles will slide about on a dowel of this size, but you can tape strips of newspapers around it until a tight fit is obtained. Fasten the center of the net to the bottom of the bottle with double-stick carpet tape, or floral clay. The bottle can be turned as the work progresses.

To make the net in Figure 80, cut a pressed board disk ½" larger in diameter than the bottom of the container. Drill 32 equally spaced holes around the disk, ¼" in from the edge. Sand the board smooth, and finish with paint or stain.

Cut 16 lengths of cord or yarn 6' long. Fold each in half and thread ends through adjacent holes as shown in Figure 79 A. The net can be supported during construction on any kind of bottle as long as the bottom of the bottle is not larger than the wooden disk. Secure the disk temporarily to the bottle support with floral clay.

Start the net by tying each group of 4 adjacent strands in a macramé square knot. (See Chapter 2.) All other knots in the net are the same, but toward the top they are tied with 8 strands, then 16.

Use a bent-wire needle for stringing the beads. When you reach the point where a number of strands are drawn through a single bead, it may be necessary to thread only two at a time through the hole.

Figs. 78–80. BEADED MACRAMÉ NET

Fig. 78. A bottle support for working nets and soft warp baskets upside down can be made from ⅜" doweling secured in a large can with plaster of Paris.

Fig. 79A. Thread ends of each strand through adjacent holes in the wooden base. Separate into 8 groups of 4 strands each, and knot.

B. Working one group at a time, thread a bead on the 2 center strands, bring outer strands around it, and knot all 4 strands. Continue for 3 beads.

C. Divide strands into pairs and string 3 beads on each. Bring adjacent pairs together and knot. You are now back to 8 groups of strands. Knot 3 beads on each . . .

D. . . . Then bring adjacent groups together and tie in an 8 strand square knot, making 4 groups of strands. Continue the sequence of knots and beads for about 8", then bring groups together in pairs and draw through large beads.

E. Remove net from the support, and knot ends of loose strands together about 8" from the last bead, leaving one strand on each side free. Suspend the net and bind the strands into smooth ropes with the loose cords. Near the top, draw the wrapping strand through the rope to secure it, and clip short.

Fig. 80. The net will shape itself of almost any kind of container, including bottles, pots, or large bowls.

BASKETS

The basic techniques of basketmaking are used in many other Indian arts. Coiled pottery evolved from methods of making coiled baskets, and every weaving technique from simple braiding to the most complex loomed textile is founded on some principle of basketry.[3] This includes woven and netted beadwork.

We cannot be certain when or where the art first appeared in North America. We do know it existed very early. It is possible that the idea of woven containers originated from birds' nests, though many animals also build nests from fur and grasses, and certain kinds of fish tangle seaweed into barricades to protect their territories. The structural patterns of insect webs and cocoons might have been other sources for the rudiments of three-dimensional weaving.

As basketry evolved from crude nets and mats to sophisticated forms that were visual treats as well as household necessities, the act of making them acquired the aura of mystique that has always surrounded aesthetic creativity. It was practiced almost exclusively by women, particularly older women whose energies were no longer absorbed by small children. They took their work seriously, conscientiously observing the traditions and taboos that were related

[3] Most modern Indian basketmakers prefer to be called "weavers."

Fig. 81. Alaskan baskets of this style are distinguished by very thin walls and fine twining, and were usually woven with split spruce roots. Designs were made by "false embroidery," in which a third strand of colored grass or fern stems was carried along with the basic weavers. Areas of lacy eyeholes were made by crisscrossing the spokes and twining a row of weavers through the intersections. This old Tlingit basket is 7" high, 8" in diameter. *Collection, Helen Irish.*

to every phase of production.

Baskets were intimately associated with the most important stages of human life: birth, puberty, marriage, and death. In many tribes, baskets that represented a woman's most supreme accomplishments were burned with her physical remains at her funeral, possibly from the hope that their gentle spirits would accompany her to the next world.

And who can say that they did not.

Figs. 82, 83. Aleutian women made the most delicate American baskets. The upright elements were flexible grasses, and the baskets were woven upside down. Designs were made with silk threads, and the texture is so refined that it resembles petit point, yet this was a winter art, worked by the dim, flickering light of oil lamps. It is no longer practiced, and existing specimens are rare. *Collection, Nevada State Historical Society.*

SELECTING MATERIALS

The emphasis in this chapter is on basket containers, though the broad definition of basketry can include sculptural forms and textiles. But making a simple bowl will provide you with the educational tools for exploring other basket forms. Once they are familiar, you will be equipped to move in any other direction that piques your imagination.

Nothing that could possibly be useful or decorative escaped the Indian basketmakers' attention, and from the standpoint of variety alone, even a brief glimpse at their methods of harvesting and processing native materials is over-whelming. Certain fundamentals are consistent, however, and entirely logical.

Understand first that a basket is composed of two structural units. One is the framework, the other binds the framework together. Except for soft baskets, the framework materials should be sturdy and capable of holding a shape, while the

Figs. 84, 85. Old Yokut coiled baskets with willow rod foundations. Willow strips were used for weaving the white areas; brown areas were redbud bark. For black details, split roots were dyed with walnut shells. The large bowl has a whirlwind design. The smaller basket has double bands of the rattlesnake pattern, and is trimmed with quail tufts. *Collection, Rolfe Ockenden.*

binding materials must be flexible enough to bend or wrap without breaking.

In some cases, they can be the same. For the most part, however, you will use two or more different materials in a single basket, perhaps even combining commercial products with those you process yourself.

Contemporary Indian weavers do not hesitate to substitute modern for traditional materials, as long as the decorative effect remains consistent. Though they may continue to use roots and grasses for the exposed weavers, many now choose rattan instead of willow for the concealed framework.

Among materials that have been used since earliest times are sedge roots, bulrushes, willow branches, oak splints, cornhusks, cornstalks, cattails, bear grass, sweet grass, rice stems, fern roots and stems, spruce roots, pine needles, sea grass, yucca fibers, palmetto and palm fronds, cedar bark, honeysuckle vines, redbud bark, and incredibly, poison oak, which I do not recommend.

But even without access to rural areas, you can make baskets from yarn, rope, raffia, string, commercial cane and rattan, broomstraw, twisted crepe paper, discarded nylon stockings, raveled burlap, or strips of fabric. In other words, there are no rules against any combinations that achieve the effect you want.

PREPARING MATERIALS

Though it takes time to collect and prepare native materials, the task is greatly satisfying. Proper drying is very important since organic matter shrinks as moisture evaporates from the tissues. If it is used too soon, the walls of the basket will eventually loosen and fall apart.[4] These fibers swell again when they are soaked in water, and the same problem can be caused by oversoaking.

The Indian basketmaker never dips her basket in water nor allows her weavers to become soggy. She keeps the working strands flexible by moistening them regularly with her fingers, and fits the movement of her hand to and from the bowl of water into the total rhythmic pattern of weaving.

A few of the most common basketry materials to collect, grow, or buy are described here. Instructions for processing can be applied to others that have similar physical characteristics.

Processing Materials

Sedge and Bulrush Roots

Bulrush roots are brownish, and Indians usually dyed them with walnut shells to make black designs. They grow in marshy areas and harvesting may require pulling them from under the water. They are processed like sedge roots.

Preparing sedge roots can be a test of your patience, but they are worth the trouble. They are tough, extremely pliable, and have a beautiful texture.

---

[4] On certain kinds of baskets, yucca, palmetto, palm, and coconut fronds can be used green.

The so-called roots are actually rhisomes—long, horizontal, underground stems that send out sprouts on the top side; true roots on the bottoms. Usable segments are in between the two terminals, and average lengths are 15″ to 3′ or more.

Sedges grow along sandy borders of streams and the roots can be gathered at any time. Fall is preferable to spring since they will have reached a full season's growth, and will have fewer shoots. Pomos avoid digging from late spring to fall because of the danger of snakes. The policy is recommended, even for non-Pomos.

The roots grow straighter where the sedges are thinned by regular harvesting. Pointed stakes, trowels, gardening forks, and other digging tools are useful for loosening the sand around the plants. You will usually reach a scaly brown root a few inches below the surface. Dig a trench and follow its horizontal path to obtain a segment as long as possible. Often you will uncover several in a single trench. Cut them away and place in a plastic bag.

Before they get dry, start at the tip (smallest) end, and strip away the outer bark. (Indian women expose the white core, secure it between their teeth, and peel the bark downward with their fingers in a rapid, graceful movement.)

Make a split in the tip and open it gradually until the root is halved. If you keep the split centered, it will follow the natural growth of the fibers. If not, it will peel to one side and you will be left with short strands.

Tie roots into loose coils with an identifying date, and store in a cool, dry place. They must cure for at least a year.

At this point, they will be sorry-looking things—twisted, knotty, and rough. Soak a strand at a time in water for about 15 minutes, stretch them to straighten out the kinks, and trim off shredded, fibrous tips. Working from the stem end, start reducing the thickness by peeling off thin layers of the inner core, in long pieces if possible. These are called "culls," and can be used for the central knot in a Pomo coiled basket. Indian women make the initial split with a knife, hold the opposite end between their teeth, and separate the fibers by pushing upward against the break with one hand, while the other pulls downward to keep the V of the split narrow. A narrow V is the secret of successful splitting.

You can also thin the roots by scraping away excess inner wood with a sharp knife, though this destroys the culls.

Since roots taper from stem end to tip, you must trim the edges to make a strand even in width. Use a very sharp knife and trim with the grain, not against it. Pare away any nodes, then run the strand between your fingers to find thick places, and work them down. It should be scarcely thicker than construction paper.

Indian weavers polish prepared roots with shredded culls. You can also draw them several times through a wad of nylon net or a nylon burnishing pad. Taper the stem ends to blunt points to use as needles.

The roots can be dyed to make contrasting patterns.

When you are ready to weave, resoak a root for a few minutes and keep it flexible thereafter by stripping it between moistened fingers as you work. If it is kept wet for too long, it will turn dark. The flat side goes against the foundation rod.

Redbud

Redbud trees are widely distributed over the United States, and the glossy, mahogany brown bark has been used for contrasting patterns in baskets by many tribes. October, November, and December are the best months for harvesting. At that time the branches have matured, yet the wood has not hardened to the point of brittleness.

Cut the bark, plus a thin layer of white wood, in long strips from the branches. Tie the strips into coils, store, and cure for a year as described for sedge roots.

The dried strips are very tough and must be soaked for several hours before they are thinned and trimmed. Oversoaking, however, may cause the brown bark to peel away from the strip. If this should happen, the white strand can still be refined and used for stitching.

The refining process is the same as for sedge roots with one important difference. You must slant your knife toward the woody side when trimming the edges; otherwise the thread will have a white border, like apple peelings.

No protective finish is necessary on baskets made from sedge, willow, bulrush, or redbud, and similar materials. From time to time wash them with castile soap and warm water to remove dust and freshen the fibers.

Figs. 86–91. PROCESSING SEDGE ROOTS AND REDBUD BARK

Fig. 86. "Sedges have edges" goes an old rhyme, and one way to identify the plant is to draw your hand gently along the slender blades. A sedge will feel rough in one direction, smooth in the other. Sedges grow around creek banks, but rocky areas are difficult to dig. Look for sandy spots.

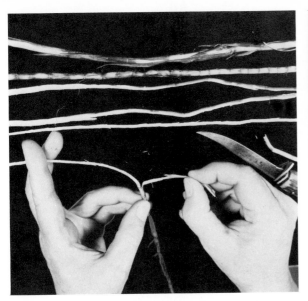

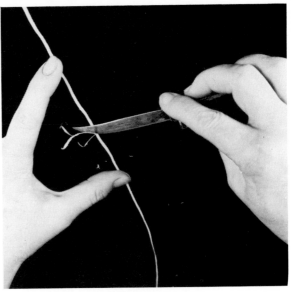

Fig. 87. Peel off the scaly bark while the roots are fresh. (The two at the top have not been stripped.) Split the roots in half vertically, and cure for at least a year.

Fig. 88. After soaking a cured strand for about 15 minutes, peel away the inner wood to reduce some of the thickness. Further refinements can be done with a knife.

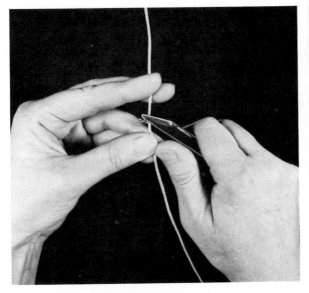

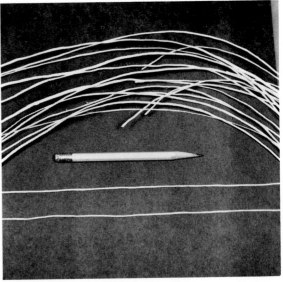

Fig. 89. Working with the grain, pare edges and nodes until the strand is perfectly even in width. It should remain the same throughout the basket. About 1/16" to 1/8" is average, though many California baskets have threads no wider than embroidery floss.

Fig. 90. Cured, unrefined roots are shown at the top. The two at the bottom are ready to use. The pencil indicates comparable sizes.

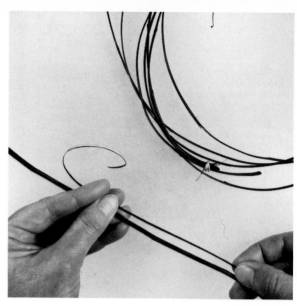

Fig. 91. Redbud bark is refined the same way, except that edges are slanted toward the back side to eliminate white borders. Compare the width of the upper refined strand with the untrimmed strip at the bottom.

Agapanthus Stems

Agapanthus, commonly called lily-of-the-Nile, is a sturdy perennial that is popular for commercial landscaping as well as home gardens. By late fall to early winter the seeds have developed and the thick stems are hard, hollow, and light tan in color.

Cut the dried stems as long as possible and snip off seed heads. Spread them on newspapers and store in a dry, cool place for several months.

Soak cured stems in warm water for about an hour, then split them in half vertically with a sharp knife. Subdivide the halves into 3 or 4 strips, according to your preference, then resoak them a short time.

Remove the slippery outer membrane with a paper towel or wad of nylon net, scrape away the pith, and trim edges as described for sedge roots. Much less trimming is required, however. You can quickly obtain smooth, fine-textured ivory-colored weavers.

When you are ready to work, soften them in a solution of 2 parts glycerin and 10 parts water. Use the solution thereafter to keep the strands moist.

Pine Needles

Gather needles in the fall as soon as they drop to the ground and spread them out on newspapers to dry for several weeks. Tie the dried needles into neat bundles with boot ends together, and store in plastic bags.

Needles 8″ to 12″ long are best, since coils need not be spliced as frequently as those made with shorter lengths.

Pine needles change color as they age. If they are cured in the sun, they turn red brown. Cooler browns are obtained in the shade. Many basketmakers like to expose their finished baskets to bright sunlight for a few weeks to fully develop the color.

When you are ready to work, soak needles in warm water for about an hour, then pull away the boots with a quick twist and roll the needles in a damp towel. (For shaggy effects, the boots can be left on, but this was not traditional with Indians.) Soften only what you can use in a single day. They will rot or mildew if kept damp too long.

A protective finish for pine needle baskets is recommended. Brush inside and outside surfaces with 2 coats of shellac diluted with alcohol, dull sheen varnish thinned with turpentine, or a solution of 1 part matt acrylic medium and 1 part water.[5]

Broomstraw

It may be difficult to find broom corn in its natural state, though bundles of cleaned, trimmed straw can sometimes be purchased from small companies that manufacture kitchen brooms. An inexpensive broom, however, can provide you with enough material to make several small baskets or table mats. It needs no further processing for a bundle foundation, and can be handled like pine needles. It does require more soaking. Small coils are easiest to handle, and the greenish golden color is particularly handsome with raffia stitching.

New Zealand Flax, Yucca, Palmetto, Palm, and Similar Fronds

Although palms are native to tropical and subtropical climates, they are surprisingly adaptable, and domesticated varieties have become widespread over North America. Yucca is abundant in desert states, but is also cultivated in home gardens where temperatures do not get too low. These, and similar fronds, can be harvested at any time. The longer fronds are usually the best, but young fronds have a finer texture. Even brown or yellowed leaves that have dried on the tree can be used if they are not too discolored or brittle.

Trim off ragged ends and hang the fronds upside down by the stems to dry for several weeks. For bundle foundations, shred them fine with a pin from central rib to tips. For stitching threads, split into wider strips, then trim into even widths with scissors. Soften in water and scrape away some of the fiber from the back sides.

Discard tough edges and ribs.

When you are ready to work, soak the strips for about 30 minutes, then roll in a damp towel for several hours or overnight. This allows the tissues to become moist, without absorbing too much water. (The glycerin solution noted earlier is also good for frond stitching strands.)

[5] See "Supply Sources" in the Appendix for a mail order source for pine needles.

It is best to dye these materials after they have been processed, since light fibers will be exposed on trimmed edges. Fast color fabric dyes can be used. Heat dye bath to just below the boiling point. Immerse a few strands at a time, stir until they begin to absorb color, then remove from the heat and let them soak until the water is cold. Rinse thoroughly.

Figs. 92–97. PROCESSING OTHER NATURAL MATERIALS

Fig. 92. Soak dried agapanthus stems for about an hour. Split them into equal strips and resoak until the pith and slippery outer membrane can be scraped away. Refine the strips as described for sedge roots.

Fig. 93. Harvest pine needles as soon as they drop to the ground. Soak only what can be used in a single day. Hold the tip of the boot in one hand; needles in the other. Make a quick twist, pulling at the same time, and the boot will slip off.

Fig. 94. Shred finely New Zealand flax, yucca, and similar fronds for bundle foundations. For a stitching material, trim strands to even widths with scissors, and scrape some of the fiber from the back side. Taper stem ends to use as a needle.

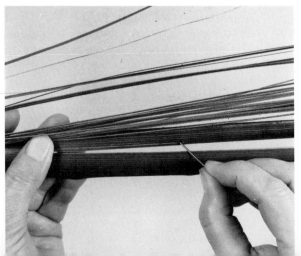

Fig. 95. Cut off hard tips and ragged stems of palm fronds. Make shredded bundle foundations and stitching materials as described for flax.

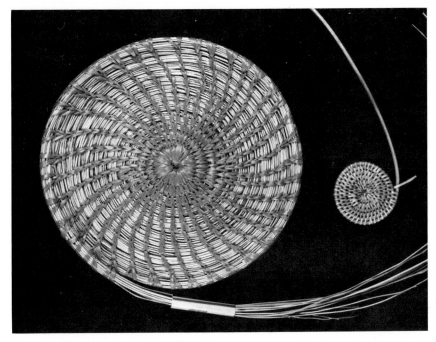

Fig. 96. The bundle foundation of the larger basket under construction is broomstraw. Raffia is used for stitching. Split broomstraw, softened in glycerin, is the stitching material for the base of the single rod miniature.

Fig. 97. Inexpensive rice straw and sea grass mats can be unraveled to obtain fibers for coiled bundles, or for forming the central knot in a Pomo-style basket. Freshen fibers in water before using.

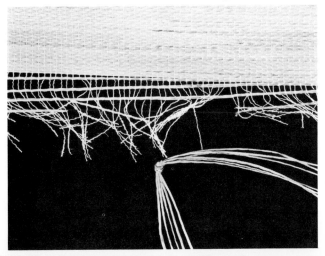

Rattan Reeds

Center cane reeds (or rods) are the cores of long shoots from the rattan palm. They are commonly used for plaited wicker baskets, and make superior foundations for coiled baskets. The most versatile sizes are #1 rod for fine coils, and #2 rod for larger coils.

If rods are to be exposed, polish them with fine sandpaper, steel wool, or a nylon burnishing pad. They can be dyed, or colored with wood stains.

Chair Cane

Chair cane and rattan reed are different parts of the same plant. When it is processed, the tough outer bark of the rattan shoot is discarded, and the long glossy skin, or cane, is peeled from the core in long strips. It can be combined with reeds for certain kinds of wicker baskets, and a few minutes spent on further refining the product are worthwhile, especially if you want to use it for stitching.

It is not as flexible as sedge roots, and has a hard surface that resists softening. It is also punctuated by joints that are easily broken if they are bent too sharply when the cane is dry. But with a little effort, these problems can be minimized, and since the cane is inexpensive and readily available, it deserves investigating.

For plaited baskets, trim away ragged fibers and draw it several times through a folded burnishing pad. To make superfine cane into a stitching material, soak it for an hour in warm water, then trim the edges with a knife so that they bevel back slightly from the glossy side. This can be done quickly, and will reveal the direction of the grain. The fibers peel toward the stem end, and this must serve as the needle. If you stitch from the opposite end, the edges will quickly ravel. Strip the cane between your fingers to find thick places and scrape them smooth on the underside.

Fold a strip of newspaper in half and slip in a small piece of paper toweling to protect the glossy side of the cane. Draw the cane through it several times from alternating directions. Buff with a burnishing pad, and soak for half an hour in the glycerin solution mentioned earlier.

It may be best to use another stitching material on the first few coils.

Raffia

Raffia is a leaf of the Madagascar palm. The stem end is thicker and wider than the tip, and this is threaded in the needle. All stitching materials are subjected to considerable abrasion, particularly those that involve a steel needle. From time to time, slide it up on the raffia about an inch to keep the foldback from becoming frayed.

You can also make the stem into its own needle by dipping it in white glue and twirling it to a point. When hard, it can penetrate holes opened through the foundation with an awl.

Split raffia into strands that are as equal in width as possible. Since a certain amount of tapering is unavoidable, trim away tips where they narrow noticeably. Most craftsmen prepare separate bundles that are graded by widths so that they can immediately select the size appropriate for a particular project. Even very fine threads can be put to good use.

The proper degree of dampness is determined more by feel than actual timing, and will require experimentation. Soak strands in warm water for a few minutes, then roll in a damp towel until moisture has penetrated the fibers evenly. When it is perfect for stitching, it can be drawn smoothly through the foundation. If it is too wet, it will drag. If it is too dry, it will be harsh, crinkly, and may squeak when the stitches are pulled tight.

DECORATIVE PATTERNS

Some Indian basket designs grew out of linear patterns that were automatically created when the materials were interlaced in various ways. Others were inspired by nature and traditional tribal symbols.

Many nature sources are recognizable, but when motifs have been abstracted from some small part of a shell, leaf, insect, bird, fish, reptile, or plant, the connection between the two may become evident only after the information is provided.

Pomo basketmakers had names for about twenty-six traditional designs, and the individual weaver usually combined several, or added special touches to make her work distinctive. Some names, such as "quail plume," "starfish," "grasshopper-elbow," "mosquito," and "bear foot," were related to the source of inspiration. More intricate designs, such as "design empty in the middle ants close in a row," and "arrowheads in the middle zigzag stripes," identified certain arrangements of motifs.

Names of designs may change from weaver to weaver over periods of many years until the original reference is completely forgotten. (A parallel can be found in the names of old patchwork quilt patterns that have been passed from one generation to the next.) To further confuse the picture, merchants and traders have been guilty of arbitrarily attaching magical powers to certain designs, hoping to make them more valuable to prospective customers. The late Tom Bahti dismissed such assumptions as "products of the white man's imagination." [6]

Crosses appear in almost all the Indian arts and have been given various meanings, including a crossing of trails, a star, or a battle. The swastika cross is one of the oldest symbols in the history of man, and was known in ancient Egypt and India, as well as in many primitive cultures. It is a common symbol on

[6] Tom Bahti, *Southwestern Arts and Crafts* (Flagstaff: K. C. Publications, 1966), p. 3.

Apache baskets and Navajo rugs, and was also painted on the walls of cave dwellers, who had vanished from America countless years before it was "rediscovered" by Spaniards.

Except where baskets figure in religious ceremonies and the symbolic

Fig. 98. DESIGNS FROM ALASKAN BASKETS
Tlingit women sometimes wove realistic motifs into their baskets, but they are best known for frets, zigzags, and other geometrics. Arrangements of triangles in the three lower borders are called "Head of the Salmonberry" by some authorities. They are almost identical to certain California patterns, where they are called butterflies and arrowheads. Different styles of weaving, however, set them completely apart in character.

elements have remained consistent for some time, only the weaver herself can interpret an abstract pattern. It may mean nothing but that she found the arrangement of colors appealing. On the other hand, it may have a highly personal significance that is too intimate to discuss with an outsider.

Fig. 99. The simple cross, and its many variations, is probably the most universal design element in Indian arts. These old Alaskan baskets were woven with very flexible materials and had to be closely compacted to make a firm structure. Like the Aleuts, Haida and Tlingit women wove them upside down. In late periods, Tlingit weavers sometimes temporarily stitched firm cardboard to the bases to keep them flat. *Collection, Helen Irish.*

Fig. 100. LARGE APACHE STORAGE BASKET

The Apaches used realistic subjects on their baskets, as well as geometric shapes and crosses. Romanticists are fond of speculating on ways the swastika cross might have been passed from one culture to another, but it is more realistic to assume that it appeared spontaneously, like other forms of cross designs. *Collection, The Millicent A. Rogers Memorial Museum.*

Figs. 101, 102. COILED TULARE BOTTLENECK BASKET

The borders on the sides of this large, elaborately patterned basket are typical among several tribes of California and Nevada, but decorations on the shoulder and neck are so unusual that we can only speculate on their meanings.

Some of the letters on the neck are arranged upside down or sideways, suggesting that they were copied from a billboard or newspaper, and used simply as designs, without regard for literary significance.

Large scarablike beetles around the shoulder dominate the tiny human figures between them. At the lower left, a figure and a beetle are joined, as though they are making some mysterious journey together. *Collection, Rolfe Ockenden.*

Fig. 103. The figures on this beautiful Yokut basket have the stylized simplicity of paper doll cutouts. It was made before 1890 from willow and redbud. *Collection, Rolfe Ockenden.*

Fig. 104. FIGURE DESIGNS ADAPTED FROM CALIFORNIA/NEVADA BASKETS
Bands of alternating male and female figures are called "friendship" designs in some tribes. In others, the pattern is related to ceremonial dances. Representations of human figures were taboo among traditional Pomo weavers.

77

Fig. 105. This is an exceptionally fine old Apache tray with a classic star, or flower design. *Photographed by permission of the Millicent A. Rogers Memorial Museum.*

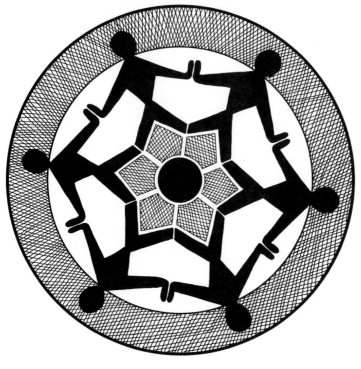

Fig. 106. Contemporary versions of western basket designs can be used for appliqué, needlepoint, embroidery, or rugmaking.

Fig. 107. These designs can also be painted on woven mats and baskets. Northwest Coast hats and textiles were often painted to reproduce the curving lines of totemic designs that could not be obtained with weaving.

Fig. 108. *Left:* Origins of designs from butterflies, cacti, and other plants are sometimes clearly evident, as illustrated by these motifs from California and Nevada. *Right:* In other cases, designs have been so abstracted that sources are obscure unless a basketmaker provides a clue. Here are two versions of the "quail tufts" pattern.

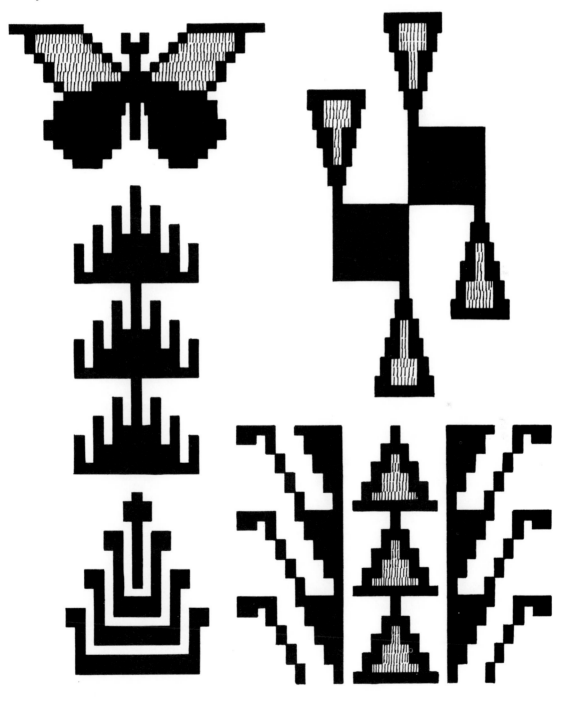

Fig. 109. Some butterfly designs only suggest the outline or decorative pattern of a wing. Others are highly stylized impressions of swarms of flying butterflies.

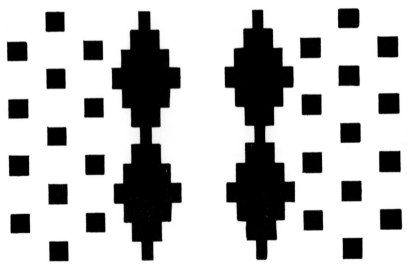

Fig. 110. Dat-So-La-Lee, the famous Washo (Nevada) basketmaker, gave this design the poetic name "Myriads of Stars Shine over the Graves of Our Ancestors."

Fig. 112. Basketry and textiles have common roots, and many of their designs are closely related, even though they might have been developed thousands of miles apart. These patterns are adapted from baskets, but similar motifs can be found on woven beadwork and Navajo rugs, as well as in Hungarian, Russian, and Czechoslovakian stitchery and weaving.

Fig. 111. Dat-So-La-Lee was one of the few basketmakers to attain national and international recognition during her lifetime. Her perfect forms and fine stitching set a standard of excellence that is admired all over the world. This basket, called "The Talisman," has a shape similar to old burden baskets. *Courtesy, The Nevada State Museum.*

BASKETMAKING TECHNIQUES

Woven Baskets

Indian basketry techniques can be loosely divided into two categories, woven and coiled, but there are many variations in each group.

Plaited and twined baskets are the most common forms in the woven class. Although their vertical and horizontal parts can quite accurately be called warp and weft, as are the lengthwise and crosswise threads of woven textiles, every craft has its own language, and it is less confusing to use basketmakers' terms where they establish a clearer mental picture.

In this section, the framework parts are called *stakes, spokes,* or *splints,* when they consist of firm, resilient materials. They are called *warps* only when they are very flexible. The moving strands that interlace the framework are called *weavers.*

Plaited and twined baskets can be started alike and finished alike. Both involve the same problems of splicing the weavers, and increasing or decreasing the spokes to make the form larger or smaller.

Starting a basket is the hardest part, for you are faced with a handful of unruly spokes that must be attached together in some fashion before the weaving can begin. Two of the easiest methods are shown in Fig. 113.

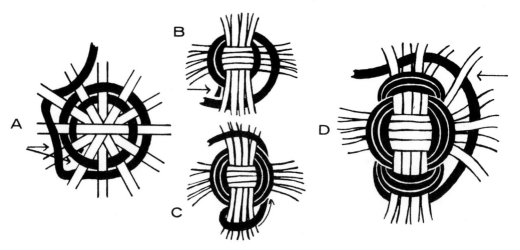

Fig. 113. STARTING PLAITED OR TWINED BASKETS

Method #1 A. Crisscross the centers of flat splints and hold together with your left hand. Tuck a weaver under a spoke, and weave over alternate spokes until you are back at the starting point. Go over two spokes (see arrows) before making the next spiral. For plaited baskets, wedge an extra spoke through the center cross after three rounds. Adjust spacing, and continue weaving. The sequence will now remain consistent.

Method #2 B. Divide spokes into two flat equal bundles of three to six strands. Stack one on the other so that the centers cross at right angles. Hold together in your left hand and tuck, or tie, a weaver under the lower spokes (see arrow). Wind around the cross over the upper spokes for three rounds.

C. Reverse direction of the weaver and wind over alternate groups of spokes for three rounds.

D. Fan out spokes and weave as shown in A for several rounds, adjusting spacing evenly as you go. For plaiting, wedge an extra spoke (see arrow) in a corner so that the over/under sequence will remain consistent.

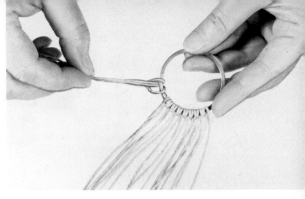

Fig. 114. Method #3. Soft warp baskets can be quickly started by tying the warps to small curtain rings or friction rings with Lark's Head knots.

Method #1 is most often used for flat, firm splints. Soft weavers must be tied or glued at the starting point. Method #2 can be used for either soft or rigid materials, but again, soft weavers must be tied on, or glued.

A controlled form is not necessarily symmetrical, but there is a great deal of difference between a basket that is accidentally lopsided and one that has been deliberately deformed for sculptural purposes. Shaping is not as mysterious and difficult as it might appear. Plaited and twined baskets are shaped primarily by the tension of the weavers. To curve walls inward, draw the spokes more tightly together. Clip out selected spokes at evenly spaced intervals if the weaving becomes too compacted. To curve walls outward, insert extra spokes to increase the circumference.

If your basket starts to lean, no amount of optimistic tugging will coax it back into symmetry. The only cure is to unwind the weaver back to the point where the shape became uneven, and try again.

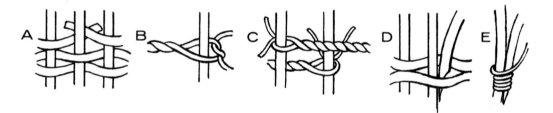

Fig. 115. SPLICING AND INCREASING
A. When you reach the end of a firm weaver, tuck it behind a spoke. Insert new weaver behind the same spoke and pack down. Clip off protruding ends on the inside when the basket is finished.
B. On a plaited basket, separate the strands of a soft weaver and tie around a spoke to be woven "over." Pull knot to the inside and tie again. Put a dab of white glue on the ends and push under the woven section. Tie new weaver above it and pack down. The ends will be concealed by the next row of weaving. Tie raffia and similar materials flat, without splitting.
C. On twined baskets, tie off soft weaver as in B. Tie new weaver on the preceding spoke and put a dab of glue on the knot. Plan splices so that they do not always occur on the same spoke. Where weavers are different colors, clip a few strands from an end of each, add a bit of glue and twist them firmly together. When dry, slip over a spoke and push end under the weaving.
D. As the circumference increases, sharpen ends of new spokes to tapering points, then at regular intervals, wedge them firmly into the woven "tunnels" beside existing spokes. To decrease, weave two spokes together for several rounds, then clip one off.
E. Additional soft warps can be tied on with glue and fine sewing thread.

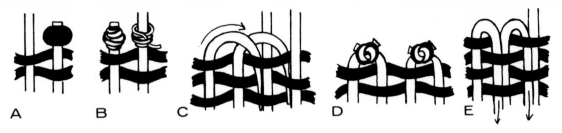

A B C D E

Fig. 116. FINISHING THE EDGE

A. Spread a drop of white glue on the spokes just above the last row of weaving. Thread spokes through wooden beads and clip short.

B. Spread glue on the spokes and wind knobs of yarn, cord, leather thongs, or other decorative materials around them. Feathers and dangles can be woven in at the same time.

C. Trim ends of firm spokes to tapering points. Carry in front of one or two adjacent spokes and wedge firmly into weaving tunnels.

D. If there is an even number of soft warps, they can be knotted in pairs and clipped short.

E. For the neat finish on many Indian baskets, thread soft warps in a curved upholstery needle and draw through adjacent tunnels. (Pliers may be needed to pull them through if the weaving is tight.) Taper ends and push out of sight with an awl.

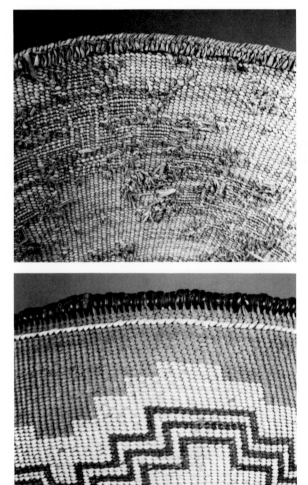

Fig. 117. The inside of this large burden basket reveals the labor involved in tying off and rejoining weavers of different colors to make an intricate twined design. The edge was finished by folding the spokes inward, stitching them down, and clipping the ends. Many baskets that were not intended for heavy use were finished by simply trimming the spokes evenly.

Fig. 118. This is a detail of a large milling basket used in the preparation of acorn meal. The spokes were trimmed, reinforced with a heavy rod, and bound tightly to make a strong, rigid rim. *Collection, Helen Irish.*

Left, top:
Hooked rug from old wool blankets, worked by Bessie Long. The design is a composite of elements from Navajo blankets.

Left, bottom:
Coiled mat and twined jute bottle, Mary Lou Stribling. The mat has Seminole/Papago basketry stitches, and the bottle design was made by Hoopa twining techniques.

Right, top:
Plaque with embroidered tin inlays, Mary Lou Stribling. The design was adapted from an old Mimbres bowl.

Right, bottom:
Left: painted gourd pendant, Mary Lou Stribling. *Right:* wooden cross decorated with split straws, Josie Ward Cox. Ornamental strawwork was brought to the upper Rio Grande Valley by Spanish artisans, and was practiced in a few Southwestern tribes, notably the Santa Ana.

◀ Necklaces, Mary Lou Stribling. *Left:* shell pendant mosaicked with eggshells after the style of old pueblo turquoise mosaics. *Center:* the large dentalium shells are painted with Carrier phonetic symbols, and the cone shell pendant has designs from Eskimo engravings. *Right:* painted beach stones, beads, and Indian tin cones.

▼ *Top:* clay owl and gourd pot, Mary Lou Stribling. *Bottom:* clay pot with water serpent design, Margaret and Luther Gutierrez, Santa Clara Pueblo.

◀ *Left:* earth painting, Pablita Velarde, Santa Clara Pueblo. *Right:* beaded hanging, Mary Lou Stribling.

◀ Patchwork bag, Mary Lou Stribling. The lower border was made by a Seminole patchwork technique. The palmetto fiber doll in traditional costume is from the Seminole reservation.

Petitpoint and embroidered pendants, ▶ Mary Lou Stribling. The same Acoma bird design was used for both techniques.

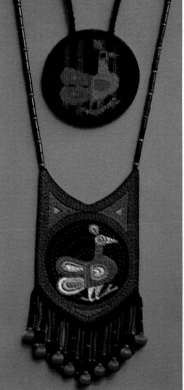

► Feathered macramé necklaces, Joan Sestak.

Very old and unusual examples of Apache beadwork. The doll-shaped awl case has hands and feet made with tin tinklers and horsehair. The pouch is attached like a locket to a long double-strand necklace of brass beads and 1½" bone hair pipes. Photo, Cloyd Sorensen, Jr.

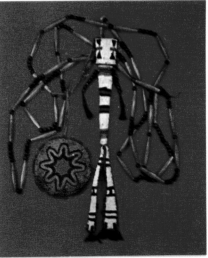

Necklaces, Mary Lou Stribling. *Left:* pennies, cupped brass buttons, small bronze beads, agate beads, and beads made from driftwood twigs engraved with a wood-burning tool. *Right:* sea urchin spines, antler tips, bone disk beads, mother-of-pearl chips, and agate beads.

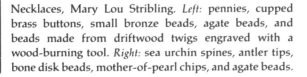

Tufted wool hanging, Mary Lou Stribling. The eagle design was adapted from an appliquéd Haida dance shirt.

Felt-on-felt appliquéd hanging, Mary Lou Stribling. The design derived from a hummingbird motif on a Zuñi pot. Photo, Rudy Muller.

Large multilayered woven hanging, Evelyn Gulick. The design was inspired by a dragonfly symbol on a Zuñi ceremonial vessel. Photo, Sidney Gulick.

Cotton weft brocade woven strip, 4" by 6½", Jacquetta Nisbet. The strip was woven on an inkle loom. Photo, artist.

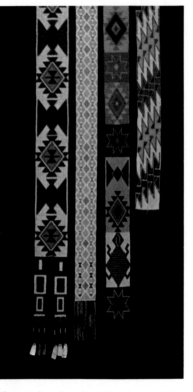

Plains beadwork. Courtesy, The Nevada State Museum.

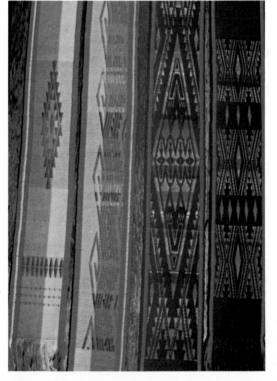

Cotton and wool brocade woven strips, 5½" by 6½", Jacquetta Nisbet. The designs were inspired by Southwestern textiles, and were woven on an inkle loom. Photo, artist.

Wool embroidered bag, Mary Lou Stribling. The design was adapted from Huron moosehair embroidery and beadwork. Photo, Rudy Muller. ▼

Top: wool patchwork floor pillow, quilted by Katimae Barnette. *Bottom:* appliquéd and embroidered throw pillow, Mary Lou Stribling. The bird design is from an old Acoma pot.

Pillow with ribbon appliqués, and wool pueblo-style embroidery in progress, Mary Lou Stribling.

Tufted hanging, Mary Lou Stribling. The butterfly design is a combination of scroll elements from Zuñi pottery. The central medallion is an elongated version of a Zuñi rosette.

Wool area rug from carpet scraps, Mary Lou Stribling. The design derived from elements of Sioux beadwork.

Navajo rug. Courtesy, The Nevada State Museum.

Southwestern embroidered throw. Courtesy, The Nevada State Museum.

Reverse appliqué quilt, Catherine Gibson. The designs are from North American petroglyphs. Photo, Verne Gibson.

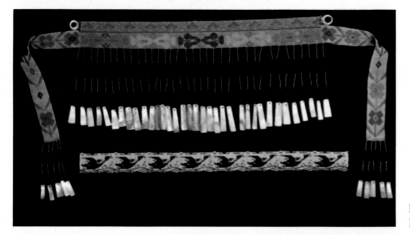

Plains beadwork. Courtesy, The Nevada State Museum.

Plaiting

In textile making, when the crosswise threads consistently pass over every other warp thread, the weaving pattern is called *plain,* or *tabby.* This is also the simplest pattern for plaited baskets, and the same terms are applicable.

It was used very early by Indians to make functional containers, game fences, and fish traps. Hopi basketmakers sometimes decorated plaited baskets after they were woven by overlaying the surface with short dyed stems. The colored elements were driven vertically between the weavers so that the ends were concealed on the inside. This suggests possibilities for changing the character of a plain commercial basket.

The most common plaited patterns require an uneven number of spokes if a continuous weaver is used. If the weaver is flat and stiff enough to hold a shape,

Fig. 119. Iroquois cornhusk masks are worn by the Society of Husk Faces, and are said to represent spirits who brought farming to the Indians. The eyes and mouth are formed separately from long braids stitched together in cupped spirals. The pieces are then joined, and the openings in between are filled in with other braids. *Courtesy, Bureau of Indian Affairs.*

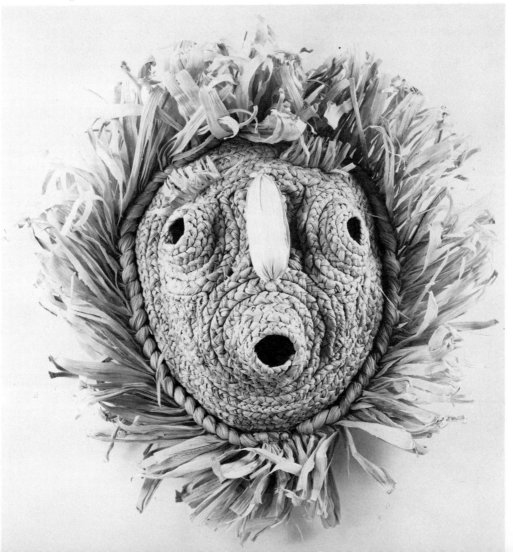

each round can be worked separately, and there can be an even number of spokes. The weaver is tucked under a spoke to begin the circle, then the end is slipped under the same spoke when it is terminated. The next row is started under an adjacent spoke so that the over/under sequence alternates.

This produces checkered designs when the spokes and weavers are different colors, but are the same width and thickness. Some of the checkerwork patterns in Chapter 4 can be worked on baskets if each row has a separate weaver.

Diagonal, or twilled, patterns are made by passing the weaver behind, or in front of, two or more spokes, such as: over two/under one, or over one/under two.

Since these techniques have been well covered in a number of publications, only a brief introduction is included here.

Making a Soft Plaited Basket

Basket-covered bottles are more interesting to make than ordinary wicker containers, and they can be used as samplers to try out several weaving patterns. The character of the weaving can be changed dramatically by combining materials of different weights and textures.

Weave baskets with flexible spokes upside down as described in the section on nets. The support in Fig. 78 is entirely satisfactory for bottle foundations. A wooden disk nailed on top of a 4" × 4" wooden post is a possibility for other kinds of soft baskets, and has the added advantage of enabling you to secure the bottom of the basket to the disk with a small nail. A turntable of some kind is handy for revolving the basket as the work progresses.

To start with a woven bottom, cut 8 warps from jute twine (or other flexible materials) about three times longer than the length desired for the finished basket. (Include length of suspension for hanging bottles.) Bind warp centers together and add an extra warp as shown in Figure 113 B–D. Continue weaving until you have a firm mat that covers the bottom of the bottle. Slip bottle over a dowel support. Attach mat to the bottom with glue, double-stick carpet tape, or floral clay, and weave the sides as described in Figures 120–125.

You can also start with a base cut from pressed board or a tin can lid. (Wooden coasters fit many common bottles.) Cut the base ¼" wider in diameter than the bottom of the form and drill an *odd* number of evenly spaced holes around the rim. The holes should be no larger than necessary to accommodate the warps. Finish the base with paints or stains, and proceed as described in Figures 120–125.

Figs. 120–125. MAKING A SOFT BASKET OVER A BOTTLE

Fig. 120. Drill 17 evenly spaced holes around the edge of a wooden coaster or pressed board disk. Cut jute warps 1½ times longer than the length desired for the finished piece. Thread through the holes from the bottom, and knot.

Fig. 121. Turn the base over and knot warps again, using your finger or a nail as a slide to draw knots against the base.

Fig. 122. Slip bottle over a dowel support and attach base to the bottom. Dampen a length of colored raffia, tie it to a warp, and tape the short end to the base to mark your starting point. Work several inches of plain weave. From time to time, pull warps straight down while you straighten and pack the rows of weaving with a blunt needle or nail. Always begin a new color or new pattern on the same warp.

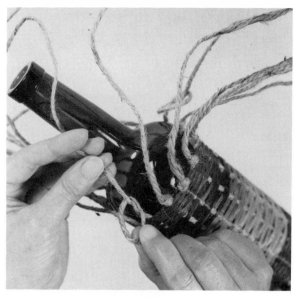

Fig. 123. Change to a twilled pattern by weaving over 2/ under 1 for several inches, then change to an over 1/ under 2 sequence. Finish with several rows of plain weave. Remove from the support and knot each warp firmly against the last row of weaving.

Fig. 124. Divide warps into two bundles. (The extra warp in one bundle will not be obtrusive.) Tie ends together and fluff fibers into a bristly pompon. Suspend, and tie sides together with a short length of string.

Fig. 125. Wrap bundles smoothly up to the pompon, and remove string ties. Combinations of smooth and furry materials would be an interesting variation.

Twining

Two or more weavers are worked simultaneously in twining. For plain two-ply twining, a pair of weavers is twisted in half-turns between each spoke so that they cross each other, and alternate from front to back. It is suitable for either firm or soft materials, and any number of spokes can be used.

Diagonal twining requires an odd number of spokes, and encloses two or more at a time. It produces a very tight construction, and was used for many Ute and Apache water jugs. Often these jugs were sealed further with pinion pitch, a technique that dates far back, even to the Tusayan, who were ancestors of the Hopi.

The pitch was smeared inside the baskets as they were woven, then they were coated on the outside to complete the seal. Canteens were carried over the shoulder on a leather strap. Some had pointed bottoms shaped like hornets' nests; others were rounded.

Fig. 126. Paiute and Apache water bottles were designed with small necks and wide shoulders so that, if they were accidentally dropped, they would immediately tilt upward. The bottle on the left is coated with piñon pitch. The uncoated bottle on the right is 12″ high, 26″ in circumference, and averages 6 stitches per inch twined around double warps. *Collection, Helen Irish.*

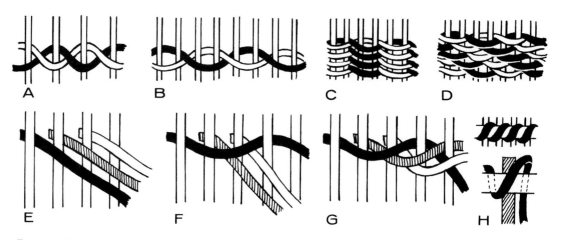

Fig. 127. TWINING TECHNIQUES

A. For plain two-ply twining, twist a pair of weavers between each spoke so that they alternate from front to back. Any number of spokes can be used.

B. For double two-ply twining, enclose two spokes between twists. An even number of spokes is required.

C. Double two-ply twining makes a ribbed pattern of vertical stripes when the weavers are different colors.

D. Diagonal twining requires an odd number of spokes so that the twists around two ribs do not occur directly above each other. Spiraling bands are produced when the weavers are different colors.

E. For three-ply twining, insert three firm weavers behind three adjacent spokes.

F. Carry the first weaver in front of two spokes and behind the third.

G. Repeat for the second weaver, then the third. Pick up the first weaver again and continue in successive order. Pack down to make a firm braid. Pomos favored this braid to make a level base, even though they might use other twining techniques on the rest of the basket.

H. For wrapped twining, hold a firm rod against the inside or outside of spokes. Wrap a flexible weaver around it in between each spoke. This is an excellent device for strengthening the rim of a basket, or for reinforcing the walls of an open construction.

Figs. 128–134. MAKING A TWINED BOTTLE

Fig. 128. Tape strips of newspaper around the dowel support in Fig. 78, and wedge it inside the neck of a half-gallon bottle. Using Lark's Head knots, tie 41 double warps of waxed twine around a 1¾" friction ring. Secure it temporarily to the bottle bottom with floral clay. Tie on a single weaver and work two or three rows of tabby over double warps, then separate warps and continue as shown in Fig. 113A.

Fig. 129. When the concave area is covered, change to a wrapped warp weave to make a heavy foot. Bring the weaver over a pair of warps . . .

Fig. 130 . . . go completely around it to make a loop, and pull tight. (This is sometimes called a "Soumak" knot in textile weaving.)

Fig. 131. At the edge of the bottom, tie on a second weaver and twine the two around double warps. Continue down sides. Hold each pair of warps taut with one hand, and twist the weavers around it with the other. Solid bands result when both weavers are alike.

Fig. 132. Diagonal lines are made when they are different colors. Combinations of the two are being worked here. At the end of a working period, secure weavers with an alligator clip or spring clothespin to keep them from unraveling.

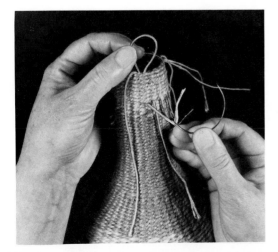

Fig. 133. When the bottle narrows into the neck and warps become closely spaced, cut one strand from each pair and continue weaving. At the rim, thread each warp in a curved needle and carry through the tunnels of adjacent warps. Use pliers to draw them through several rows of weaving. Clip ends on a slant and push out of sight.

Fig. 134. Half-gallon bottle covered with twined jute in natural, black, dark red, and light green.

Figs. 135, 136. HOOPA (CALIFORNIA) TWINED BOTTLES

These bottles are covered with two-ply twining over single warps. For the large dark patterns and wide diagonal stripes, new weavers of contrasting colors were tied on at intervals in each row. The small patterns on the neck of one bottle were made by simply using two weavers of different colors, and varying the placement of the twists. *Photo, Jim Toms; courtesy, The Nevada State Museum.*

Fig. 137. If the starting point of a basket is thick, it can keep the basket from standing level. On these examples, the problem was solved by molding the bottoms slightly inward.

Fig. 138. *Left:* Hoopa women wore rounded, snugly fitting basket caps to protect their foreheads from being chafed by the carrying straps of burden baskets and cradles. *Right:* This coiled basket has a "foot" made from a heavy rod attached by wrapped twining. *Collection, Helen Irish.*

Fig. 139. A foot can also be made from rings cut from tin cans and other containers. A small embroidery hoop was used here. Fifty-nine rattan spokes were lashed together with damp raffia, and a base was woven with jute to fit inside the hoop. The hoop was attached to the spokes in several places with fine sewing thread, then was secured with wrapped twining. Several extra wraps were made in between the spokes completely to cover the hoop.

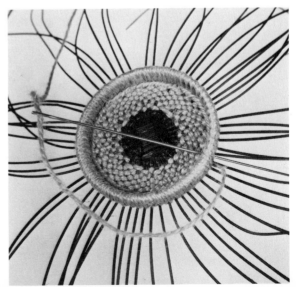

Fig. 140. Plain two-ply twining was used up to the patterned border, where two weavers of different colors were twined over two spokes to make diagonal lines. To reduce the spokes to an even number for the vertical ribs in the center, three spokes were enclosed at one spot in the circle. The rib is wider at this point, but the change is not obtrusive, and the principle was almost universally followed by Indian weavers.

Fig. 141. Indian weavers spaced their designs by eye, not mathematics. When repeat designs did not exactly fit around a basket, selected sections were altered slightly, or something entirely different was introduced. The vertical design on the coiled Washo basket at the left was repeated precisely except in one place.

Fig. 142. Here, it was changed to keep the spacing even. This beautifully woven basket has 26–28 stitches to the inch. *Collection, Helen Irish.*

Fig. 143. *Left:* Twined Hoopa cap. *Right:* Coiled Pomo bowl. *Collection, Helen Irish.*

Fig. 144. Washo coiled-willow cooking basket. *Courtesy, The M. H. De Young Memorial Museum.*

Coiling

Coiled baskets do not have a fixed framework of spokes or stakes. The foundation winds around itself in a continuous spiral that is bound together by a flexible weaver. The foundation, or *core,* can be a single rod, or several rods. When it consists of shredded materials or multiple strands, it is called a *bundle.* There are many ways of manipulating the weaver to create textures and surface patterns. These are called *stitches,* whether or not a needle is involved. Since the stitches move vertically and color changes can easily be made, a great variety of decorative patterns are possible.

Single Rod Cores

Rattan is one of the best choices for a single rod basket if the core is to be exposed. The rods should be polished, however, and perhaps stained or dyed, if they are intended to contribute something to the design. For baskets with a free, primitive character, experiment with flexible shoots that have interesting bark.

Fig. 145. SINGLE ROD CORES

A. With pliers, gently flatten the last inch of the rod to reduce its springiness. Hold one end of the weaver against it and wrap several times. Reverse direction, and wind tightly over the end of the weaver.

B. Bend the tip of the rod inward to start the coil. Keep spirals moving counterclockwise so that the free end of the rod is out of the way. Thread weaver in a large-eyed needle and wrap figure-eight stitches around the center.

C. When the center is established, the spacing between stitches can gradually become wider. Bring needle from the center, go over two coils, around and under one, over two, and so on. This is a version of the lazy stitch.

D. A regular over two/under two sequence without additional wraps in between will form a pattern of diagonal ridges when the stitches are separated. (See Fig. 180.)

E. When they are closely compacted to cover the core, an even, all-over texture results.

F. There are many ways of adding new weavers, and each basket may call for a different solution. When the core is exposed, bring end of old weaver (1) down through lower stitches on the *inside* of the basket. Thread new weaver (2) through same stitches and come out on the front side so that the pattern is not interrupted. Add glue if necessary to hold the ends securely.

G. The end of a firm weaver (1) can be bent to the inside and tucked under adjacent stitches. Carry the new weaver (2) through one or two stitches on the lower coil and out to the front side.

H. When the core is concealed by closely wrapped stitches, lay new weaver (2) against it and wrap old weaver (1) over the end for several rounds. Hold old weaver against the core, pick up new weaver, and continue the stitching pattern.

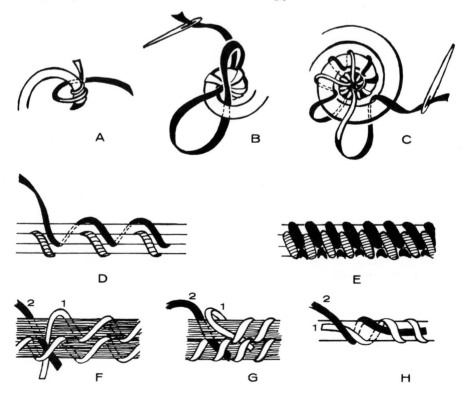

A   B   C

D   E

F   G   H

On certain trees and bushes, the bark will peel or crumble when it becomes dry, and an examination of dead twigs will provide some insight.

Although most instructions for splicing hard rods follow the old principle of lashing together tapered ends, the Pomo method described later in this chapter is infinitely superior. When the core is exposed, plan the splices to occur in areas where they will be concealed by stitching.

Sash cords (preferably uncoated) and other kinds of ropes also make useful cores. They are more difficult to splice than hard cores, and it is best to work with a piece that is long enough for the entire basket. Wind up and secure excess material with a rubber band or gardening tie to keep it out of your way.

Indian basketmakers used an awl to pierce stitching holes through dense materials. Rope is not easily penetrated, so you will be largely restricted to wrapping methods for lashing the coils together. This is not as limiting as it may sound, however, for inventive shapes, trims, and combinations of colors and textures are the ingredients that make baskets unique.

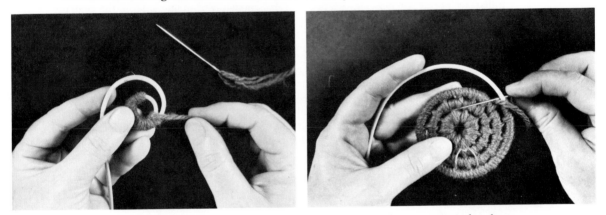

Figs. 146, 147. The center can also be formed by winding the rod into a tiny circlet, then wrapping the weaver around it until the circle is covered. Wrap weaver twice around the rod, then go through the center and back. Mark your starting place with a short piece of thread. On the second coil, wrap three times around the rod between stitches, and on subsequent coils, increase the number of wraps to four or five so that stitch lines alternate evenly. Coils will be slightly separated when rods are firm, and heavy materials are used for stitching.

Figs. 148, 149. A four-to-five-inch base is large enough for the average basket. Begin shaping the sides directly out from the beginning of the first coil. For a rounded form, lay the rod slightly inside the base so that the spirals begin to cup inward. Hold the rod in position between the fingers of your left hand. For a cylinder, bring the rod sharply upward and place it directly on top of the base coil. Bring weaver over two coils, around one, and wrap as many times as necessary to keep the long stitches evenly spaced. You can stitch from back to front, or the reverse. This is a version of the lazy stitch.

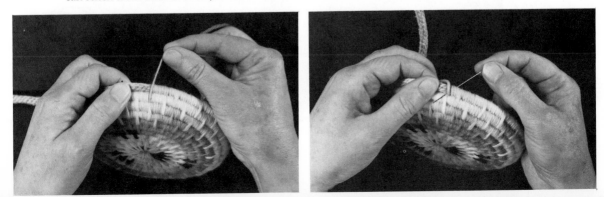

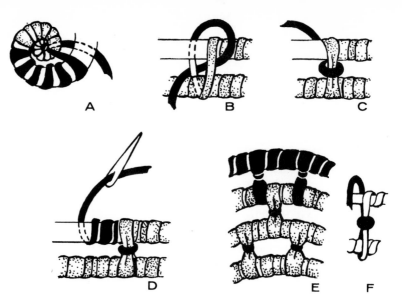

Fig. 150. OPENWORK

A. Coils can be separated by tying knots around the long lazy stitches. This is an ancient Indian technique for weaving sifters or similar openwork containers. Form the center, then wrap weaver four or five times around the rod. Carry it through the center and out the back side.

B. Holding the coils slightly apart, bring weaver around outside coil and behind the two connecting strands. (If you only take in the single long stitch, the structure will be weak.)

C. Make one or more loops around the middle of connecting strands, depending on how widely you want the coils separated. Pull tight.

D. Carry weaver under the outside coil and wrap four or five times. Carry it over two coils again, and continue.

E. Adjust spacing on subsequent coils so that knots are not directly above each other. For variety, use a contrasting color on the edge coil, then rebind knots to match.

F. To substitute wooden beads for knots, pick up a bead on the long stitch, and go back through it after encircling the lower coil.

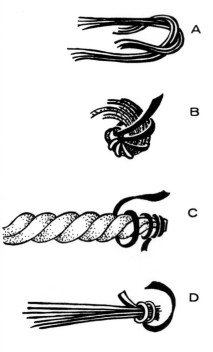

Fig. 151. BUNDLE CORES

A. When core materials are flexible, the basket can be started with several strands loosely knotted together. Turn ends backward to form a loop, and hold together.

B. Insert weaver through the bundle, bind over the short end, and continue wrapping the loop to complete the circle.

C. Taper the ends of a twisted hemp bundle. Hold the weaver against it and wrap several times. Fold the tip inward and continue as shown in Figure 145 until the center is established.

D. Traditionally, pine needle baskets are started with three to five well-soaked needles. Bind the weaver around the blunt ends, fold inward, and make a circle of stitches around the center.

E. Increase size of core several needles at a time until it is about the size of a pencil. A wrap stitch is the simplest method for binding the coils together. Bring weaver around the new coil and through several strands of the old.

F. Space new stitches in between the stitches of the previous row. Add extra stitches regularly as the circumference of the basket increases.

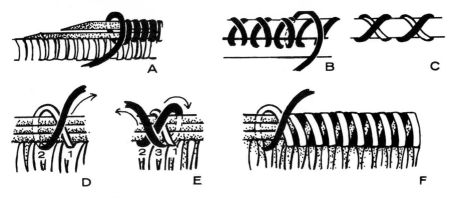

Fig. 152. EDGE FINISHES

A. The last coil should always be ended directly opposite the beginning of the first coil. Taper the core so that it blends smoothly into the underlying coil. Closely spaced wrapped stitches were most frequently used by Indian basketmakers to finish the edge.

B. Cross-stitches are also attractive. Go around the edge coil with widely spaced slanting stitches. When you return to the starting point, reverse direction for another row.

C. A top view of the cross-stitches.

D. Navajo wedding plates have a distinctive herringbone edge that resembles braiding, but is made with a single weaver. Bring weaver through the old coil at 1. Carry it forward, go around the core, and come out at 2.

E. Draw weaver backward, go around core, and come out between the first two stitches at 3.

F. Continue the forward/backward/forward rhythm until the circle is completed.

Fig. 153. NAVAJO WEDDING PLATE

Replicas of Navajo wedding plates are produced today by the Paiutes, but old specimens like this are rare. In traditional marriage rites, the basket was filled with a thick cornmeal porridge decorated with sacred pollen. After the porridge was ceremonially tasted by the bride and bridegroom, it was turned over to guests. The basket was kept as a treasured keepsake until the death of one of the partners. At this time it was supposed to be burned. The pattern represents the mountains and valleys of the lower (earth) and upper (spirit) worlds. The opening to the center is sometimes called a "spirit break." According to legend, it provided a path for the soul of the dead to travel from earth to the spirit world. The last coil around the basket was always ended just opposite the break. *Collection, Helen Irish.*

Fig. 154. PAPAGO BASKETMAKER The Arizona Papagos are the most prolific basketmakers in America today. *Photo, Chuck Abbott.*

Fig. 156. On this old split-stitch basket, the stitches are not separated. The weaver is brought through the middle of the stitch beneath it, splitting the fibers in half.

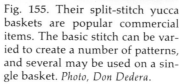

Fig. 155. Their split-stitch yucca baskets are popular commercial items. The basic stitch can be varied to create a number of patterns, and several may be used on a single basket. *Photo, Don Dedera.*

Fig. 157. PAPAGO AND SEMINOLE STITCHES
A. Bring weaver out at 1, make a long slanting stitch around the bundle, and come out at 2. Go completely around the bundle to make a straight stitch, coming out slightly below 2. Continue around coil.
B. The straight/slanting sequence produces this pattern. On subsequent coils, draw the new straight stitch through the middle of the stitch beneath it.
C. Raffia, yucca, roots, and other flat materials will split more crisply than yarn.
D. By taking this sequence a step farther, another pattern is produced. Stitch around the coil as shown in A, then go back around again, making a slanting stitch in the opposite direction. When you are back at the starting point, proceed to the next coil.
E. Gradually increase the lengths of the slanting stitches as the basket becomes wider. If the rim cups inward, decrease them again. This brings about a pleasing harmony between decoration and form.
F. Stitches can also be spaced close together to create a texture rather than a linear pattern.

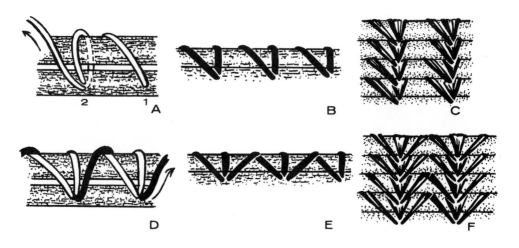

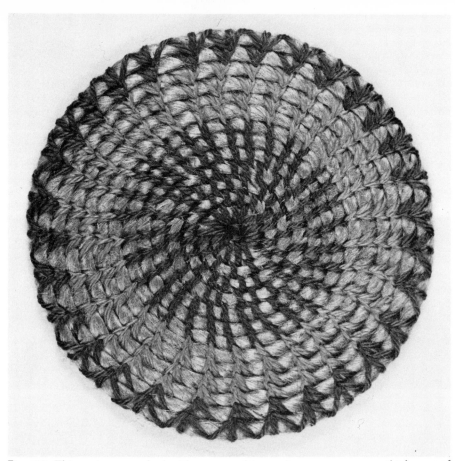

Fig. 158. This mat was worked with green and turquoise rug yarn over a thick core of light green unspun jute. Simple split stitches (sometimes called "chain" stitches) were used in the center. Slanting stitches were added as the size increased.

Making a Pine Needle Basket

Pine needle baskets can be started with a round or oval wooden base that is completely concealed by the coiled sides.

Cut the base from ½" pine or 3/16" plywood. About ¼" from the edge and ½" apart, drill a circle of holes a little larger than a tapestry needle. Sand base and finish with paint or stain.

Bring raffia through a hole in the base. Hold the blunt ends of five or six needles against the edge of the base and tie raffia securely around them. Place the short end of the raffia with the needles, and wind the long end several times through the hole and around the bundle.

A 1" segment cut from a large plastic drinking straw, or piece of plastic tubing, makes a useful device for holding the bundle of needles together. It will also serve as a gauge for keeping it even in thickness. Slip it over the needles, then wedge the blunt ends of five or six needles into the center of the bundle. Slide gauge forward with each stitch to keep it out of the way.

You can use a simple wrap stitch to bind the first coil to the base, going

101

through each hole once or twice. Continue adding several needles at a time to keep the gauge comfortably filled.

When the base has been encircled, bind coils to each other as described in Figures 159–167.

Figs. 159–167. MAKING A PINE NEEDLE BASKET

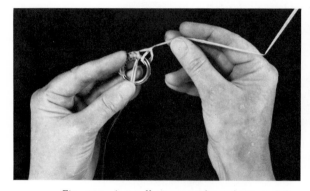

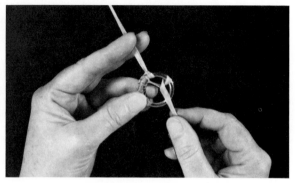

Fig. 159. A small ring can be substituted for traditional methods of starting a pine needle basket. Attach the center of a long strand of raffia to the ring with a Lark's Head knot. Bring one end up, and the other down. Carry the top strand around the ring, through the loop, and pull tight.

Fig. 160. Bring the bottom strand around the ring and through the loop. Slide against the top strand and pull tight. Continue working these double buttonhole stitches until the ring is filled, then go through the first top and bottom stitches to complete the circle.

Fig. 161. Carry the inside strand through opposite stitches to fill the center with radiating spokes. The spokes can be woven or left open.

Fig. 162. Hold a small bundle of needles against the rim of the ring and bind tightly to the top strand of raffia, going through one buttonhole stitch with each wrap.

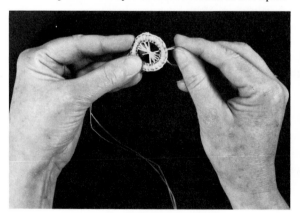

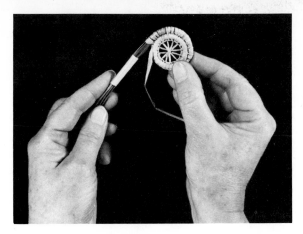

Fig. 163. Slip on the gauge, and start adding extra needles gradually until it is filled, but not packed.

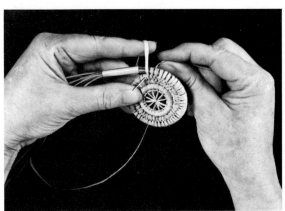

Fig. 164. A simple wrap stitch is best for the first few coils, then you can change to straight/slanting stitches, or chains. Keep the raffia flat, and control its tension with your left forefinger.

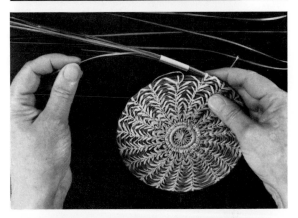

Fig. 165. Make longer slanting stitches as the circumference of the basket increases. Add needles regularly to the center of the bundle so that ends will not protrude on the outside.

Fig. 166. Start shaping the basket by placing new coils slightly to the inside of the preceding coil. The raffia will become twisted as you stitch. From time to time, drop the needle and allow it to unwind. Periodically, slide the needle up an inch to keep the raffia from becoming frayed at the foldback.

Fig. 167. Gradually start tapering the last coil of the basket a few inches before its terminal. Clip needles at intervals, and push ends into the center. Secure end of raffia by weaving it invisibly through several coils. *By Mary Lou Stribling.*

Figs. 168–170. PINE NEEDLE BASKET LIDS

Fig. 168. Lids can be woven to fit over or inside the rim of a basket. A bundle of needles with the roots left on makes an interesting handle. Wrap the bundle tightly with raffia, then attach a small coil of needles.

Fig. 169. Stitch around the coil and through several needles of the handle until one round is completed.

Fig. 170. Trim ends of handle to about an inch. Slip on the gauge and start gradually increasing thickness of the bundle. For an edge trim, several short root ends can be periodically wedged into the coil at an angle, and secured by the stitches.

Pomo Basketmaking

From the eastern slopes of the Sierra Nevada and west to the Pacific Ocean, the land is full of surprises. Over a gritty desert knoll, you may suddenly find a blue lake, set like a turquoise in a ring of bare mountains that are hospitable only to lizards, snakes, grasshoppers, rabbits, and spirits.

As you move westward, the dark sand and tumbleweed merge into yellowed, grassy hills where oaks drop the bitter nuts that sustained countless generations of native peoples.

Then the dry hills end abruptly, and there are patches of dense shade, cooled by fog and ocean drafts. You may rest under a tree that was young when Christ was young. The remains of old villages that were young even earlier may be there, too, buried deep under the moist loam, redwood litter, and ferns.

This strip of land that reaches north into Oregon and south into the Baja Peninsula is called the California culture region. In prehistorical times it was occupied by many tribes who had as many differences as the land itself.

In some ways they were culturally poor. They had tribal customs, beliefs, and ceremonies, but religious practices were not as formalized nor as elaborately ritualistic as those of the peoples of the Northwest Coast, Southwest, and Southeast. They were not architects, nor farmers. But in two regards, their talents were unsurpassed: they knew how to live on whatever the land provided and Pomo women made the finest baskets produced in North America, perhaps even in the entire world.

Many California tribes specialized in one or two types of basketry, but the Pomos excelled in nearly all major forms. The art was held in such high esteem that it became surrounded by traditions, many of which have continued into modern times.

There were special songs and prayers for harvesting and preparing materials so that the baskets would be beautiful and live a long life. The true artist waited for spiritual direction before proceeding with certain forms and patterns, and often received instructions through dreams and visions. The woman weaver never touched her work during menstrual periods, nor went near another weaver. She withdrew from the rest of the family and assigned her household duties to a friend or relative, who took care of children and the preparation of food until the period had passed. This was not a time for companionship or basketmaking. It was a time for rest and contemplation, and for prayers and dreaming.

Disobedience of this ancient law could bring about disasters far more drastic than having a basket grow lopsided or sewing roots become twisted and brittle. Hands could swell and lose their suppleness. Tiny scratches could mysteriously become infected. Sudden blindness might be inflicted, or strange, lingering maladies that had no cure.

But the dedicated weaver was always rewarded. Her roots worked easily, quickly turning into even, glossy threads. Her baskets were strong, her stitches were straight, and her feather designs lay as smooth as the breast of a bird.[7]

---

[7] There are probably only five or six traditional Pomo weavers left.

Pomo Techniques

Only three tools are essential for Pomo basketmaking: a sharp knife, an emery stone for honing the edge, and a small awl. Fingernail clippers and tweezers are optional, but useful.

In early periods, basketry awls were made from slivers of polished bone, or were carved from a tough wood, such as manzanita. You can make an excellent tool from a tapestry needle and a 2″ segment of ½″ wood doweling. Drill a hole in one end of the dowel to fit the needle's eye. Spread epoxy glue in the hole, and wedge in the needle as far as it will go. When the glue has cured, sharpen the needle to a fine point. After working with the awl, you will probably want to taper the handle toward the needle to fit your fingers more comfortably.

Look for small knobbed or bulb-shaped handles in hardware stores. The awl in Figures 172 and 173 was made from the handle of a small herb pestle. You should be able to work with the awl constantly in your hand, moving it from finger to finger as necessary.

Nearly all modern Pomo baskets are made with rattan rods, instead of traditional willow. For fine coils #1 rods are used; for large baskets and coarser work, #2. Sedge roots and redbud bark are the most common stitching materials, though dyed bulrush is sometimes used for black designs.

The instructions here are for these materials; however, they are applicable to superfine chair cane, and others described earlier in the chapter. Raffia will have a different character, and must be worked with a needle.

It is important to understand that you do not perforate the rod itself on a single rod basket. The awl is slipped between the coils at an angle, creating an indentation in the softened rattan that is large enough to be penetrated by the sharpened tip of the weaver. By slanting the holes, the stitches will be straight on the surface of the basket. They should never lean. Always stitch from front to back. As the circumference of the basket increases, add two stitches in one hole at intervals to keep the spacing even.

A good Pomo basket is as perfect on the inside as the outside, regardless of how elaborate the design. This often involves tying off and adding weavers every few stitches, and the Pomos have a superlative method for concealing the ends.

The basket is started with a small bundle of culls, or shredded roots. You can use raffia, tough flexible grass stems, or shredded fronds instead. Have at hand a small bowl of water, several trimmed and refined weavers, and a rod. Soak a weaver only until it feels pliable when it is stripped between the fingers. Do not soak the rod at all. Dampen the section on which you are working a drop at a time to soften, not swell, the fibers.

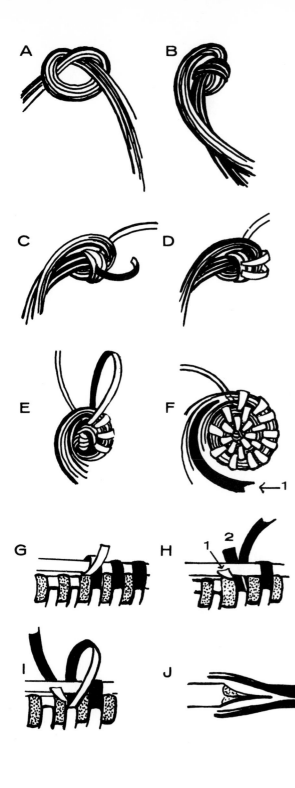

Fig. 171. POMO SINGLE ROD BASKET

A. Tie an overhand knot about three inches from the end of a small bundle of flexible grass stems, split roots, or raffia. Adjust strands until the knot is tight and smooth.

B. Coil the short end of the bundle around the knot.

C. With the awl, open a hole near the center and thread the sharpened weaver through it, leaving a tail about ½″ long. (The flat side goes against the bundle.) Bend the tail to the left and fold behind the knot. Hold it in place until it is secured by the next stitch.

D. Stitches around the center must not go through the same hole, or they will pile up and form a lump. Keep them evenly apart, leaving enough space in between for the stitches of the next coil.

E. At this point, you are quite literally hanging on by your fingernails. Periodically twist the strands of the bundle to keep them together, and clip off any ends that protrude between stitches.

F. As the coil gets larger, add extra stitches at regular intervals. When one or two inches of the bundle remain, taper the end of the rod and dampen it with your fingers. Make an opening in the center of the bundle with the awl, and wedge in the rod as far as it will go (1). If necessary, thin the bundle on the inner side to compensate for the thickness of the rod. After several stitches, trim remaining strands of the bundle to uneven lengths so that they will not make a hump in the coil.

G. To tie off the weaver, bring it over and under the rod, and pull tight.

H. Slide it to the left where it will be covered by the next stitch (1). Open a stitching hole, bring new weaver through it, then lift the rod slightly and slip the end under to the back side (2). The ends of the old and new weavers now cross each other under the rod. Pull both tight and trim (2) close to the rod.

I. Open a stitching hole, bring new weaver over the rod and through it. Trim end of old weaver if necessary. This procedure is followed when introducing colored stitches to make a design.

J. Pomos have a special technique for splicing a rod. Continue stitching almost to the end of the old rod, then force the point of the awl through the center to split it. Loosen the last few stitches, sharpen the end of a new rod and wedge it into the split. Shave the old rod with a knife until the joint is evenly thinned. Retighten the stitches and continue weaving.

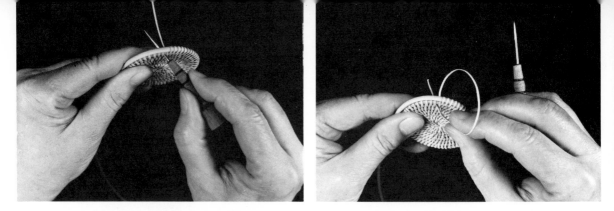

Figs. 172, 173. POMO STITCHING TECHNIQUES

Always work from front to back and make stitching holes on a slant so that stitches are vertical. Remove stitches if they start to lean, and check your spacing. Usually, you need to add an extra stitch or two. Holes dented between the damp rods can close up quickly, sometimes before the weaver can be inserted. Pomo basketmakers do not waste time by laying down the awl between stitches. They make an opening, bring the weaver into position, withdraw the awl between the last two fingers of the right hand, and immediately slip the weaver through the hole. It takes practice to master this smooth, graceful rhythm, but it soon becomes automatic. It also explains the value of a slim awl with a slightly knobbed end.

Planning a Design

Pomo weavers never worked out their designs on paper. A stitch diagram is a useful guide, however, even though changes may be necessary as the basket develops. You will probably have to count stitches for the first few rows to get the pattern started evenly. But as the basket gets larger and extra stitches are added, your eyes will be better guides.

Fig. 174. Designs for baskets based on Pomo stitching methods can be planned on graph paper. Each stitch goes over two coils. Draw one row on the lines of the paper, and the next in between. When the form curves and extra stitches are added, make the design fit the space rather than continuing a rigid stitch count.

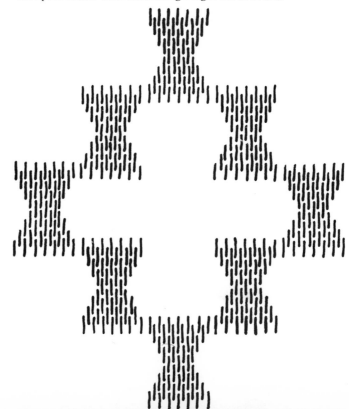

Miniatures

Pomo weavers delighted in miniature baskets, and some were almost as elaborately decorated as baskets of normal sizes. One example in the State Indian Museum, Sacramento, is the size of a large pinhead and has details that can be seen only with a magnifying glass.

Beaded baskets of all sizes were often trimmed with feathers and abalone pendants. At first they used only creamy white beads, either scattered over the basket or worked into patterns that contrasted with brown woven motifs. In later periods, colored beads were sometimes woven over the entire surface, giving it the appearance of a mosaic made of tiny, brilliant stones.

Although in some tribes, baskets were beaded after they were finished, the best bead designs were worked as the basket was woven. In one method, the beads were strung on a separate thread that was carried against the outside of the rod. The beads were slipped forward one at a time and secured by the regular stitching thread. You can identify baskets made this way by the slanting positions of the beads.

It is simpler to pick up a bead at a time with the weaver so that the beads are secured with the stitches. Pomos used their customary stitching materials. You can substitute anything that is reasonably flat, such as embroidery floss or raffia, as long as it will go readily through the beads and will cling smoothly to the rod.

Stitching can be done with beading needles if they will accommodate the thread. They are too delicate, however, to perforate their own stitching holes. This must be done with an awl. Fine sewing needles will pass comfortably through #9 and #10 seed beads and are strong enough for a certain amount of direct stitching. Even with these, you will find the awl indispensable, and after you get the rhythm of punching and stitching, you can actually work faster than by tugging at the needle to draw it through a tight spot.

It is best to work repeat patterns on baskets with fairly straight sides. Sharply curving forms involve periodically adding extra stitches that can throw the pattern out of alignment. One solution is to make the curving areas in a solid color, and work a patterned band around the middle where the wall is comparatively straight.

Fig. 175. This represents one segment of the repeat pattern on the miniature in Figure 179. Colors are indicated by different kinds of dots. Your own designs will be easier to follow if they are drafted with colored inks. A. Pick up beads one at a time with the needle. As the stitches are pulled tight, the beads will seat themselves in the crevices between the rods.

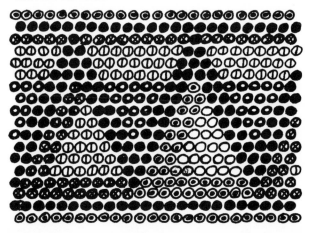

A

As a first project, you might simply work scattered motifs against a plain background, or weave a single motif in the center of the back and front. You can then increase and decrease stitches in plain areas.

To work out a pattern, count the beads on one full coil, and plot the color sequences on paper.

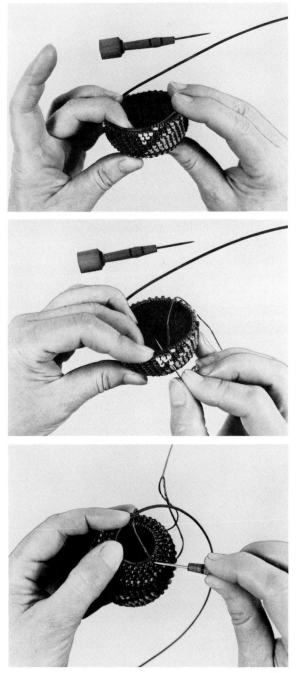

Figs. 176–179. MAKING A MINIATURE BEADED BASKET

Fig. 176. Follow the procedure in Figure 171 for starting the basket, using a fine rattan rod as a core, and embroidery thread for the central knot. When the base is about an inch across, add a bead in between each stitch. From the fifth coil on, add a plain stitch in between each beaded stitch to make a tighter construction. It will also serve as a cushion to keep beads vertical. Hold the basket between thumb and second finger.

Fig. 177. Bring the forefinger on top of the rod to control the shape. Moisten the rod regularly to keep it pliable. If beads start to lean in a design area, plain stitches can be added at intervals without distorting the lines.

Fig. 178. If the basket has a small neck, place your little finger under the bottom, and hold the rod in place with your thumb and forefinger. Finish the top coil with closely spaced wrap stitches.

Fig. 179. This miniature was woven with embroidery floss and #9 seed beads. The technique is applicable to larger forms as well. *By Mary Lou Stribling.*

Fig. 180. Tiny baskets were made in many tribes for toys, gifts, and display. The basket on the left is woven. The coiled bowl on the right is stitched as shown in Figure 145. Origins are unknown. *Collection, Helen Irish.*

Fig. 181. Pomo feathered baskets were their highest achievements, often involving years of work. They were intended to be works of art, not functional containers. Tiny feathers from orioles, woodpeckers, flickers, jays, pheasants, and other colorful birds were stitched into the basket as it was woven, often as many as 30 to 50 per inch. They were fastened so skillfully that they cannot be pulled out. *Courtesy, The M. H. De Young Memorial Museum.*

Figs. 182–184. YARN BASKET

Fig. 182A. Many kinds of perforated forms can be resurfaced to make decorative baskets. For a furry texture, tie on a weaver and carry it around every other intersection in a back stitch, holding back loops on the top side with your left hand.
B. Wrap edges, or use some of the other finishes on Indian baskets.

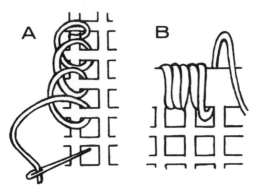

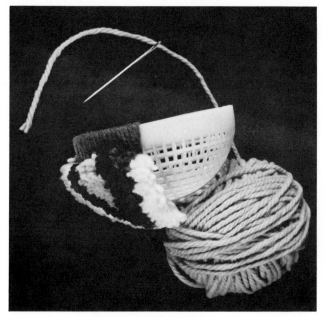

Fig. 183. Stitch as many rows between grids as necessary for a thick pile. Coat stitches on the inside with diluted rug adhesive, then clip loops and shear evenly. Plastic half-spheres used to make animals and other three-dimensional forms are available in needlework shops.

Fig. 184. To attach feather trims, shear away some of the down, dip quill ends in white glue, and wedge in between the threads. Pearl button chains have a character similar to Indian shell disk beads. This repository for reading glasses and jewelry was worked with white, black, brown, and yellow ochre rug yarn.

Fig. 185. These Apache burden baskets are modern, but the style is quite old. Dangling leather fringes were added after the baskets were woven, and tin can cones were crimped on the ends, as much for their tinkling sounds as their appearance. *Collection, Pacific Western Traders.*

Fig. 186. The idea was borrowed to give this wicker-covered bottle a different personality.

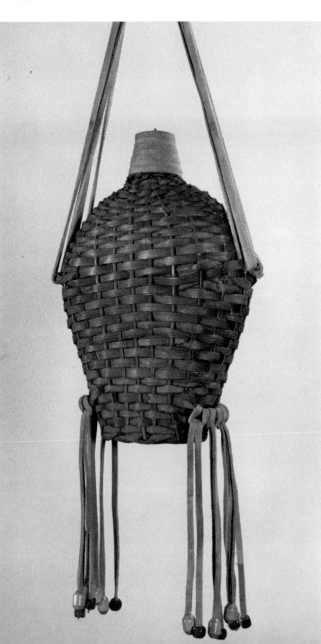

4

PLAITED AND BRAIDED TEXTILES

Plaiting and braiding do not refer to precisely the same methods of weaving, though both are forms of "finger weaving." Indians made an astonishing variety of nonloomed textiles, ranging in quality from crude plaited yucca mats to beautifully patterned braided sashes and twined bags.

PLAITING

The general category of plaiting can be defined as the over/under crisscrossing of strands so that they are interlaced into a single unit. The metal racks in dishwashers, stoves, and drains are usually plaited, as are wicker furniture, sieves, and screens. It is distinguished from braiding in that the strands are arranged to come from opposite directions and cross each other diagonally, or at right angles.

The basics of plaiting are well known, and nearly every child has made a checkerboard mat from strips of colored paper. In spite of its antiquity, however, it is still useful for many kinds of contemporary projects. Paper weaving is an excellent way to explore design possibilities. Colors will be reversed on opposite sides, and sometimes the underside will be unexpectedly better.

PLAITED PAPER PATTERNS

Cut two or three colors of construction paper into ¼" strips. Tape one set of strips vertically to a large sheet of cardboard for warps,[1] and weave another set

---

[1] Lengthwise threads are warps; crosswise threads are wefts.

Fig. 187. Twined Wasco (Oregon) Sally bag. The cylindrical twined hemp and cornhusk bags of the Wascos can be classed as either textiles or baskets. The design here is a repeat pattern of stylized human heads turned sideways. An engraved version of a typical figure design is on the handle of the digging stick in Chapter 1. *Courtesy, The Oregon Historical Society.*

through them from the opposite direction. A regular over/under plain weave produces checkerwork, but the monotony of the grid can be altered by weaving every other row in a different color, or by alternating each row with a strip of the warp color. It can be further changed by crossing over two or more warps in between the rows of plain weave.

Try, also, using ½″ strips for warps, and ¼″ strips for weavers, or the reverse. In Figure 188 B, identical double rows were woven, though wide weavers would produce the same effect.

More complex figures are formed in Figures 188 A and C by crossing over selected warps in units that change with each row until the figure is completed. Designs of these kinds can be plotted on graph paper, but they should be tested with paper strips, since sometimes a drawing will not indicate that certain weaving sequences fail to adequately interlock all the strips together. (You should avoid crossing over or under more than four warps to make a design, unless the weaving is to be bonded to a foundation.)

A file of these samplers makes a good reference when you are ready to execute them in more permanent materials. If you make them from fade-resistant papers, they can also be used for table mats and coasters. Glue them to thin sheet cork and seal the surface with five or six coats of clear acrylic medium.

After working out plaited designs with strips arranged vertically and horizontally, tape a set of warps running diagonally, and work weavers from the opposite diagonal. The same patterns will appear quite different.

Figs. 188, 189. PLAITED DESIGNS FOR STRIP WEAVING

Fig. 188. Variations of these plaited designs were made by many tribes, sometimes in a single color. Multicolored designs were woven on Southeastern baskets, especially by the Choctaws, Atakapa, and Chitimachas.

A. Row 1. Under one/ over two, under three/ over two.
   Repeat.
   Row 2. Over one/ under three. Repeat.
   Row 3. Over one/ under two/ over three/ under two. Repeat.
   Row 4. Go under two. Start unit with over two/under one/ over two/ under three. Repeat.
   Row 5. Under one/ over two/ under one/ over one/ under one/ over two. Repeat.
   This brings you to the center of the top figure. To complete it, weave rows 4, 3, 2, and start at the beginning again.
B. Rows 1 and 2. Under one/ over one/ under one/ over three. Repeat.
   Rows 3 and 4. Over three/ under one/ over one/ under one. Repeat. Go back to row 1 and continue.
C. Row 1. Over one/ under two/ over two/ under one / over three/ under one/ over two/ under two. Repeat.
   Row 2. Over two/ under two/ over two/ under one/ over one/ under one/ over two/ under two/ over three/ under two. Repeat.
   Row 3. Under one/ over two/ under two/ over two/under one/ over two/ under two/ over two. Repeat.
   Row 4. Under two/ over two/ under two/ over three/ under two/ over two/ under three. Start unit with over two and repeat.
   Row 5. Over one/ under two/ over two/ under two. Repeat.
   Row 6. Over two/ under two/ over two/ under three/ over two/ under two/ over three. Start unit with under two and repeat.
   Row 7. Under one/ over two/ under two/ over two. Repeat.
   Row 8. Over one/ under one/ over two/ under two/ over three/under two/ over two/ under one. Repeat.
   To weave diamond figures, weave back through rows 7, 6, 5, 4, 3, 2, 1.

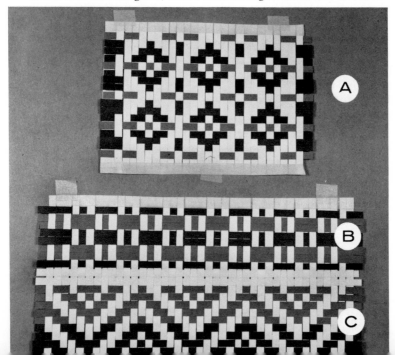

Fig. 189. This Choctaw twilled design is basically an over two/ under two sequence to the center, where a diamond is worked, and the weaving sequence is reversed. Each row advances a single strip to produce the diagonals. It can be continued to complete as many diamonds as you wish.

STRIP WEAVING

Firm, nonraveling materials are recommended for strip weaving, and there are many choices. Vinyl, leather, and Naugahyde are useful for making table mats, beach bags, belts, purses, desk pads, outdoor pillow tops, chair seats, coverings for wastebaskets, planters, and other things where a durable or waterproof surface is a practical consideration.

These materials are tough, and can be sliced into very thin strips for fine designs. If they are not too thick, the foundation can be cut to size, slashed, and woven as shown in Figures 190–193. There are certain advantages to this method, though the design must be carefully planned so that the weft strips exactly fit within it. For mats, stitch across the fringed ends of the completed weaving, and trim evenly.

To cover a cylindrical form, cut the foundation piece to fit, then cut a matching piece of graph paper. Work out a repeat design in equal units so that the seam can be covered without a break in the pattern. Mark the required number of warp strips on the foundation and slash with a straightedge and a sharp craft knife.

When the weaving is finished, smooth a band of white glue around the top and bottom of the can, and press the unfringed borders into it. Tape the seams securely until the glue is dry, then weave in the fringed ends. If you have planned the design properly, the seam will be invisible.

118

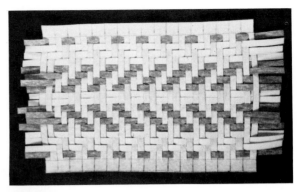

Fig. 190. Mark guidelines for warps on the underside of vinyl with a waterproof pen. Slash with a sharp knife, turn over, and work weavers from the top side.

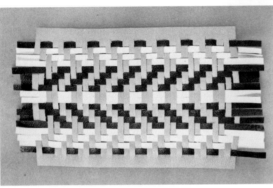

Fig. 191. Simple over two/under two twilling can be varied by using weavers of different colors. This pattern is made with dark red and white weavers, and yellow ochre warps.

Fig. 192. Glue solid borders to the form and allow to dry, then weave in the loose ends of the wefts across the seam, one at a time.

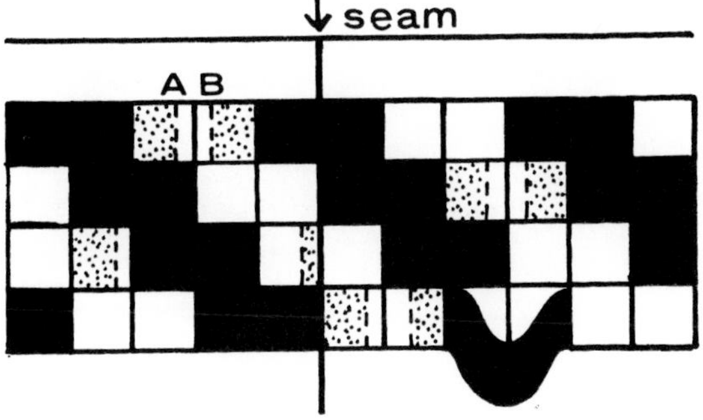

↓ seam

A B

Fig. 193. The black blocks represent weavers. Their ends are indicated by shading and dotted lines. Starting at the top, clip left end of the weaver (A), and tuck it under a warp strip. Weave right end (B) over the seam and tuck it under the adjacent warp. Use a toothpick to slip drops of glue under the warp strips to hold the weavers in place. Repeat down the seam on alternate sides.

Braids, tapes, and ribbons eliminate the chore of cutting even strips for plaited designs. Bias tape is probably the least expensive, and is handy for certain things, even though it lacks the body of firmer grosgrain and wool. Since it is ½″ wide, large pieces work up quickly.

Cut warp strips to equal lengths and arrange them side by side on a sheet of cardboard. Bond lengths of tape across the top and bottom with a fusible netting. You now have a structure similar to the slashed vinyl in Fig. 190. Fasten the top edge to a celotex board with masking tape, and weave as previously described, using a T pin to lift selected strips so that the weavers can be slipped under them.

Adjust each row evenly as you go, and secure the ends with pins. When the weaving is finished, remove the pins and bond tape across the fringed sides to match the top and bottom. The piece can then be trimmed, and stitched or bonded to a lining. Additional tape borders can be added if desired.

The intense colors and soft matt texture of felt make beautiful plaited designs, but since it has no spring it is a bit difficult to handle. It has an elegance of its own, however, and samplers can be made from the small inexpensive squares available in fabric shops. These are large enough for pattern experiments, and the

Fig. 194. Plaited samplers from felt strips (*top*), and bias tape (*bottom*).

Fig. 195. Designs for plaited strips are also useful for beadwork and loom weaving.

finished samplers can be bonded to a backing and put to a practical use. The small units are especially attractive when they are joined together with narrow wool braid into plaited mosaics. These reconstructed textiles can be made into table runners, wall hangings, bags, jackets, and vests.

Long felt strips should be marked with a ruler and pen before cutting. Short strips can be cut more quickly by attaching a sheet of ruled paper on top of the fabric with double-stick tape, and using the lines as a cutting guide.

Fig. 196. "Stele" wall hanging, 6' × 15". Peruvian pebble weave in wool, woven on a floor loom. *Weaving and photo, Jacquetta Nisbet.*

Fig. 197. Woven strip, 1½″ × 6′. Peruvian pebble weave in cotton, woven on an inkle loom. *Weaving and photo, Jacquetta Nisbet.*

Fig. 198. Wall hanging, 15″ × 2′. Peruvian pebble weave in wool, woven on a floor loom. *Weaving and photo, Jacquetta Nisbet.*

PLAITED CORDS

By working several successive rows alike, designs similar to those in Figure 195 can be woven with yarn or other cords. The warps cannot hang free, however, or they would become hopelessly entangled with the crosswise threads. A simple support for holding them taut can be made from notched cardboard, or nails driven into a board, but this goes into an area that is not generally classed as finger weaving.

Belts and other kinds of useful bands can be plaited by a technique that requires no support except a nail or hook from which to suspend the vertical strands. The key element is a heavy material for the warp, and finer material for the weft. This is the reverse of most weaving procedures. Decorative cording is especially appropriate, though fine yarns can be used if they are grouped into bundles.

Work narrow bands first until you are familiar with the simple process. They can be stitched together to make a wider fabric. After a little experience, you will be able to comfortably handle a surprising number of warps and still keep the weaving even. The thickness of the warps almost completely eliminates the problem of "waistlining," or drawing in, that is present in so many processes of handweaving.

For plaited belts that are simply tied around the waist, hand- or machine-stitch across the ends of the woven section, and knot the remaining warps into a fringe.

If a buckle is to be used, attach it first. To your waist measurement, add an allowance for an overlap or fringe, plus two or three inches for take-up of the weaving. Cut lengths of cording until they snugly fill the crossbar of the buckle. Remove an inch of the filler from one end of each cord. Fold these ends over the crossbar, and stitch neatly on the underside. Tie a weaving thread to the first right-hand cord and hang the buckle from a nail. Weave over/under across the band, go around the far left cord, and return. Keep spacing and tension even, and pull warps periodically to keep them straight. Tie on new weavers as needed, keeping knots on the back. When the belt is finished, thread the loose weaver ends in a needle, and work them invisibly into the back of the strip.

Machine-stitch (or hand-sew) across the end of the woven section, and knot the remaining warps into a fringe.

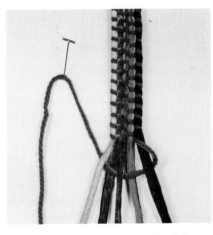

Fig. 199. Plaited belt from heavy yarn and velvet cording.

Yarn bundles can be worked the same way, but instead of sewing the ends to the buckle, cut double lengths and attach centers to the crossbar with Lark's Head knots. For firm, compact bundles, use three strands doubled of Lopi or other heavy yarn, two strands doubled of rug yarn, and five or six strands doubled of knitting worsted.

Fig. 200. PLAITED BELTS FROM YARN
A. Bring ends of yarn bundles together, and attach centers to the crosswise bar of the buckle with Lark's Head knots.
B. Tie the weaver on the back side of the first right hand bundle, and weave back and forth across the band.
C. For a different texture, arrange an even number of firm cords side by side, and weave an over two/under two sequence, back and forth.

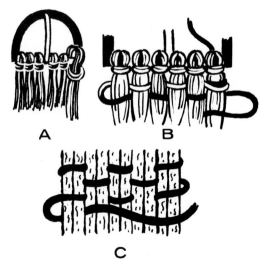

BRAIDING

Braiding is a category of plaiting, but only one set of strands is used and they all originate from the same direction. It can be done with as few as three strands, and as many as your fingers can manipulate.

The technique is so old and widely distributed that we cannot assign it a history. The Southwestern Basket Makers braided fine sashes from animal hair at least 2,000 years ago. Their antecedents, the pueblos, continued the fashion almost unchanged, and braided excellent functional heavy duty straps and ropes as well.

Most tribes throughout the eastern and central areas of North America used braiding to make bags, belts, and wide girdles, the most notable of which had variations of the arrow design described later in this section.

In spite of many modern techniques and devices for textile making, such crafts from the past as braided rugs continue to have a large and dedicated following. The very fact that they are old-fashioned may contribute to their popularity.

Simple three-and four-strand braids need no explanation, and instructions for making braided rugs can be found in many craft books. In some Indian tribes, where braiding was highly developed, several bands were braided simultaneously and joined together at the same time by interlinking the end strands. This produced a better integrated textile than the familiar spiraled single braid, and there was less chance of puckers along the seams where tensions are not always exactly even.

This is a somewhat tricky technique to master, but the idea of laying out and braiding a number of strands at once has excellent application for making small square or rectangular rugs or mats from fabric scraps, worn blankets, and outmoded wool clothing.

The technique used to make the belts in Figures 201 and 202 is commonly called Osage braiding, and though that tribe produced some fine examples, it was not confined to that area. It has a long history in the Southwest, as well as among the Algonquians and other groups who lived around the Great Lakes.

Simple forms of this braiding can be picked up very quickly, but it can also be expanded into a sophisticated art form. Some museum examples are made of hundreds of strands braided into complex designs, often with beads woven along their outlines.

As an introduction to the process, follow the instructions in Figure 203, using from twenty-two to thirty strands of cotton rug yarn. Resist the temptation to use too many colors. The results will be tweedy and disappointing.

Alternate rows of several strands of the same color create diagonal stripes similar to those on the left braid in Figure 201. But something will happen, no matter how they are arranged, and it is often more exciting to group them at random and see what develops than to follow a prescribed sequence.

Two shades of turquoise in the order shown in Figure 203 produced the subtle pattern in Figure 202. It is more dramatic when worked in black or brown, and white. Twenty-two strands of rug yarn make a 1½" band; thirty-two strands will equal 2½". The weaving take-up in length is about double.

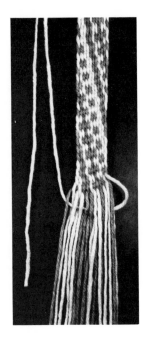

Fig. 201. Diagonal and chevron braids in three colors. *By Joan Sestak.*

Fig. 202. Diagonal braid in two colors.

Fig. 203. DIAGONAL BRAIDING

A. Cut yarn about double the length desired for the finished braid, plus allowances for fringe, buckle overlap or other methods for finishing. Wind each strand once around a pencil or short length of doweling, and tie in a single knot. Draw short ends together, tie in an overhand knot, and suspend from a nail or a T pin on a Celotex board. To set strands in order, twine a length of yarn through them just under the stick, and knot.

B. Start with the first row on either side. Weave under one/over one across the row, and hang the weaver (1) over the end of the supporting stick.

C. Go back to the same side, pick up the next strand and weave across the row. Bring old weaver (1) down over weaver 2 to return it to the warps. Hang weaver 2 over the end of the stick. Adjust the tension by drawing on weaver 1 until the threads are even. Continue the pattern. If weavers become too short to reach the stick, hang them on the edge of the woven area with a pin or piece of tape.

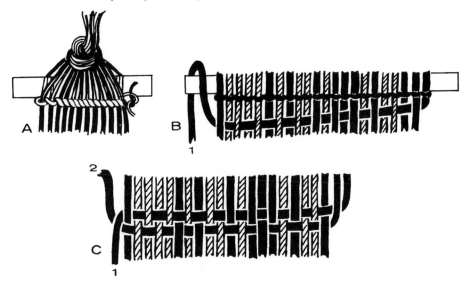

CHEVRON BRAIDING

The setup for chevron braiding is essentially the same as for diagonal braiding, except that an even number of strands is required, and colors must be arranged in the same order on each side of the center.

The center point is very important, and it is a good idea to mark it on the supporting stick with a short length of yarn in a contrasting color. If each new row of weaving does not start with crisscrossing the two central strands, the pattern will become distorted.

To reverse the chevrons on each end of the braid, start in the middle and braid one end, then remove the twined stay, turn the braid around, and weave the other end.

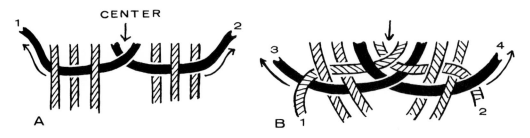

Fig. 204. CHEVRON BRAIDING, METHOD #1
A. Set up twenty-four to thirty strands of rug yarn as described for diagonal braiding, using the same number of strands and the same color order on each side of the center. Gather one side in each hand. Take the first strand to the right of the center (1) and weave it over and under the strands to the left. Hang it over the end of the stick. Take the first strand to the left of the center (2) and weave it under and over the strands to the right. Hang it over the end of the supporting stick.
B. Go back to the center and repeat. Pull old weavers (1 and 2) to adjust the tension, and return them to the warps. Hang new weavers (3 and 4) on the stick. Threads are shown separated here for clarity. They should be drawn close together to make a firm braid.

CHEVRON BRAIDING, METHOD #2

As an alternate to Method #1, start with the first strand to the right of center and weave over one/under one to the left edge. Hang up the weaver, then turn the stick around so that you are facing the back side. Pick up the first strand to the right of the center, and weave over one/under one to the left again. Turn the stick back to the front and continue. By turning back and forth, the weaving sequence is automatically reversed. There is no special advantage to this method unless you feel more comfortable with weaving in one direction, but it can be very helpful preparation for the arrow design.

Fig. 205. Osage woman's sash, double diamond pattern. *Courtesy, Osage Tribal Museum, Arts and Crafts Center, Bureau of Indian Affairs.*

ARROW DESIGN

Some of the finest braided textiles produced in North America had variations of the arrow and flame designs, and a comparatively few examples are still in existence. The famous "Assomption" sashes were made from fine yarn by Northeastern French Canadians, who picked up the technique from the Hurons.

You should practice the chevron braid until you are completely comfortable with the basic process before starting the arrow design. Although the arrow involves only slight changes, you must constantly concentrate on keeping the strands in the proper order. Like complicated knitting or crochet designs, however, it will capture your total attention, and you may find it more interesting than simpler techniques. You will also have the satisfaction of participating in an old art form that is nearly extinct.

Begin with heavy yarn in two strongly contrasting colors, one arranged as a central stripe, the other forming narrow stripes on each edge. The center point is again very important, and the size of the arrow will be determined by the width of the central stripe.

As an example, let us assume that you are using forty strands of brown and white yarn to make a band about three inches wide. Starting at the right of the center, tie on sixteen strands of brown, then four strands of white. Repeat the order to the left.

As described in Method #2 for the chevron braid, you must braid alternately from the front and back sides to keep the sides of the arrow symmetrical. As in most weaving projects, the first two or three rows are the hardest because the thread order is not clearly established. But once the pattern begins to emerge, your eyes will tell you where the strands have to be twisted, and you will no longer have to actually count.

At the end of each row, pull down on each warp thread in turn to keep them straight and adjust the tension. If your arrow begins to look lopsided, you have either lost the center, or have broken the weaving sequence by crossing over or under two threads instead of one. Unravel it until you find your mistake.

Fig. 206. ARROW BRAIDING
Mark the center and gather the side threads in each hand. Draw out the first thread to the right and weave over/under to the left until you reach the end of the central color group. (Fifth from the edge in this diagram.) Bring this thread under the weaver in a half twist, drop the old weaver, and continue to the edge with the new weaver. Hang it over the stick and turn the braid to the back side. Repeat, using the first strand to the right of the center again.

The slanting edge of the arrow is formed by advancing the twist one thread on each row, as shown by 5, 6, and 7. Keep the weavers in proper order, and continue the pattern until the twists reach the center. The colors will then be back together again. Start the pattern over, weaving the first strand to the right out to thread 5, and so on. One arrow will be completed when you have worked back to the center.

Fig. 207. To use three colors for arrow braiding, make each half of the central stripe a different color, and keep edge stripes alike. The heavy green worsted and charcoal Lopi used here do not separate in a black and white photo, but they can be identified by the different textures. A green strand is being woven to the left.

Fig. 208. When the white threads are reached, the green weaver is twisted, returned to the warps, and the weaving is continued with the grey thread.

Fig. 209. The weavers control the tension. At the end of a row, pull on the old weaver before bringing it over the new weaver and returning it to the warps. This color order will make arrows half grey and half green on a white background.

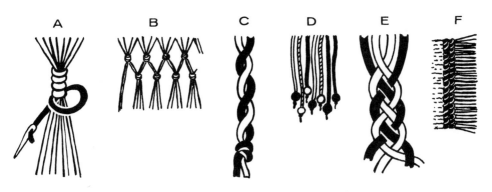

Fig. 210. END FINISHES

A. Divide strands into even bundles. Tie a length of yarn around them, wrap tightly several times, then draw the yarn downward through the last wrap.

B. Tie even bundles with an overhand knot. Adjust threads, then subdivide the bundles and tie in between the knots of the previous row.

C. Draw out adjacent strands. Twist one tightly until it begins to kink, then pin it to a board or have someone hold it. Twist the other strand, bring the ends together, and knot. When they are released, they will wind together into a neat cord.

D. Tie beads, bells, shells, coins, or tin cones on the ends of the strands.

E. Many Indian fringes have three- and four-strand braids combined with twisted cords.

F. Several rows of twining make a good finish for a short fringe.

CONTEMPORARY APPLICATIONS
FOR PLAITED AND BRAIDED BANDS

Plaited and braided bands make excellent straps for guitars and other musical instruments, and can add a custom touch to sweaters, jackets, and vests. Indians joined the edges of a number of bands to make wider textiles for girdles, sashes, and bags.

To divide long strands into shorter lengths, mark terminal points so that the patterns can be matched, and make two rows of machine stitching across them, ½" apart. Cut between the rows of stitching. The segments can be invisibly whipstitched together, or they can be joined by decorative lacing.

Other suggestions are shown in Fig. 211.

Fig. 211. USING PLAITED AND BRAIDED BANDS
A. Cut long bands into segments, and join edges together with the patterns aligned. For a simple tote, use one long band in the middle as a handle.
B. Mark the center of a hemmed length of fabric and whipstitch one end of a band to it (1). Whipstitch edges of the band over each side edge of the fabric. Bring opposite end over to the other side of the fabric, and repeat.
C. Braid each end of a wide band, leaving the center threads free. Machine-stitch across terminals of each segment. Using separate lengths of yarn, tie together alternate bundles of threads. (See Fig. 210A and B.) Fold the braid in half lengthwise, and whipstitch each side over the vertical edges of the hemmed fabric (1). Hand-stitch invisibly across the bottom of the fold to close it.
D. For small throw rugs and pillow tops, join a number of bands together, matching patterns. Secure the ends with machine-stitching, and knot into a short fringe.
E. Use fine yarn for braided necklaces. Knot one end of the bundle, arrange colors symmetrically on each side, and work chevron braiding without crisscrossing the center strands. This will result in a split. When it is long enough to go over your head, crisscross the center strands and continue the normal chevron pattern.

5

TEXTILE-
MAKING
SPECIALTIES

Navajo rugs are the best-known North American textiles, yet they are less than three hundred years old. They were preceded by a long history of weaving discoveries, some of which may be even more remarkable when they are evaluated against the time and culture when they occurred.

There was first basketmaking, then finger weaving, accompanied by the discovery that colored fibers could be arranged in certain orders to create designs. But there are only a limited number of ways that free-hanging threads can be manipulated, and the search for greater flexibility led to devising a support for the warps (lengthwise threads).

At first, it was simply two upright stakes with crossbars at the top and bottom between which the warps were stretched taut. This permitted the colored wefts (crosswise threads) to be interchanged as they crossed, opening up many new design possibilities.

This was just a frame, not a machine, but a fixed warp is essential for true weaving, and it needed only a few refinements and a heddle for separating alternate warps simultaneously, to become the loom still used by the Navajos today.

THE VILLAGERS AND THE RAIDERS

Before the Spaniards arrived, the tribes in the Southwest could be loosely divided into two culture groups: the villagers and the raiders.

The villagers, or pueblo peoples, were farmers and had settled around the

131

New Mexican Rio Grande Valley, and at Hopi, Zuñi, and Acoma. They had a precarious security that allowed time for the development of many arts. They carved, made pottery and baskets, and wove cotton into textiles in much the same way that their ancestors had done as early as A.D. 700, possibly even earlier in Arizona.[1]

The precariousness of their security was partly due to periodic droughts, plagues, and other natural disasters. But it was mainly caused by the borrowing habits of the raiders, notably the Apaches and the Navajos. These were semi-nomadic peoples who grew no crops. Instead, they hunted for food, both in the open country and in the farms of the pueblos.

The Navajos had wandered down from Canada a few generations earlier, absorbing an ethnic mixture along the way. They were quick-witted and observant, and in their raids on the pueblos not only picked up food, livestock, slaves, and sometimes wives but also ideas that could be turned into profitable commodities.

Although they had probably made some functional textiles by plaiting and braiding, there is little doubt that the art of loom weaving was one of the ideas they borrowed. Very likely, they periodically borrowed a few weavers along with the idea.

Only by establishing themselves on defendable sites and building fortified communities were the villagers saved from extinction by the raiders. But they were no match for the Spaniards, who arrived in the mid-1500s with guns and horses.

[1] We do not know exactly where cotton was first developed, though most authorities agree that it came from Peru or Middle America.

   Charles Avery Amsden, *Navajo Weaving* (Glorieta, N.M.: The Rio Grande Press, Inc., 1971), p. 21.

Figs. 212, 213. NAVAJO RUGS
The idea of rugmaking came from traders when handmade blankets could no longer compete with manufactured goods. But the upright loom and basic weaving process are of native origin, and go back much further than the period when they were picked up, and eventually improved on, by the Navajos.
   The exact origin and date of these rugs is unknown. *Collection, Elizabeth Craster.*

It was not in the Spanish plan to exterminate them. It was more profitable to allow them to live and to return the favor by paying heavy taxes of labor and salable goods, including cotton cloth.

The elusive Navajos occupied lands to the north of pueblo settlements, where they were not hemmed in by Spanish posts. They not only managed to evade the ever-widening net of Spanish domination but, characteristically, profited from it. There were now horses, sheep, and new weapons to be borrowed on raiding expeditions, and they made possible a gradual change toward a pastoral way of life.

For about a hundred years the Spanish military and church governments kept the pueblos suppressed, but their increasing demands finally became intolerable. In 1680 the village tribes united in a massive rebellion and forced out the intruders. They kept control for twelve uneasy years, and the history of the West might be completely different if ancient grievances had been set aside and the raiders had added their support against a mutual enemy.

But the pueblos had wounds that were very old and deep, and the Navajos were prospering from the weakened situations of foreigners and villagers alike. It was more profitable for them to operate from a neutral position—a position they demonstrated by raiding both Spaniards and pueblos with equal fierceness and frequency.

It soon became painfully clear to the villagers that their independence was doomed. They could either resubmit to Spanish oppression, or seek refuge with their traditional enemies.

Many chose the latter, exchanging their identity for survival. All necessary elements were then present for the development of Navajo weaving—looms, wool, and a permanent supply of instructors.[2]

Navajo women continued the traditions of the pueblo weavers for some time. The first major change occurred when traders brought in a red wool cloth, called *bayeta*. Since there were no good red native dyes, they eagerly unraveled the cloth and retwisted the threads to use in their blanket designs.

Traders next introduced bright aniline dyes, commercial yarns, and designs that were directed toward the tastes of the white market.[3] The results were often busy and cluttered. The chemical colors were garish, and lacked the natural compatibility of the early combinations. Weaving quality deteriorated rapidly, and from about 1890 to the early years of the twentieth century, Navajo weaving fell to the level of tourist art. Machine-made products were not only better but cheaper, and there would have been little incentive to keep the craft alive if traders had not come up with the idea of rugmaking.

The first attempts at heavier textiles were not very successful, but technical

---

[2] The Navajos were finally conquered by American troops in 1863–1865, and imprisoned at Bosque Redondo. After four miserable years, during which thousands died, they were allowed to return to their homeland, where their reservation is today.

[3] Some of these designs were copied from Oriental rugs that had been brought to America by early immigrants. Their influence can still be seen in many Navajo patterns.

Fig. 214. This old and very rare blanket has an unusual style that is much less familiar than patterns that are popularly identified with the Navajos. These textiles were made primarily for their own use, not for trade. *Collection, The Millicent A. Rogers Memorial Museum.*

Fig. 215. The Yei rugs were woven for sale, and, though they had no place in Indian ceremonies, the designs were copied from sandpaintings used in sacred religious rites. The practice met with strong tribal disapproval at first, but it soon dissipated when the patterns proved to be popular on the market. This unfinished example is still on the loom and shows how the design was woven horizontally. One side of a "rainbow" guardian symbol is at the bottom and was intended to be completed on the other end. *Collection, The Millicent A. Rogers Memorial Museum.*

problems were gradually solved. From the efforts of a few sincerely dedicated traders, weavers abandoned the harsh colors, and in many cases, went back to natural wools and vegetable dyes. Some of the most beautiful rugs being woven today have designs in creamy white, earthy browns, and a range of terra-cotta reds that reflect the colors of Southwestern landscapes.

Fig. 216. The design of this small Navajo rug is very similar to some of the California basket designs. The colors are golden brown, dark brown, red, and natural. Its origin and date are unknown, though it has certain characteristics of the throws woven in the area of Gallup, N.M.

Fig. 217. A fine example of Navajo weaving, possibly dating from the Classic period, about 1850–1870. Measurements are 46″ × 30″. *Courtesy, The M. H. De Young Memorial Museum.*

Figs. 218, 219. The design on the square Navajo saddle blanket is typical, but the flying birds on the rug are unusual. *Photos by Jim Toms, courtesy, The Nevada State Museum.*

136

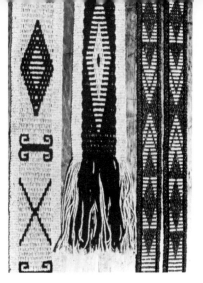

Fig. 220. Woven sashes and strips in wool, using Hopi and Navajo warp-faced pickup techniques on an inkle loom. *Weaving and photo, Jacquetta Nisbet.*

CONTEMPORARY TEXTILES FROM SOUTHWESTERN AND PLAINS DESIGNS

A Navajo loom is a simple piece of equipment that is little more than a bundle of sticks when it is dismantled. It can be easily constructed, and detailed instructions can be obtained from references in the Appendix.

Their designs, however, are also appropriate for contemporary methods of textile making, and they have a timeless quality that is compatible with any style of furnishings.

Fig. 221. DESIGNS ADAPTED FROM NAVAJO BLANKETS AND RUGS

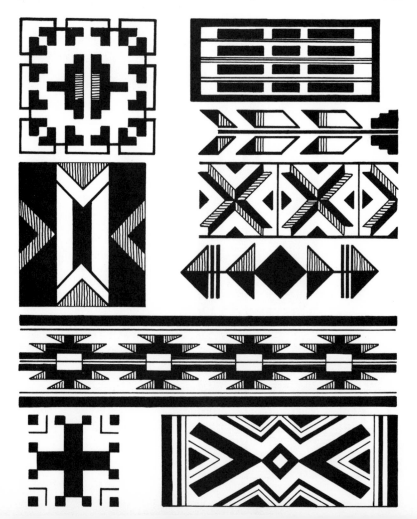

Unlike painted designs that can be freely drawn on a finished surface, woven designs are a part of the basic construction. Early Navajo designs were simple crosses, squares, rectangles, and stripes. Later, as their techniques improved, zigzags, diamonds, and diagonal elements were woven in by jogging the color lines a block or row at a time. This produced characteristic stepped, or "terraced," designs.

Adaptations of these patterns can be worked out on graph paper, and they lend themselves well to textiles that are assembled from woven, knitted, or crocheted units, and to rugs and tapestries that are made on fabric foundations.

Fig. 222. Knitted, crocheted, or woven squares in solid colors can be arranged in many ways to make border patterns or geometric designs. This unit in cobalt, turquoise, light green, and medium green knitting worsted has five squares to the side and makes a 20″ × 20″ floor pillow top. The squares were woven on an inexpensive needle loom. More complex designs can be made by weaving some of the squares on a half-size loom.

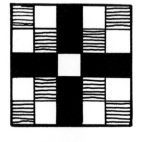

Fig. 223. By eliminating one row of squares between each unit, the same pattern can be used for a V-shaped shawl. Four units will make a straight stole 68″ long, not counting fringe. Other ways of combining three and four colors are shown at the left. These contemporary fashions are not too different in style from the Navajo wearing blankets and poncho/serapes of the pre-reservation period.

HOOKED TEXTILES

Hooking is one of the easiest and most practical techniques for rugmaking, and is another old art that will probably live forever. The nubby, slightly irregular character of the surface texture is especially suited to Southwestern designs.

Traditionally, hooked rugs were made from old clothing or blankets cut into strips, and this material is still favored by many craftsmen. Colors can be freshened with dyes, and often, interesting shades can be obtained with laundry bleaches. Old wool khaki-colored army blankets can be bleached to subtle avocado greens. Unexpected things can also happen to rusty blacks and faded browns when they are treated with bleach. If nothing does, you can still try dyes.

In earlier times, the fabrics for rugmaking were laboriously cut by hand into strips from ⅛" to ¼" wide. Now there are cutting instruments that will slice several strips at once. Electric scissors are also very helpful.

Rug canvas, heavy burlap, or commercial jute backing can be used as a foundation, and it must be stretched in a frame of some kind. Although lap frames, easels, and adjustable folding frames that allow you to roll up finished sections of the rug can be purchased, you can improvise a frame for small throw rugs or floor pillows from inexpensive stretcher bars. For large rugs or tapestries, where it would be difficult to reach the center area, an adjustable frame is a good investment.

Some experienced rugmakers sketch their designs directly on the backing and indicate colors with acrylics or indelible inks. You will have fewer problems, however, if you first work out a pattern on graph paper. By marking the backing with an equal number of larger squares, the working drawing can accurately be transferred a square at a time. This is especially recommended for large pieces where transferring a full-size drawing with many pieces of carbon paper or a perforating wheel is very tedious.

Standard rug hooks can be obtained from shops carrying needlecraft supplies, as can instructions for using them. The 39" × 68" rug in Figure 226 required about three-fourths of a twin blanket in each color (dark red, white, rust, olive) for a thick pile. To estimate the amount of rug yarn needed for the same size and design, hook a sample swatch 1" to 2" square, then pull out the yarn and measure it. By adding up the number of square inches in each color section, you can approximate the total yardage.

The design is worked from the top side. Fabric strips or rug yarn is held on the underside with the left hand, and the hook is positioned above it on the top side. One loop at a time is pulled up.

It takes a little practice to keep the loops even in height, but a certain irregularity is attractive. It is easy to pull out new rows of loops to correct a mistake, but as they become packed in by rows on each side, it is more difficult to make changes.

Fig. 224. Although Navajo weavers work entirely from a mental image of their design, most of us need a fairly accurate pattern drawn to scale on scored paper. This design is a combination of elements from old Navajo rugs.

Fig. 225. Mark the rug backing into squares that are equal in number to the squares of the pattern (shown at the left). Fill in color areas with washes of acrylics or indelible markers. Allow at least 2″ of backing around all sides of the design for hems.

Fig. 226. Start at one end of the rug and hook the design horizontally. Trim uneven ends. Coat the back side of the worked area with rug adhesive, and, when dry, hem the edges. *Worked by Bessie Long.*

PUNCH NEEDLE TEXTILES

Similar looped textiles can be made with a punch needle instead of a hook. They are available in several sizes, for fine yarn as well as heavier rug weights. The most versatile styles can be adjusted to obtain loops of different heights.

The amount of rug yarn needed for a project will vary according to weight, lengths of loops, and spacing of stitches. As a rule of thumb, when the punch needle projects 1½″ (the #9 setting on an adjustable needle), 1½ yards of cotton or acrylic rug yarn will fill a one-inch square that has six stitches to the side. It is always wise, however, to work your own test swatch, and purchase extra material so that dye lots will be consistent.

The same backings noted for hooked rugs can be used, though for fine yarn the weave must be fairly tight to keep the stitches from slipping out. The backing can be stretched in an embroidery hoop for small designs. For large tapestries and rugs, it can be stapled or tacked to a stretcher bar frame, and worked in either lengthwise or crosswise sections. Start with one end or side. When this is completed, remove tacks and restretch the adjacent section. To elevate the frame high enough from the worktable to accommodate the downward plunge of the needle, place books, bricks, or sections of 4″ × 4″ blocks under each end.

Allow from two to four inches around all sides of the design area for hems, and for attaching in the frame.

Punch needle designs are drawn and worked on the back side. Hold the needle upright on a pattern line so that it is perpendicular to the backing, and plunge it straight down as far as it will go. Bring it up so that the tip barely skims the surface, and move it forward to the next stitch. If it is pulled up too high, it will draw the loop along with it. Make stitches with fine and medium weight yarn about ⅛″ apart. With rug weights, stitches can be from ¼″ to ⅜″ apart.

It is important to keep several yards of yarn pulled out of the skein at all times so that it trails freely behind the needle. Even the slightest tension can cause the loops to be irregular in height. Try to hold already worked loops out of the way with your left hand, but some intermeshing is likely to occur, especially when filling in enclosed areas of the design. Separate the loops with a toothpick, row by row. If they are not corrected, the lines of the design will be distorted.

Uncut loops have a pebbly texture. For a smooth, velvety pile, pull the loops straight up between the blades of scissors, and clip before proceeding to the next row. When the piece is finished, use a vacuum cleaner to draw up yarn ends that might be buried beneath the surface, then carefully shear the tips with scissors held horizontally. Vacuum again to remove clippings.

Pin the textile face down on a flat surface and coat the back side of the worked area with rug adhesive.

For tapestries, trim margins down to two inches. Hem long vertical edges, then hem top and bottom, leaving ends open to make a casing for supports of wood molding. Fringe can be made from rug yarn cut into twenty-four-inch lengths. Thread two lengths at a time in a tapestry needle, and attach at the bottom with Lark's Head knots. Divide the fringe into equal bundles, and tie into tassels.

Fig. 227. Coils and scrolls are used in almost endless combinations on pueblo pottery. "Rain Bird" designs on Zuñi water jars often feature an unusual pointed scroll that is reversed, doubled, or repeated in many different ways. A similar element also appears on the pottery of other pueblo tribes.

Two of these scrolls placed back to back form a stylized butterfly. They will resemble a fleur-de-lis if they are arranged facing.

Fig. 228. This 15″ × 54″ tapestry was worked with a punch needle. The outlines were worked first, then enclosed areas were filled in. On the butterfly's wings, two rows of stitches (⅜″) were used on the narrow outlines; three rows (½″) on the wider lines. The central medallion is an elongated version of a Zuñi rosette that is believed to represent either the sun or a sunflower.

Rugs from Carpet Scraps

Figure 229 illustrates a different approach to rugmaking. All the larger areas, including the lighter background stripes, are carpet remnants. The dark outlines and dark stripes are worked with wool rug yarn and a punch needle, in order to obtain contrasting colors that are not readily available in carpeting.

Designs that are made up of straight lines are recommended for this technique, since accurate curves are difficult to cut from heavy carpeting. Use a heavy jute or canvas backing, and mark the pattern with waterproof ink or acrylics, leaving a margin of two to four inches on all sides.

Figs. 229, 230. The dark stripes and dark outlines of this area rug were worked with a punch needle. Other sections are carpet remnants. The central motif has a smooth, velvety pile, and, for contrast, the lighter carpeting stripes have both cut and uncut loops. The design was inspired by Sioux beadwork.

Stretch the backing in a frame with the design side up, making sure the pattern does not extend over the frame. This will be the *back* side of the finished rug.

Adjust punch needle for loops the same height as the thickness of the carpeting. Work all the punched lines, clipping loops row by row as you go.

Cut out paper patterns for the carpeting sections, then trim off ⅛″ on all sides to allow for the spread of the pile. Mark patterns with an arrow to indicate the direction of the carpeting nap. It should be consistent on all pieces.

Turn the rug to the front side and lay paper patterns inside the punched outlines to check for accurate fits. Flip patterns over, and place on the back of the carpeting with straight edges aligned with the grain and arrows aligned with the nap. Trace around them, then use a very sharp craft knife to cut out the carpet pieces.

Cover your worktable with plastic wrap or cleaning bags. Set the still framed rug on it, front side up. Starting in the center, smooth back the punched outlines, and liberally brush both the foundation backing and the back of the carpet pieces with rug adhesive. Wait a few seconds for some of the adhesive solvent to evaporate before pressing the carpeting in place. (If the pile is very thick and springy, lay masking tape along the top edges of the punched outline and press it back out of the way.)

Continue with adjacent sections. After all carpet sections are positioned, cover rug with a large sheet of heavy cardboard or plywood, and weight overnight with books or bricks.

Coat the back side of the worked area with rug adhesive and allow it to dry before removing the rug from the frame. Shear irregular threads. Trim margins down to two inches, and fold to the back side for hems.

CARPETING MOSAICS

The headboard in Figure 232 is made entirely of carpeting, attached with white glue to a framed backing of ¼″ pressed board. Vertical strips of one-inch molding were incorporated into the design for extra bracing. Frame the backing first, then mark it in 1″ squares and transfer the pattern with waterproof ink. Secure the molding strips with small brads and glue, and paint frame and molding.

Cut carpet sections to fit, with the nap running downward if it is directional. Attach them one at a time with white glue, except for the two sections at the top indicated by C on the pattern. Drill holes on each side at these points for fastening the board to the wall with toggle bolts or long screws. Glue the remaining segments of carpeting over the bolt heads after the piece is installed.

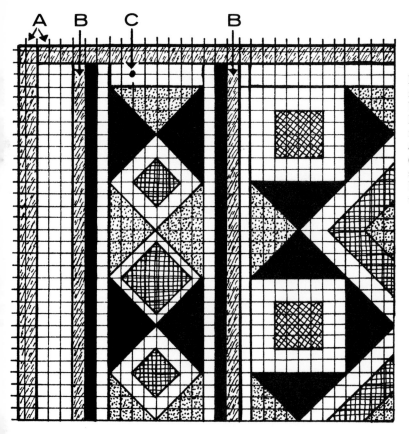

A B C B

Fig. 231. This represents one-fourth of the pattern for the head-board in Fig. 232. 1 square = 1". Frame the backing with 1½" wood molding (A), transfer the design, and attach 1" wood molding strips (B) before setting in the carpet segments. (C) indicates where the board will be bolted on each side to the wall.

Fig. 232. Queen-sized headboard from carpet remnants of varying heights and textures. The depressed areas are indoor-outdoor carpeting; the raised areas are wool and nylon pile. The design from Sioux beadwork is in shades of red, olive green, and ivory. *By Mary Lou Stribling.*

Fig. 233. This large curtain is a variation of the design in Figure 230. It is made from olive green burlap, stretched between two spring tension rods. The design was outlined with chalk, then two rows of machine-stitching were made around sections to be "unwoven." The weft threads were carefully clipped just inside the stitches and were pulled out, leaving only the vertical lines of the warp.

Woven Form from a Pottery Design

The beautiful hanging by Evelyn Gulick in Figures 234 and 235 illustrates how inspiration from Indian designs can emerge as a completely original art form. Of impressive dimensions, about 93″ × 68″, the multilayered weaving uses shades of charcoal on the body, head, tail, and upper wings. The underwings are brilliant contrasts of red, black, and white. Most of the materials are shaggy—horsehair, brushed mohair, goat hair, roving, and plain wools. Bright red rayon and smooth wools are used in the underwings.

For the interest of experienced weavers, the artist provides this technical information:

"The length is all on one warp, threaded on twelve harnesses to make manipulation of the layers possible. There are three tubes for the tail, changing to one tube for the lower body. The body has three layers, crossing in the center. At the base of the neck, four layers separate into two layers for the wings. There are two layers for the neck and head. The neck becomes tubular and the head is tubular, separating into three tubes for the pronged topknot. The upper wings remain two layers each, extending to the full wingspan of 68″. The lower wings have four layers—two red, one white, and one black. The layers are switched at the stripes so that red layers are inside at the open edges of the wings, and the red warp shows in the fringe with the black. The lower wings are tied and tacked in place onto the hanger under the upper wings."

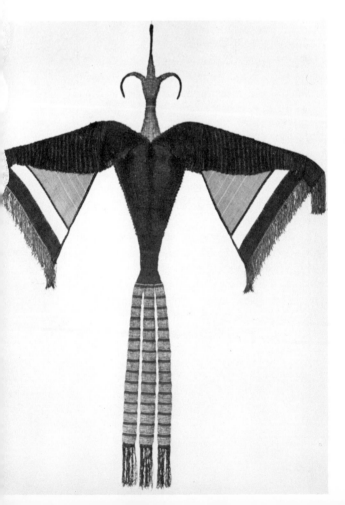

Figs. 234, 235. The design of this multilayered weaving by Evelyn Gulick was inspired by a dragonfly symbol on a Zuñi ceremonial vessel. A closer view shows some of the technical details of the construction. *Photos, Sidney Gulick.*

NORTHWEST COAST TEXTILES

The dry air in the Southwest has preserved many ancient artifacts that have established a fairly clear chronological history of the arts of that area. By comparison, information on early cultures of the humid Northwestern Coast is skimpy.

Tools can tell us a great deal about the art techniques of specific periods, but little about the development of designs. The textile arts were already highly advanced when Captain Cook reached the Northwest Coast in 1778,[4] and at that time a sophisticated decorative style had become standardized. It is safe to assume that this could have come about only after a long period of growth.

This narrow strip along the northern Pacific Ocean must have been settled very gradually by many different tribal families. They were not farmers, but the necessity for storing dried fish and meats during seasons when they were abundant restricted their mobility and led to established communities.

Although the true loom was unknown in this region, the Salish wove fine fabrics on frames that held the warp threads taut. Along with utilitarian bags, blankets, and clothing, they made unique ceremonial robes with designs worked in feathers. They also bred small furry dogs that were sheared like sheep to obtain wool.

The Chilkats, who were a branch of the Tlingit tribe, wove many kinds of excellent textiles for shirts, bags, and mats, but they are famous for their distinctive ceremonial blankets. Nothing like them was produced anywhere else in North America.

Their development cannot be traced. They were so highly valued that they became a basic unit of exchange. The worth of a carved box or a slave, for example, would be figured on the basis of an equivalent value in blankets.

The Chilkat weaving frame consisted of a horizontal bar attached across the tops of two poles. The poles were set upright into blocks of wood, and were braced with wedges so that the frame could be moved about if necessary.

Loomed textiles are always woven from the bottom up, since it is easier to pack in the wefts by drawing a beater toward the body. The Chilkat blankets had a loose warp, and like braided and plaited textiles, were woven from the top down.

The most common blanket materials were wool of the mountain goat, softened and shredded bark, and sinew, in dyed and natural colors of white, yellow, black, and bluish green. The weaving process was a curious mixture of twining and tapestry techniques.[5] The designs were woven in separate sections, then were joined together. Although it is often difficult to find the seams, they are clearly visible on the old blanket in Figure 236.

Unlike the Navajo weavers, who worked from a mental picture and made no two textiles alike, Chilkat women worked from patterns that were painted on

[4] Loom weaving was known only in the Southwest.
[5] See "Twining" in Chapter 3.

boards by men. The designs had ceremonial significance that presumably the women were not entitled to fully understand, nor accurately document. Since the pattern boards were preserved, the same designs were woven over and over, with occasional color changes or minor rearrangements.

The pattern drafters were concerned about keeping traditional symbols consistent, not with the materials or methods used to reproduce them. So where Navajo designs were based on the right-angle crossing of warp and weft threads, Chilkat designs had the same curvilinear shapes and free-flowing lines that were typical of paintings on housefronts and storage boxes.

Some old blanket designs were also painted, not woven. The earliest woven designs were geometric, but the most familiar Chilkat specialties feature abstracted animal symbols. The occasional rare example is asymmetrical, but usually half the design was painted on the pattern board and the other half was duplicated in reverse.

Animal symbols often suggest the internal anatomy as well as the exterior shape. These details are highly abstracted, however, and may be recognizable only after study and comparison. The patternmakers also had a compulsion to cover the entire surface with some kind of decoration. Spaces that were isolated and could not be related to the portrayal of the figure were simply filled in with compatible shapes.

These fillers in time became standardized, though they were used in many combinations. Rounded rather than angular shapes were preferred, and most blankets were liberally studded with oval "eye" forms. These were often positioned at the joints of the animal's skeleton, where it is generally assumed they represent sockets. Real eyes can be identified by the points on each side that suggest lids.

Fig. 236. Old Chilkat blanket with typical symmetrical design of animal symbols. *Courtesy, The Museum of Northern British Columbia.*

Fig. 237. Chilkat blanket from Ksan Village, British Columbia. The House of Treasures in Ksan Village serves as a repository for the tribal heritage of Indians in that area. They are kept on display when they are not being used for special events and ceremonies.

Fig. 238. Characteristic space fillers from Chilkat blankets.

Fig. 239. Ksan Village, British Columbia. The designs on Northwest Coast totem poles and housefronts are clearly related to the designs on Chilkat blankets.

CONTEMPORARY TEXTILES
FROM NORTHWESTERN DESIGNS

Carved poles, posts, rattles, masks, and ceremonial dishes are good sources for sculptured textile designs. They can be worked in carpet remnants by shearing the pile along the edges of the separate sections before gluing them to a backing. They can also be worked with a punch needle, like the bear mask in Figure 243.

Figs. 240–243. SCULPTURED TEXTILE MASK

Fig. 240. Draw the pattern on a coarse linen or canvas backing, and indicate the colors with acrylic paints. Leave a border from ½″ to ⅜″ wide around separate parts of the design to facilitate shearing the pile. Set the punch needle to make a row of short loops around each section, then adjust it for longer loops and fill the inside areas. Clip each row of loops as it is worked.

Fig. 241. Coat the back of the yarn stitches with rug adhesive. When it is dry, separate the pile along the borders between color sections and shear it into smoothly rounded contours.

Fig. 242. Cut away unworked margins of the backing.

Fig. 243. Mount the sculptured mask on a matching shape cut from pressed board, or a felt-covered plywood backing. Although this design was inspired by a carved bear on a ceremonial rattle, very similar faces can be found in Chilkat blankets. Colors are gold, turquoise, red, and black.

Figs. 244–246. EAGLE TAPESTRY

Fig. 244. Eagle design adapted from a Haida dance shirt.

Fig. 245. The dramatic simplicity of the eagle design makes it a good subject for sculptured effects, but it is also effective in a flat, thick, velvety pile.

Fig. 246. A dense pile has a tendency to curl unless it lies flat on the floor. Hangings should be braced on the back sides with strips of ⅛" pressed board. Attach the bracing with white glue or rug adhesive, and weight with bricks until dry.

Figs. 247, 248. Hooked tapestry by Harold B. Balazs. It is difficult to pinpoint the factors that contribute to the "Indianness" of this handsome contemporary tapestry. Of magnificent scale, it covers an entire wall in the Appaloosa Room of Kah/Nee/Ta Lodge, Warm Springs (Oregon) Reservation. Some elements, such as the owl at the upper left in the detail, and the fish at the lower left and right, suggest totemic carvings and basket designs. Others have the feeling of plant forms and petroglyphs.

6

APPLIQUÉ AND PATCHWORK

Decorative appliqués were made in many areas of North America, but they differed greatly in style and the materials from which they were made.

The resources of the Eskimos were considerably more limited than those of tribes who lived in temperate climates, especially before trade goods were introduced. They were remarkably inventive, however, with such unlikely animal by-products as birdskins, fishskins, and the intestines of seals, otters, bears, and reindeer.

The intestines were first cleaned, inflated, and dried, until they became tough and parchmentlike. They were then cut into strips and fashioned into waterproof wearing apparel, dolls, game equipment, and appliqué patches. Sometimes the appliqués were painted and joined with furs in alternating stripes.

On the cold, foggy Aleutian Islands, where vegetation is limited to a few species of low bushes, mosses, and dwarfed trees, fishskin work became a fine art. The skins were often dyed with bark, colored clays, or metallic oxides, and were appliquéd to contrasting foundations in geometric arrangements that reflect a Polynesian or Asian influence, possibly dating back to early immigrants. Some appliqués were made with perforated strips that were layered to expose underlying colors in the openings. The essentials of this technique are similar to ribbonwork, described later in this chapter, but the membranous texture and unique trims of small tufts of fur, shells, sea lion whiskers, polished animal teeth, and feathers set it completely apart in decorative impact.

Printed calico brought by traders appealed to the Aleuts' love of color, but since it lacked the durable, waterproof qualities of fishskins, they combined the two, using the skins for practical foundations, and the fabric for decorative bindings and linings.

On the Northwest Coast, dance kilts, robes, and other ceremonial costumes were made from Hudson's Bay Company blankets appliquéd with flannel cloth. (Some modern versions are made from canvas, and the designs are painted, instead of appliquéd.) Typical animal designs were split down the centers of the bodies with the halves folded out and joined to a common head and tail. The same space fillers, eye shapes, and rounded rectangles that were noted on Chilkat blankets were used in appliqué designs.

Early appliqués were often outlined with rows of dentalium shells, but small pearl buttons were readily substituted when they became available.

Fig. 249. Old chief's robe trimmed with pearl buttons, from Ksan Village, British Columbia. The symmetrical bird design is typical of Northwest Coast totemic symbols, but the repetition of the bird's head in the eyes and center of the body is an interesting variation, as is the figure in the upper left corner.

Fig. 250. A more contemporary chief's cloak from Ksan Village has appliquéd bands around the edges, and rows of buttons down the front sides.

RIBBON APPLIQUÉS

The ribbonwork of the North Central and Midwestern tribes cannot be classed as aboriginal, since it originated from exposure to foreign materials, tools, and tastes. According to some authorities, the style is of Spanish origin and reached the Indians through Spanish missionaries, yet it emerged distinctly "Indian," in both technique and design.

It is a modern art, dating from the late 1700s. Osage, Winnebago, Menomini, and Delaware women are especially well known for the work, but it was widely practiced throughout the Plains and Woodlands areas. Certain refinements were added to it in different groups, though it retained the special flavor that distinguished it from its European ancestors.

In its simplest form, pink, yellow, red, purple, blue, and other brightly colored silk ribbons were appliquéd in stripes to a dark foundation, or were arranged to crisscross in imitation of commercial plaids. Eventually, geometric and floral designs from traditional beadwork and moosehair embroidery became popular.

Really fine work was made by cutting shapes from the ribbons, then hand-stitching both the cutouts and the strips from which they were removed to a contrasting backing, creating positive-negative designs of the kind shown in Figures 251 and 252. Elaborate examples might involve multiple rows of appliqués, each made up of several layers that exposed sections of different underlying colors. The combined widths of as many as ten ribbons might be required to make a twelve-inch border.

They were worked on broadcloth, woolen goods, and occasionally on leather. (Thrifty seamstresses sometimes made them on separate strips of material so that they could be removed from a worn garment and added to a new one.) They were most commonly used around the bottom and down the side flap of women's wraparound skirts, and along the edges of shawls and robes, but they were also added to leggings and moccasins for both sexes and to shirts, doll clothes, and bags.

Figs. 251, 252. Ribbon appliqués on leggings; details. Delaware ribbonwork was often edged with beads, or combined with sewn bead motifs. Leggings were held up by garters tied above the calf. *Researched by Ty Stewart, courtesy, Indian America.*

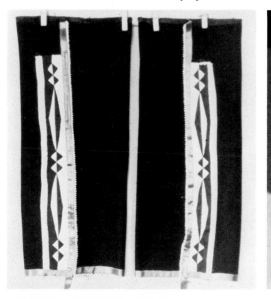

Fig. 253. The appliqués on this Micmac (Eastern Woodlands) skirt were made from ribbons and silk fabrics. Although the design is simpler than the better-known ribbonwork, the effect is quite elegant. The pointed hood is beautifully decorated with a classic double-scroll design of small beads. Beads are also stitched along the edges of the appliqués, and embroidered in the pattern of the upper printed border. Bead dangles are attached between the points. The costume was made in the early part of the twentieth century. *Collection, The Nova Scotia Museum.*

Small bells, beads, and dangles of various kinds were sometimes sewn down the centers or along the edges of ribbon borders, and in certain tribes, the silk cutouts were combined with beadwork. In later versions, taffeta or satin textiles were substituted for the narrow ribbons so that the designs could be worked faster and on a larger scale.

Obviously, this type of decoration was fairly fragile, and was not intended for everyday garments.

Ribbon appliqués are being revived again in certain Plains areas, notably Oklahoma, where contemporary needleworkers use grosgrain ribbon instead of silk. They often attach it with a zigzag sewing machine stitch to eliminate the chore of turning under the edges. This also allows for a greater freedom of design, and the simple geometric, floral, and leaf motifs that were favored in earlier periods are being replaced by curving patterns of great complexity.

Fig. 254. The idea for this pillow top with maroon, red, pink, and orange ribbons appliquéd on raw silk was borrowed from early Indian appliqués that did not use cutout patches. The design, however, was adapted from Southwestern sun symbols.

Fig. 255. Ribbonwork and beadwork have common design roots, and many of the same patterns can be found in both. Ribbonwork designs were simplified, since the edges of the silk had to be turned under to prevent raveling. Geometric shapes were widely used, but stars, maple leaves, and double hearts were very popular.

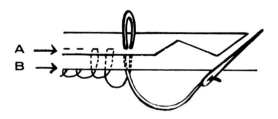

Fig. 256. Ribbonwork appliqués are made up of two elements: the design ribbon (A) and the foundation ribbon (B). The background ribbon is sewn to the foundation fabric first, then the cut edges of the design ribbon are turned under and secured with tiny stitches that create rows of regular indentations along the edges of the design. The best needleworkers used a back stitch that was more durable than running stitches.

Felt, blanket cloth, double knits, pile fabrics, and other nonraveling textiles are easier to appliqué than ribbons, since the edges do not have to be hemmed. Not all of these fabrics are alike on both sides, and the cutouts cannot be flipped over for positive/negative designs. For repeat patterns, cut half the units from the front side of the pattern, then turn it over and cut out the rest. A complete unit can then be assembled with one piece from each group.

A spray pattern holder can be applied to the backs of the appliqués so that some, if not all, of the basting can be eliminated. It also allows you to easily remove and rearrange the pieces if necessary.

APPLIQUÉD TOTE BAG

It was not practical to include pockets in garments made from skins or coarse fabrics, and the Indians devised many kinds of bags and pouches to take their places. Early bags were usually simply two rectangular pieces stitched together on three sides with the top opening closed by a drawstring, though a flap was sometimes folded over the top and fastened with a thong or shell button.

Plains women made tulip-shaped bags from hides and decorated them with beads and long fringes. They also used cloth bags of various shapes that were trimmed with ribbonwork.

Instructions for making simple bags can be found in many clothing pattern books, but it is easy to draft your own to the exact proportions needed for a special design. Except for the handles, the bag in Figure 258 is constructed like the patchwork bag shown later in the chapter.

Chalk the outlines of such bags on the fabric, then work the decorative designs and carefully align them with the pattern before cutting them out. This keeps the edges from becoming frayed or stretched, especially if an embroidery hoop is required.

Fig. 257. Brown and rust felt design on gold wool, adapted from Delaware ribbonwork. The design is divided down the center, and has six separate units and a border on each side. The units were cut out on the pattern lines, and the cutout sections were flipped over to the opposite side.

Fig. 258. A basic pattern for making the bag is in Figure 277. To adapt it for wooden handles, cut additional strips for top casings. Before stitching, the appliquéd fabric was 14″ long, 11″ across the top, and 16″ across the bottom.

Fig. 259A. Attach the bag to the handle by folding in seam allowances on each end of the casing, and machine-stitch it to top outside edges of the bag. Slip casing over the handle to the inside, secure with pins, and blindstitch in place.
B. On bags with rigid handles of this kind, leave the edge seams open about 4½″ down from the top so that it can be opened wider.
C. Turn in seam allowances of the bag and lining on the unjoined edges, and whipstitch invisibly together.

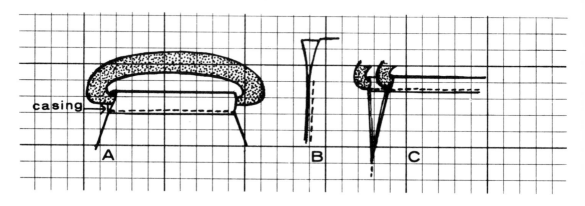

CONTEMPORARY APPLIQUÉ DESIGNS
FROM OTHER INDIAN ARTS

Many designs from the arts in other chapters are suitable for contemporary appliqués, and their classic dignity is a pleasant change from cute and sentimental subjects. Northwest Coast masks and animal figures are especially rich when worked in soft pile fabrics. Synthetic furs can be used for appliquéd bedspreads and throw rugs.

The hanging in Figure 261 is 15″ × 38″, and is made from gold, white, red, and black felt layered on a brown felt foundation. To use the pattern in Figure 260, draw design to size, then cut the foundation piece, allowing two inches at the top for a casing, and ten inches at the bottom for fringe. Measure and mark the foundation with long running stitches on the dotted vertical and crosswise lines as guides for positioning the appliqués. (Chalk marks are difficult to erase from dark felt.)

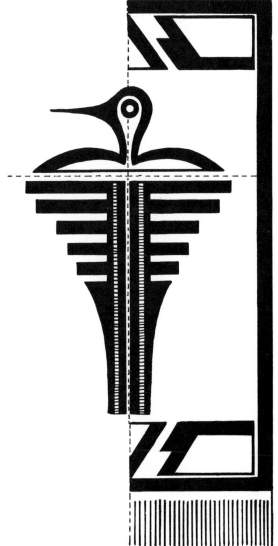

Fig. 260. This hummingbird design is a free interpretation of a painted motif on an old Zuñi pot. Many of their designs were completely abstract, and when birds or other realistic subjects were used, they were presented as decorative symbols rather than naturalistic pictures.

Make paper patterns for the appliqués and cut them out. (Refer to the photo in the color pages for the colors used here.) Center the white head and shoulder section just above the crosswise line. Baste it in place, or use a pattern holder. Position and baste the white body parts next, then stack the colored sections of the bird in proper order. Use short, evenly spaced running stitches of knitting worsted to attach the appliqués to the foundation. Repeat for the borders.

Add extra rows of stitching at the bottom of the design, the center of the bird's body, and in the borders, as shown in Figure 261. Cut vertical slashes ¼″ apart in the remaining felt at the bottom for fringe. Fold back two inches at the top and hem, leaving the ends open to form a casing for a decorative rod.

Fig. 261. Layered felt hanging stitched with wool worsted.

Figs. 262, 263. This handsome quilt by Catherine Gibson is made by the reverse appliqué method used for San Blas molas. The lively and colorful designs are based on North American petroglyph and pictograph symbols. Details show the textural interest created by the tiny quilting stitches. *Photo, Verne Gibson.*

Fig. 264. Plains men often used the walls of their tipis as canvases for painted scenes of brave deeds and triumphant hunts. Their animal figures are distinctly different from Northwest Coast and Southwestern figures, but are equally suitable for appliqués in nonraveling fabrics.

SEMINOLE PATCHWORK

Seminole patchwork was developed in the late 1800s after the introduction of hand-cranked sewing machines. The basic concept of pieced textiles was borrowed from colonial quilts, but the Indian method of forming the designs is entirely original.

In the Seminole technique, fabrics are cut or torn into narrow strips, and seamed horizontally to make striped bands. The bands are then sliced vertically or diagonally into equal segments and restitched together in new arrangements.

By turning alternating segments upside down, or sliding every segment up an inch or more to interrupt the rows of colors, many unusual border patterns can be created. Other designs can be made by combining segments from two or more different striped bands, or by alternating striped segments with solid colors.

Part of the characteristic flavor of Seminole patchwork derives from the practice of using a number of different borders on a single garment. The effect is not disorderly, for they are separated by bands of a single solid color, traditionally dark red, navy, or black. The borders are also sometimes appliquéd on top of a solid piece of fabric. In earlier periods, they were set off by several narrow rows of solid color on each side, but in recent years, rickrack braid has become an increasingly popular substitute.

The textiles are used for men's overshirts and jackets, baby clothes, caps, aprons, bags, and especially for the long, full skirts that have become a tribal trademark. The skirts are worn with soft, loose, capelike overblouses, often of some sheer material, and many short strings of brightly colored glass beads.

This unique art almost disappeared a few decades ago, but has been revived on the Seminole reservation in Florida.

168

Fig. 265. Seminole dolls became a commercial product in the early 1940s when a few tribal craftsmen founded the first cooperative marketing enterprise for Seminole crafts. Simple armless and legless bodies are made from the brown fibers at the base of palmetto fronds. Faces are suggested by embroidery. Similar full capelike overblouses are still worn today, but they are usually made from voile or other sheer materials, with opaque borders around the edges. The doll's hat is also traditional.

Figs. 266–268. MODERN PATCHWORK APRON FROM THE SEMINOLE RESERVATION.

Fig. 266. Although a great deal of time might go into assembling some of the more elaborate borders, combinations of the simpler patterns can be equally attractive.

Figs. 267, 268. Seminole patchwork designs look bewilderingly complex until the basic steps of construction are understood. The right sides of the apron have been folded over to show the number of seams in the patterns. They are not, however, made one at a time.

Fig. 269. Patchwork jacket with traditional Seminole designs, by Jerry Zarbaugh. *Photo, Scott Zarbaugh.*

EXPERIMENTING WITH SEMINOLE PATCHWORK

It is more practical to work out Seminole designs with paper than with fabric. Glue colored strips to construction paper to make the basic bands, then cut them into segments and experiment with ways of reassembling them.

The basic band can be cut at almost any angle as long as it remains consistent. A drafting triangle is handy for establishing the slant of the first cut. You can make a pattern as a guide for successive segments, but it is faster to mark them with a transparent ruler and a waterproof felt-tipped pen.

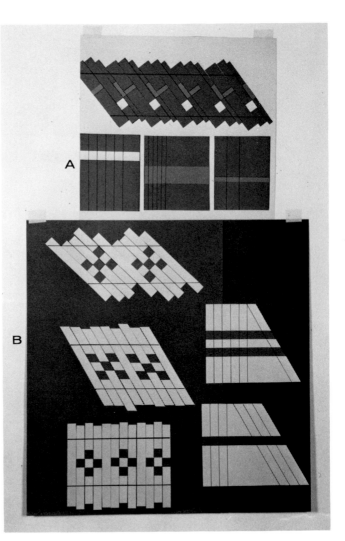

Fig. 270. To work out Seminole designs with paper, glue colored strips to construction paper for basic bands, then cut them into segments, and experiment with ways of reassembling them.

A. The upper border requires three bands and is more complex than the designs in B. The stripe on the first band is ½″ wide, and is slashed vertically into ½″ segments. The stripe on the second band is 1″ wide, slashed into ¼″ segments. The stripe on the third band is ¾″ wide, slashed into ¾″ segments. They are assembled in numerical order.

B. The two bands at the right were used for the patterns on the left. Top and bottom designs were made with vertical segments. In the center design, segments were slashed diagonally.

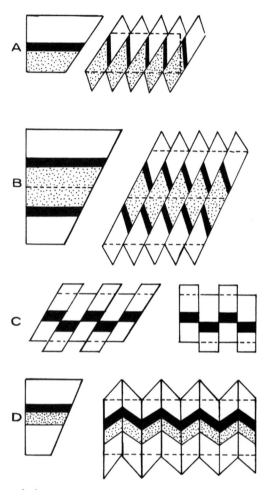

Fig. 271A. The sawtooth design is one of the easiest. Make a basic band of three stripes, and cut it diagonally into equal segments from 1½″ to 2″ wide. Reassemble by slipping each segment up 1″ to 1½″. The dotted lines indicate how to trim the edges and ends.

B. The basic band can also be designed to make two borders at once. After slicing and reassembling the segments, cut the borders apart in the center.

C. The pattern is completely changed when every other segment is slipped up the width of the central stripe. On the left, the segments were cut diagonally. At the right, they were cut vertically.

D. For a zigzag pattern, make two identical striped bands, then slice them so that diagonal lines are reversed. Reassemble the pieces as shown here.

Fig. 272. SEMINOLE PATCHWORK BORDERS

Once the designs have been worked out with paper, add ¼" seam allowances, and use extra fabric on the edge pieces for trimming the borders evenly. Using a short stitch, sew segments together in pairs, and press seams to one side before stitching them into a continuous row. Bias tape can be used for narrow stripes.

A. For band #1, make the narrow stripes half the width of the wide stripes. The single stripe in band #2 equals two wide stripes and three narrow stripes in band #1. Assemble diagonally.

B. For band #1, the narrow stripe is half the width of the wide stripe. The stripe in band #2 equals two wide stripes and one narrow stripe in band #1. Assemble diagonally.

C. Make basic band in three colors. Assemble diagonally with colors reversed on adjacent segments. A different pattern can be made from the same band by adding bias tape between each segment.

D. The stripe in band #2 is three times the width of the stripe in band #1. Assemble vertically.

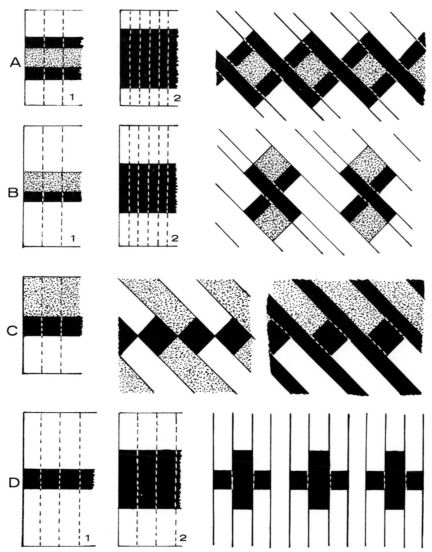

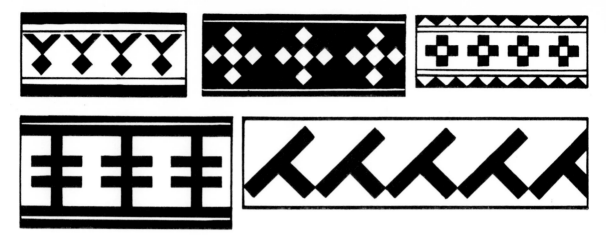

Fig. 273. TRADITIONAL SEMINOLE PATCHWORK PATTERNS

USING SEMINOLE PATCHWORK

Seminole patchwork has been almost exclusively associated with costume arts, but it is equally useful for making throw pillows, table runners, place mats, tablecloths, and café curtains. Worked on a larger scale, the patterns can be used for distinctive bedspreads, coverlets, and quilts.

Cotton percale or fine cotton and synthetic blends are best for narrow borders. Medium to large designs can be worked with heavier fabrics. Although it is not traditional with the Seminoles, combinations of printed and solid colors are very effective. Ribbons, braids, and tapes can be substituted for narrow strips of fabrics as long as they are compatible with other materials, and the use for which the piece is intended.

Figs. 274–278. PATCHWORK BAG AND UMBRELLA SHEATH

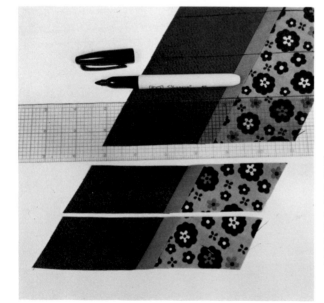

Fig. 274. All measurements allow for ¼″ seams. Cut a strip 3½″ wide from a printed and a solid color fabric, and stitch them on each side of bias tape to make the basic band. Mark a 45°-angle across one end, then measure and cut the band into 1½″ segments. Slide each segment up 1½″ and stitch together as shown in Figure 271A, until the patchwork is 36″ long. Trim edges to make a border 4″ wide.

174

Fig. 275. Stitch upper edge of patchwork border to fabric strips and ½" bias tape in the following order: solid color fabric—1¼" wide; bias tape; solid color fabric—1¼" wide; solid color fabric—2" wide; bias tape; printed fabric—1½" wide; bias tape; solid color fabric—2¼" wide. Press, trim edges, and cut in half vertically. Turn pieces so that the sawtooth borders are facing, and stitch them to each side of a strip of solid color fabric 2½" wide. Trim solid strips with rickrack braid, matching colors on each end.

Fig. 276. The tote bag can be made from one side of the textile; the umbrella sheath from the leftover strip. The construction of the sheath is similar to Indian methods for making rifle scabbards, bow cases, and arrow quivers.

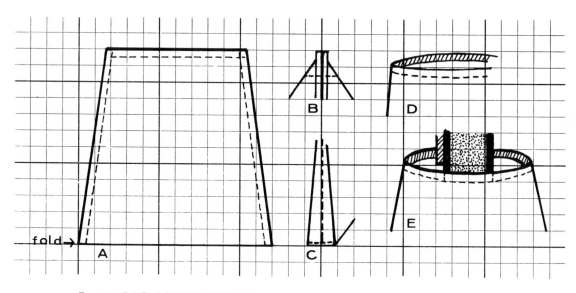

Fig. 277. BAG CONSTRUCTION

A. Cut a pattern for half the bag from wrapping paper, allowing ½″ seams as indicated by dotted lines. Fold fabric in half and place bottom of pattern on the fold to cut out the bag in one piece. Mark bottom line on the wrong side. Stitch side seams, clip at the fold, and press open.

B. Fold corners so that the seam is directly on top of the bottom line. Pin in place, and stitch straight across the seam 1½″ down from the point.

C. Trim away about ¾″ of the point, and slash folds so that the corners will lie flat against the bottom when the bag is turned right side out. Use same pattern for cutting out a lining, and assemble, taking slightly wider seams.

D. Bind top of bag with bias tape. Turn under seam allowance at top of lining and baste.

E. Cut 3″ × 13″ strips of fabric and lining material for the handle. Pin together, right sides out, and bind long edges with bias tape. Trim with tape and rickrack braid, cut to proper length, and blindstitch inside the top edge of the bag. Insert lining, and blindstitch in place.

Fig. 278. UMBRELLA SHEATH CONSTRUCTION

The patchwork strip left over from the bag can be lengthened or shortened in the center if necessary, to adjust it to different umbrella lengths.

A. Measure furled umbrella from the metal tip to ½″ above the rib ends (1). Measure loosely around the top (2) and bottom (3). Add seam allowances and draw pattern on paper.

B. Fold pattern in half, place on a lengthwise fold of the fabric, and cut out. Stitch narrow hem facing to the right sides of cut vertical edges (4).

C. Fold facing to the wrong side, crease on the seam line, press flat, and blindstitch.

D. Finish top and bottom edges the same way, or bind with bias tape.

E. Roll newspapers tightly and tape to make a cone approximately the size of the umbrella.

F. Fit sheath around the cone, right sides out, using tape to temporarily hold it in place. Blindstitch open edges securely together. Use the paper cone as a pad to press the seam.

G. Cut a strip of fabric and matching lining 1½″ to 2″ wide, and 14″ long. Make a handle as described for the bag. Turn under raw edges on the ends, and blindstitch inside top of the sheath.

H. For an alternate method, machine-stitch the vertical edges, finish seams with seam binding, then hem the top and bottom. Straighten a length of coat hanger wire and bend one end into a small loop.

I. Slide the wire inside the sheath with loop at the bottom, and attach it to two sides of the fabric with safety pins. Gently draw the wire upward to turn the sheath right side out. Attach handle as described.

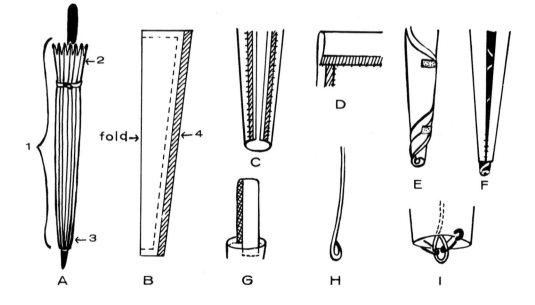

CONVENTIONAL PATCHWORK FROM INDIAN DESIGNS

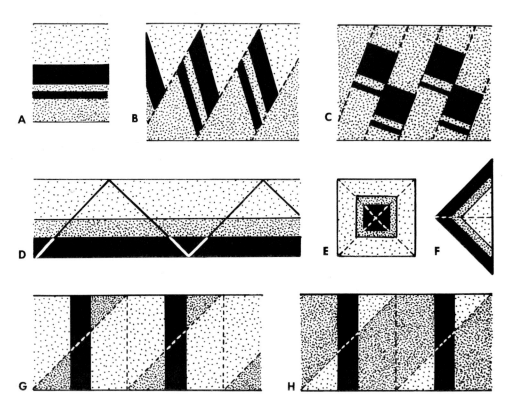

Fig. 279. The concept of Seminole patchwork has many applications. A single basic band is used for traditional patterns B and C, but it can also be used for nontraditional designs. In D, a band is cut into equilateral triangles with the hypotenuse on the straight edge. The triangles on one side have a different color arrangement from those on the other. Matching triangles can be joined into squares (E), or they can be joined in pairs to make larger triangles with a border around two sides (F). Other patterns result when equilateral triangles are cut with the hypotenuse on the bias. Matching triangles can be assembled as shown in G. When the remaining triangles are assembled the same way, color areas are reversed (H).

Fig. 280. Prints of all kinds can be combined as long as their colors are compatible. Often, stripes of solid colors will pull them together. Large equilateral triangles were cut from the multistriped band at the top and joined as shown in Figure 279E, to make a square pillow top. The patchwork was basted over bonded Dacron batting and a soft lining, and was quilted with colored embroidery thread.

Fig. 281. This design for a large floor pillow is based on Figure 279F. On a small scale it could be repeated for a border design. Seam allowances must be carefully planned so that the points of the triangles are not cut off when stripes are added on each side (A).

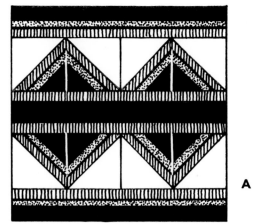

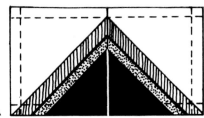

A

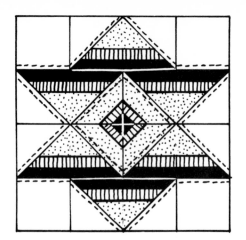

Fig. 282. Loomed beadwork is an excellent source for patchwork designs made from striped triangles and squares. The patterned pieces here are formed from the cuts shown in Figure 279 (D, E, and F). They are combined with background triangles and squares in a solid color.

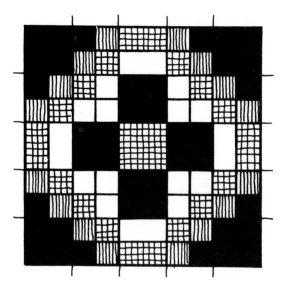

Fig. 283. A practical system for seaming the pieces together is an essential part of designing for conventional patchwork. This plan for a large floor pillow top is based on five horizontal rows of five blocks, some of which are made up of four patches, others two, others one. The blocks can be scaled to any measurements. Allowing ¼" for seams, 5½" blocks will finish 25"; 4½" blocks will finish 20". You can also assemble the patchwork in squares, then trim the outer edges to form a border of rectangles. (See color pages.)

Fig. 284. Stitch the small pieces together until all the blocks are assembled, then join them into horizontal strips. Sew strips together with the seams aligned. This design is a variation of the woven pillow top in Chapter 5, and was made from scraps of old wool blankets.

7

QUILLWORK AND BEADWORK

QUILLWORK

Although cousins of the American porcupine are native to other parts of the world, quillwork was developed only on this continent. It was practiced wherever the animal lived throughout Canada and the northern forested regions of the United States, and in adjacent areas where its quills were obtained through trade.[1]

It was probably the most laborious of the applied arts. The quills were cleaned, sorted by sizes, and stored in separate containers. Sometimes they were dyed with colors from roots, mosses, berries, flowers, and bark.[2] When they were ready to use, they were softened in the mouth, and flattened by drawing them out between the teeth or fingernails. Once they were attached to a foundation and had become dry again, their new positions were permanent.

Most tribes specialized in only one or two methods of working the quills, but many different designs were obtained by folding them in various ways, or by manipulating more than one at a time.

The wrapping technique was used on cylindrical handles and fringes. Plaited decorations were made in strips, then were wrapped around some object, often a pipestem. The quills were not independently plaited, as in textile making. They were folded around two taut parallel lines of sinew. The quill was placed under the threads, then alternate ends were bent toward the center and under

---

[1] Bird quills were also worked to a limited extent, mainly by Alaskan Eskimos.
[2] Commercial dyes were substituted when they became available.

the opposite thread, creating the effect of a tiny braid. Short ends were bent to the back side and covered with the next quill.

Sewn quillwork involved both of these techniques, and others, but was made directly on a hide foundation, using sinew to anchor the quills. Sometimes parallel lines of sinew were attached and the quills were folded over and under them from opposite sides, or were wrapped around them in parallel rows. Checkerwork patterns were also sewn to leather foundations. For fine curving lines, a single thread was stitched to the hide and used as a core for wrapped quills. In all cases, the sinew stay was completely covered. Plains tribes are especially well known for these types of quillwork.[3]

Woven quillwork, a specialty of the Canadian Cree and tribes around the northern Great Lakes, was unquestionably the ultimate of the art. It was worked on sinew warps stretched taut between the ends of a tough, flexible shaft (sometimes called a "bow" loom). Thread wefts were then woven over and under the warps to serve as stays for the quills. The quills were woven vertically through the wefts, then they were slipped up and compacted so that all threads were concealed under the little quill humps. Ends were left on the back side. Elaborately patterned strips that resembled very fine beadwork were produced by this method.

[3] These techniques are fully explained in a number of old publications, some of which have been reprinted. See the Appendix.

Fig. 285. Quills from the American porcupine average from 1″ to 4″ long. The finest come from the stomach and were used for delicate work on small objects. The largest come from the tail and were reserved for heavier work on a larger scale.

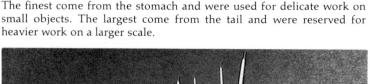

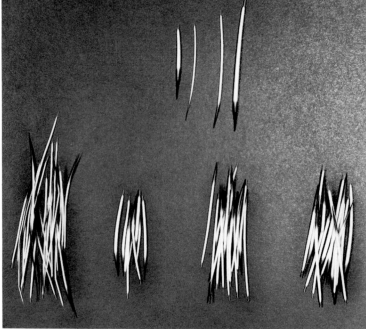

In the Northeastern areas, distinctive appliqués were made on birchbark by imprinting a design in the wood with an awl, then punching holes through it for the quill ends. As the springy fibers contracted, the quills were locked securely in place. This was a fairly fast technique that resembled satin-stitched embroidery, and was made with unflattened quills for a corrugated effect.

Another unusual variation resembles French-knot embroidery, and existing examples are rare. The quills were attached in the middle to a foundation, then the ends were bent upward and clipped short. Couched outlines of dyed grass were sometimes combined with the compacted quill dots to make floral designs.

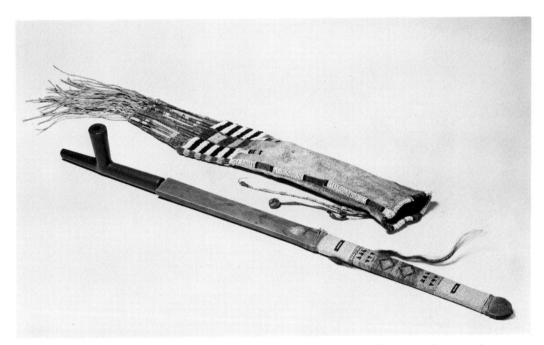

Fig. 285A. Lakota (Sioux) tobacco pipe and bag, decorated with quills and beads. A man's pipe was related to his religion, and some of its magical power derived from a beautifully decorated stem. For the most part, they were made by men, but the geometric design of this plaited quillwork indicates that it was made by a woman. Wrapped quills are used on the fringes of the bag. *Courtesy, The M. H. De Young Memorial Museum.*

Fig. 286. Micmac chair cover, made in 1893. Dyed quills inserted in birchbark. *Courtesy, The Nova Scotia Museum.*

The Plains peoples moved about constantly following game, and their arts had to be practical, not purely ornamental. To fill both requirements, they decorated nearly all their useful possessions—clothing, storage bags, weapons, even their tools and tents.

Porcupines did not live in that area, but when migrants from the East brought with them their knowledge of quillwork, it was enthusiastically accepted as a more beautiful and permanent substitute for native paints. Trading sources for materials were soon established.

Unlike many arts that were traditionally "his" or "hers," Plains quillwork was made by both sexes. The western Sioux, however, had a curious rule. Only men could make representational designs. Geometrics were assigned to the women. The custom persisted through the period when beads took the place of quills, and was not abandoned until they started producing goods for the white market.

CONTEMPORARY APPLICATIONS OF QUILLWORK

Although beads are plentiful and inexpensive today, there is a growing interest in old materials that are unlike anything that can be manufactured. The porcupine still ambles through the North American forests, and its quills are still available in shops carrying Indian craft supplies.

Few persons have the patience to explore the more complex methods that have been very briefly described here, but the technique for birchbark embroidery is quite simple, and can be made on leather.

Tint the quills with fabric dyes, keeping the temperature of the bath just below the boiling point, or leave them white. Open spaces in the pattern will add interest, as will directional changes in the quill lines. A leather medallion or inset for a box top will reveal a great deal about how the quills can be handled.

Draft a simple pattern with the style of satin-stitched embroidery. Keep in mind that the length of the quills will be reduced by ⅛" or more on each end where they are inserted into the leather. The separate quill "stitches" should not be longer than ½" to ⅝". Transfer the design to firm leather with dressmaker's carbon. Soften quills in a bowl of warm water. Use a needle awl (see Chapter 3) to perforate holes through the leather at each end of the lines. The holes should slant outward from the line-ends in opposite directions, so that the quills can lie flat. Insert the sharp (dark) ends of the quills from the back, go across top of leather and through the opposite hole. Try not to bend them—bend the leather instead, and use the awl as necessary to seat the quills in the holes. Work from the center of the design to the outside edges. When it is finished, dampen both sides of the leather with a sponge. Cover a wooden board with clean paper and tack the leather to it, quill side down. Let dry, then cut out the outline and attach the piece to a lining or other foundation with white glue.

Micmac and Chippewa quillwork are good resources for corrugated designs made with ordinary broomstraws that can be applied to boxes, plaques, and wooden pendants. Cut the straight ends of the straws into segments about 4″ long, then tint them with fabric dyes. Separate by diameter sizes, and use straws of fairly equal thicknesses on a single project.

Draw a geometric design on the foundation, cut straws to fit with scissors, and attach them one at a time with thickened white glue. Finish with several coats of clear satin finish varnish.

The easiest patterns to work are single motifs that use the foundation as a background. For very fine work, split straws vertically and attach the flat sides with glue.

To make inlaid designs on plain, flat-topped boxes, glue a border of ⅛″ square balsa rods on the top to form a recessed area for the decoration. (Balsa rods can be obtained in toy shops and hobby stores that carry materials for making model airplanes.)

Decide which parts of the design should be set in first to create outlines for enclosed areas. Glue these down, and let them dry before continuing. The thicker white glues are best for this purpose, or you can pour small amounts of ordinary white glue into a foil-lined jar lid and allow some of the solvent to evaporate. Use a brush to apply a thin coat to one section at a time.

Figs. 287–290. QUILLWORK EFFECTS WITH STRAWS

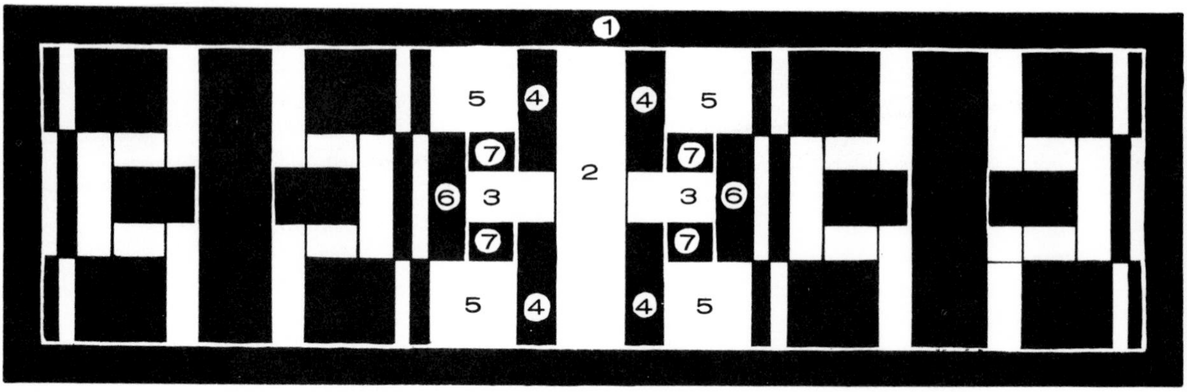

Fig. 287. This design for a box lid is to be worked with straws arranged horizontally and vertically. Attach outside borders (1) first, using random lengths of straws. Area 2 is vertical; 3—horizontal; 4—vertical; 5—horizontal; 6—vertical; 7—horizontal. Repeat the order on each end.

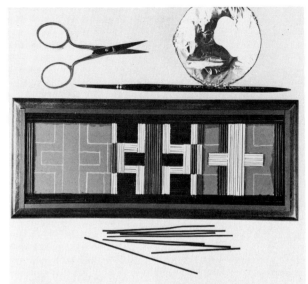

Fig. 288. Straws will not be exactly equal in thickness, so the same number may not fill areas that are equal in size.

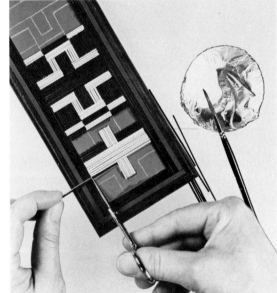

Fig. 289. Straws can be laid on the pattern and cut to fit, though once part of the design is established, it is easier to use the lines on the box as measurements.

Fig. 290. Apply several coats of clear satin finish varnish to seal the decoration. This example was worked with natural golden green and dyed dark brown straws.

BEADS

The first glass beads brought to the Americas were large, of the style that is commonly strung into necklaces. They were probably ordinary trinkets in Europe, but to the Indians they were as priceless as rare gems, for they represented an unknown, exotic world and could not be reproduced by the most skillful craftsman among them. In a short time, trading was so brisk that thousands of beads were scattered across the continent, creating a fascinating puzzle for modern collectors who try to retrace their routes back to their original points of entry.

Most of the early forms were probably made in Venice. Pony beads, named after the pony pack trains that brought them into the Plains, appeared first in the coastal areas and gradually filtered into the interior. They were about ⅛″ in diameter, somewhat irregular, but small enough to be worked into designs. Colors were limited primarily to white and medium blue, though a few tan, red, and dark blues have survived. They were used to make simple bands with geometric figures that could be attached to garments, bags, and ceremonial regalia.

The tiny glass "seed" bead did not appear until the 1800s in the East, and some fifty years later in the West. Its size and availability in quantities made possible the working of the intricate patterns that have come to be considered uniquely Indian.

BEADWORKING TECHNIQUES

Indian beadwork can be separated into three basic categories: sewn, netted, and woven. Although the techniques are different, a few general rules apply to all methods.

Seed beads come in many sizes; the higher the number, the smaller the bead. Most work is made with #8 through #12 sizes, though exquisite shadings and details can be obtained with even smaller grades.

There are irregularities in all sizes. Reject undersized, oversized, and lopsided beads. Extreme variations in hole sizes can also be objectionable, especially on loomed work. But save your rejects. Many can be used on fringes, twisted chains, and rondelles. Odd sizes are often needed for making space adjustments on netted bottles.

Your eyes will quickly become trained to spot an unsuitable bead when it is picked up on the needle, but inspect each new addition to your design. If a bad bead shows up, remove and replace that section before proceeding. A single protruding bead can spoil the effect of an entire piece.

Stretch felt, leather, velveteen, or other backings for sewn work in a frame. Small rondelles, purse fronts, and pockets can be worked in an embroidery hoop. Staple larger pieces and the ends of bands to a cheap wooden frame, or make one from stretcher bars. You may find it helpful to attach the frame to the edge of a table with C clamps (available at any hardware store), especially if you are working with two threads. This will extend the frame beyond the table so that back and top sides are accessible. It also frees both hands for manipulating thread and beads. In Figure 294, the edge of an embroidery hoop has been covered by a thin board to provide a gripping surface for the clamp.

Woven work requires a simple loom to keep warp threads taut.

Beading thread must be thin enough for three thicknesses to be drawn through the beads, since even in sewn work, some beads are passed through twice. There will then be the original thread, plus the new thread and the tail that doubles back from the eye of the needle. The thread should comfortably fill the holes, however. Otherwise, the beads will be loose and inclined to tilt.

Linen thread is the strongest, though heavy-duty sewing threads and dental floss are useful. Waxed thread will wear longer and is less inclined to tangle. It can be purchased, or you can wax your own thread with beeswax cakes available in fabric shops. Draw the thread across it several times until it is slightly stiff.

Long, thin-eyed beading needles are necessary for loomed work, but they are too delicate for sewn work. This requires fine sewing needles, usually in sizes from #5 to #8. Packets of assorted sizes are available in variety stores and fabric shops.

SEWN WORK

Spot Stitching

Indian overlaid, or "spot stitched," work is made with two threads. The beads are strung on one, laid along the lines of a design, then are attached with a tiny stitch of the second thread between every two or three beads.

Fig. 291. Buckskin gauntlets with spot-stitched beadwork, from Warm Springs, Oregon. The maker presented them as a gift to Cyrus W. Walker, a pioneer, in 1838. *Courtesy, The Oregon Historical Society.*

This is a couching technique, and it undoubtedly derived from earlier hair embroidery. It was most useful for curving designs, and was favored in the Northeastern and Great Lakes regions where floral designs were popular. It was used to some extent by all beadworking tribes, however, at least during early periods.

Floral beadwork has never had the art status of geometric designs, and is often dismissed as a gaudier version of colonial embroidery designs. Curiously enough, like some Navajo textile designs, many geometric patterns derived from Oriental rugs brought by the colonists. So, a preference for one over the other should not be based on which is most authentically Indian.

Fig. 292. Breech clout that belonged to Chief Turtotte, a North Dakota Chippewa. An outstanding example of overlaid floral beadwork. *Courtesy, The Oregon Historical Society.*

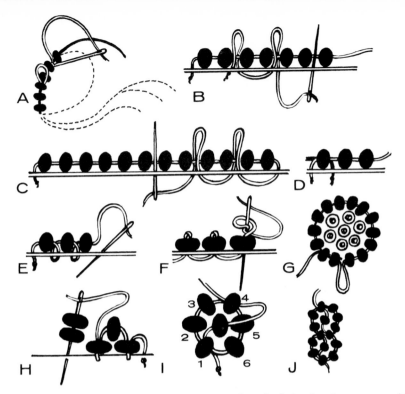

Fig. 293. A. Traditional spot-stitching requires two threads. String beads on one, and lay it on a line of the design. With the stitching thread, secure the bead thread to the foundation between every two or three beads, keeping the stitches on the guideline. This top view shows beads separated, instead of being pushed close together as they would be in actual work. The outlines of most Indian floral designs were worked first, then centers were filled in, but there were many exceptions.

B. Side view of two-thread spot-stitching. Knots can be under the foundation if it is to be lined. They should be concealed between beads on the top side if it is to be unlined, or they will quickly wear off. You can hold down the bead thread with your left thumb to keep beads from sliding apart, or you can periodically anchor it to the foundation.

C. Single thread overlay is easier for certain designs. String on enough beads to fill a line, anchor the end, then work back down the row, securing it between every two or three beads. (Beads must be strung loosely enough to allow for widths of stitches.)

D. To extend the row, go through the last bead with a new thread, and continue.

E. Single-bead stitching is almost as fast and is not as difficult to control. String on a bead, go through the foundation, and take a tiny backstitch on the guideline. Add a bead, and continue. The beads will be slightly farther apart, but equally as attractive if the spacing is kept even.

F. As an interesting variation, beads can be attached flat with French knots, instead of on edge. Unwaxed thread must be used for this method or the knots will not slide. Entire designs can be worked this way . . .

G. . . . or the knotted beads can be combined with spot-stitched outlines. Close circles smoothly by carrying the thread back through the first two beads before anchoring it.

H. Many Indian bags, bands, and rondelles had a picoted bead edging. Anchor thread, pick up a bead, and take a stitch across the edge of the foundation. Go back through the bead and pick up two beads. Take a stitch across the edge, go back through the lower bead, and continue.

I. To make a daisy chain for suspending rondelles, string on six beads, and go through the first bead to make a circle. String a slightly larger bead for the center, go through bead #4 from right to left and draw thread tight.

J. String six beads and come back through bead #5 to make a circle. Add center, go through bead #4 of new daisy, and continue.

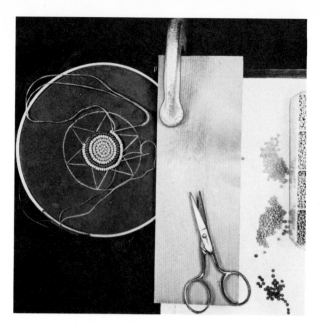

Fig. 294. Felt or other nonraveling fabric can be used as a foundation, though the soft suede shown here is even better. Transfer the design with a perforated pattern (see Chapter 10), then go over the lines with acrylic paint or a waterproof marker. Lift off chalk dust with masking tape. Stitch one bead in the center, then make a circle of beads around it. Adjust them evenly and tack with the stitching thread. Continue until the required number of center rows is completed. The bead thread is shown at the top; the stitching thread is at the bottom.

Figs. 294–296. MAKING A SPOT-STITCHED RONDELLE

Fig. 295. Work rays of star first, starting and ending the rows of beads exactly on the pattern lines. (Use some of your thin rejects as necessary for a good fit.) Fill in the background, keeping the rows continuous as shown in Figure 293D, then spot-stitch between every two or three beads. Cut out finished rondelle, add fringe or a beaded tassel at the bottom, then glue it to a firm felt or leather lining.

Fig. 296. Overcast edge neatly, or finish with picoted beads. Suspend from a thong, twisted chain, or daisy chain. The rondelle at the right is a classic design in red, white, and black beads on moosehide. The beads are very small, probably #14 or #15. It was made by Bertha West, 12 years old, of the Carrier tribe, Lake Babine, British Columbia.

Lazy Stitching

The lazy stitch is a fast, easy method for appliquéing beads, though unless sinew is used, it does not produce work as durable as the spot stitch, and designs are less precise than loomed work. The beads are attached to the foundation in short, parallel rows, using a single needle and thread.

Fig. 297. Nineteenth-century Sioux dress with lazy-stitched beaded yoke. Primary design colors are red and yellow, with blue and green used more sparingly. White backgrounds were favored by the Sioux.

On the best Indian work, the sinew was moistened and pulled firmly into a leather base so that the bead rows were rigid. Fine waxed carpet warp is a satisfactory substitute, but if the thread does not adequately fill the holes, the beads may tilt out of alignment.

When threads are drawn very tightly, the bead lines bow up slightly to create a ridged effect similar to sewn quillwork. It was probably a deliberate adaptation of the earlier form. Although the technique is especially suitable for geometric designs, Indian workers often used it to fill in backgrounds around spot stitched floral motifs.

Lazy-stitched work should be made on a firm canvas, felt, or linen foundation, then appliquéd to a garment or lining. It can be tricky to draft a design that will exactly fill a specific area, since seed beads are wider than they are thick. It can be done, however, by first working a sample swatch and making a bead count vertically and horizontally as a guide for spacing. The effect is more orderly if the pattern can be divided into an equal number of rows. The rows can be made up of as many as eight beads, but five or six beads to the row is firmer.

It is practical to design a motif that can be expanded if necessary by adding borders or a solid background, a technique that was frequently used by Indians. In this case, you need only to draw guidelines for the parallel rows on the foundation, not the entire design. If your pattern has been drafted on graph paper with each bead represented by a colored dot, you can then string them in proper order by counting, as you would for loomed work.

Stitch a small sample block to estimate the number of beads required to fill a ½″ or ⅜″ square. For example, with #12 beads a block of five horizontal rows of seven beads each will equal ½″. With #8 beads, four horizontal rows of six beads will fill approximately the same space. Mark the foundation in equally spaced parallel lines and indicate the center by a perpendicular line. It is easier to keep the design straight if you start in the center and work out to the edges.

The ridged effect can be distracting on certain designs, and can be eliminated by going back through the last attached bead before adding a new row, as shown in Figure 298 C. It also makes the work firmer.

Fig. 298. LAZY STITCHING
A. Work design from the center out to the edges. Anchor the thread to the foundation, string on a predetermined number of beads, take a tiny backstitch on the guideline, and continue.
B. Grade beads carefully so that rows are even, and develop the design by counting, as you would for loomed work.
C. The ridged effect can be eliminated by going back through the last attached bead before stringing on the next row. From time to time, measure the vertical lines to make sure they do not become slanted.

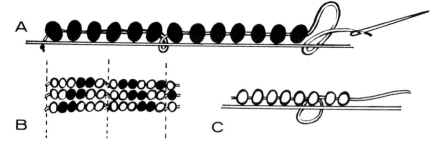

Wrapped Beadwork

Wrapped beadwork is useful for decorating handles and cylindrical objects. The form must be covered with felt or leather to provide a foundation to which the beads can be anchored. They are attached in rows by a variation of the lazy stitch.

The technique is shown here as a way of decorating a rattle handle, but the method of making the rattle itself is also worth investigating, since it can be applied to making handsome wall pots for dried plants. It was used by the Plains tribes, but similar hide forms for storing sacred meal and pollen were made in the Southwest by the Zuñis.

Figs. 299–302. MAKING A RAWHIDE RATTLE

Fig. 299A. Draw a pattern for the bulb, and scratch around it on softened rawhide with an awl. Cut out with heavy scissors, and perforate an equal number of stitching holes on each side, ½″ to ⅜″ apart.
B. Start at the top of one side, and stitch it closed with heavily waxed carpet warp or sinew. Use pliers if necessary to pull needle through the hide. Draw stitches very tight, knot at the handle end, and leave thread dangling.
C. Stitch opposite side down to the inward curve. Insert handle, then close remaining seam to fit snugly around it. Knot, and leave thread dangling. Twist out handle.
D. Pack cavity firmly with sand, and insert handle. Stand the rattle upright for several days until it is dry and hard. Remove handle and knock out the sand. Sweep the interior clean with a small brush.
E. If side seams have separated from shrinkage of the hide, start with the top stitch and draw them back together. Untie knots at the handle, take up the slack, and retie. Drop in a few pebbles and insert the handle.
F. Hold the rattle up to a strong light to locate the hole in the handle. Twist it to the center and perforate hide over it with a nail.
G. Paint other end of handle and stitch a strip of soft leather or felt around the sides.
H. Glue borders of narrow leather strips or thongs at each end, then proceed with wrapped beading.

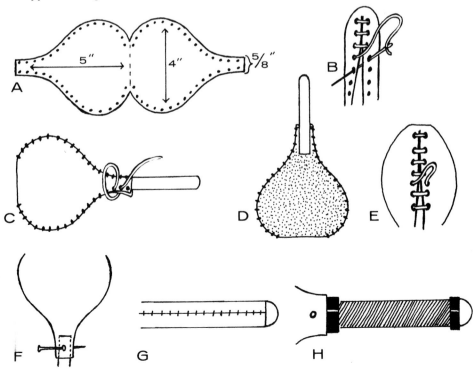

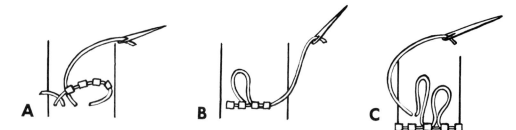

Fig. 300. WRAPPED BEADING

A. Anchor end of thread with one or two tiny stitches, instead of a knot that would make a hump. String on three or four beads and make a backstitch through the leather.

B. Pull thread tight so that beads lie flat against the handle, then bring needle through the last two beads again. String on three or four beads, and continue until the row is filled.

C. At the end of the row, bring needle through the first bead to make a neat invisible joint. Take a tiny stitch above it to start a new row.

Fig. 301. The bulb can be left plain, or painted with opaque acrylics. This design in two shades of red and black was derived from an old Southeastern pot. To finish the rattle, cut one end of a thong to a tapering point and thread it through the hole in the handle.

Fig. 302. Wrap around the handle several times, and tie. Trim ends with beads, feathers, or tin cones.

Rawhide is very tough and hard, but becomes quite pliable after it has been softened overnight in water. At this stage, it can be stretched to assume a shape, and will retain it after it has become dry again.

While the rawhide is soaking, prepare a handle from ½" wood doweling, 5½" long. Round the edges of one end. An inch from the opposite end, drill a hole through the center.

Add hot water to the soaking bath an hour before you start work. Remove the rawhide and pat it dry. It will remain workable long enough to complete the bulb of the rattle.[4]

[4] Materials for making similar rattles can be obtained from Winona Trading Post. See Appendix.

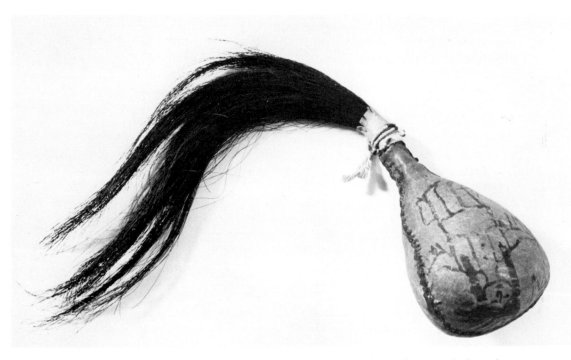

Fig. 303. Ceremonial rattle 18" long, from the central or northern Plains, made from the scrotum of a buffalo bull. The bulb has crude paintings of human figures in red and black. Further decorations are lavender beads and a hank of horsehair. Rattles of this kind were used in religious rites in which individuals solicited power from supernatural spirits. *Courtesy, The Oregon Historical Society.*

NETTING

The two most popular netting techniques progress a single bead at a time, but once the stitches become familiar, work can move quite fast.

Although the ends of each row can be attached to a flat leather or felt foundation for bags, collars, and strips, netting is most commonly used to cover handles, bottles, and other three-dimensional objects.

Beaded bottles were, and are, popular in a number of tribes, particularly in western regions. The Paiutes produce most of the bottles that are commercially available today, and prices for good work are very high.

Early beadworkers started with a tiny circlet of beads that was increased to the size of the bottom of the bottle. The netting was then continued up the sides. Later, a leather disk was used for the bottom, simplifying the process and providing a better seat for the bottle.

It is not difficult to work out the basic stitches by tracing thread lines on Indian work, but the secret of adjusting the bead rows to an irregular surface has remained somewhat mysterious. It is actually quite simple, and will be immediately apparent to anyone who has made a coiled basket, or has knitted or crocheted a shaped garment. As the bottle enlarges, the number of stitches is increased by adding extra beads. As it decreases, the beads are subtracted.

If you closely examine the peyote-stitched bottles in Figure 307, you can locate places where adjustments were made on the bottle at the right. Two rows below the lowest central diamond, an extra bead was added. Another was added just inside the diamond. Beads were subtracted in upper areas where the circumference of the bottle diminishes.

These points are almost impossible to locate on the central bottle where dark beads were used for the background—a tip worth remembering when you plan a design. As on beaded baskets, solid bands and disconnected motifs are easier to adjust to an irregular shape than a continuous pattern.

Beaded Bottles

Draw around the bottom of the bottle to make a pattern for a soft leather disk, then enlarge it slightly to allow for the thickness of the beads. Spread a thin layer of epoxy glue on the bottom of the bottle, center it on the disk, and allow it to dry before starting the beadwork.

Fig. 304. BEADED BOTTLES—NETTING STITCH #1

A. Bring thread out on the top side of the leather, and pull knot against the underside to the top. Pull thread tight and go back through the bead hole again. Continue around disk, keeping beads evenly and closely spaced.
B. When you reach the starting point, go through the first bead again to close the circle.

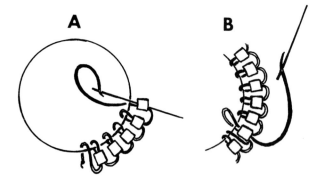

A   **B**

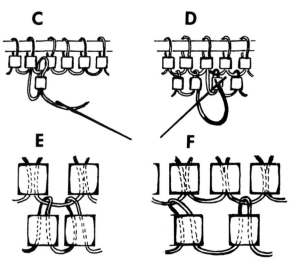

C. The same stitch is used on successive rows, except that beads are suspended from the thread loops between beads on the previous row, instead of the leather.

D. At the end of each row, bring thread over and behind the starting loop and pull tight before moving to a new row. After the second row is strung, it is easier to go through the loops if the bottle neck faces outward.

E. As the circumference of the bottle increases, string two beads to a loop wherever stitches become too widely separated. Do this in solid areas, rather than on lines of the design. Often, two thin beads will fit more smoothly than two of regular size.

F. If the circumference of the bottle decreases, subtract beads by skipping loops of the previous row.

Fig. 305. In netted work, beads are staggered like the stitches of Pomo coiled basketry. This is the basic unit of the pattern being worked in Figure 306.

Fig. 306. Choose small bottles with uncomplicated contours for introductory netting projects. Long, flexible beading needles are easier to slip through the thread loops than short sewing needles.

Netting stitch #2

Most Indian techniques have several regional names, but this distinctive netting process is most commonly called "peyote stitching." It was widely used among the Plains tribes for decorating fans, rattles, and other ceremonial paraphernalia connected with religious rites, where trances and hallucinatory visions were induced by the ingestion of peyote.

It is easy to understand the basic structure if you think of it as a row of little hills, each separated by a valley. Additional beads fit into the valleys and become the hills on the new row.

The regularity of the serrated line is periodically interrupted when there is need for increasing or decreasing the number of beads to a row. For example, by adding two beads in a valley, you will have two hills without a valley in between.

Fig. 307. Paiute peyote-stitched beadwork. Since early times, Indians decorated their baskets with beads. Although traders were responsible for the idea of covering bottles with beads and woven fibers, it was actually an extension of the older art form. *Collection, Pacific Western Traders.*

This is corrected on the next row, and though it creates a tiny break in the surface texture, it will be unobtrusive on the finished bottle.

With the peyote stitch, it is particularly important that beads be closely compacted from the beginning. Otherwise, the design will begin to spiral, making numerical adjustments difficult. Some Indian workers spaced the first row of beads far enough apart so that the second row would exactly fit in between, as can be seen at the base of the central and right bottles in Figure 307. It is probably safer for the beginner to make the beads on the first row as close together as possible.

Figs. 308–311. NETTING STITCH #2

Fig. 308. Peyote stitching can be used for flat work, as well as three-dimensional surfaces. Anchor thread at one end, and string the entire row. At the other end, go through the foundation and come out on top in position for the next row. String on a bead, go through the second bead of the upper row, string on a bead, and continue. A pattern of little hills and valleys will emerge. Each new bead fits into a valley and becomes a hill on the new row.

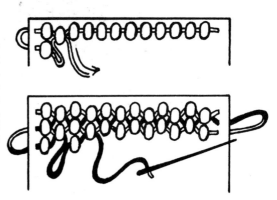

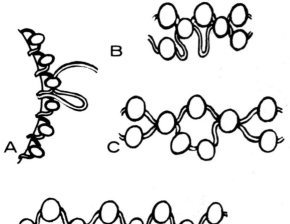

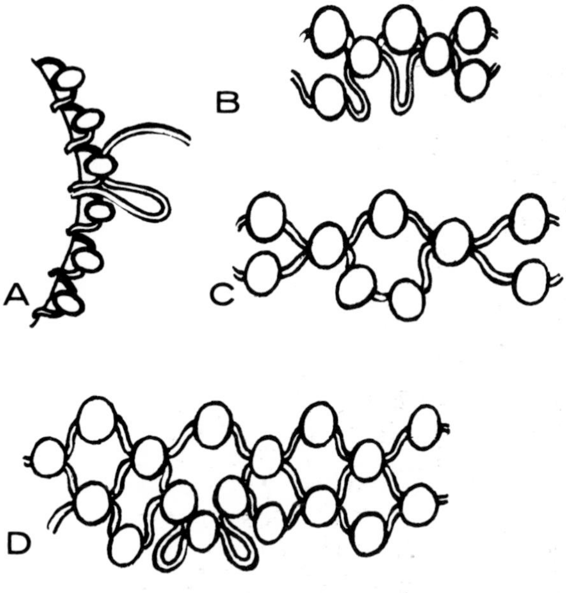

Fig. 309A. For bottles, make and secure a leather disk to the bottom as described in stitch #1. With an overcast stitch, anchor the first row of beads as close together as possible. Close the circle by going through the first bead again.

B. Continue as shown for flat work. To conform the netting to irregular contours, skip a bead when they become crowded.

C. Add an extra bead when they become too widely spaced. This will make two adjacent hills . . .

D. . . . but the sequence will become regular again on the next row when a bead is added between them. Subsequent work will smooth out the texture.

Figs. 310, 311. In netting stitch #1, the bead holes are vertical. In stitch #2, they are horizontal. In both, however, the beads are staggered. When you are ready to work in a design, mark the end of a row with a piece of thread, and count the beads around it. You can then work out a design on graph paper as described for beaded baskets in Chapter 3.

Fig. 312. Old peyote-stitched pouch and woven decoration from a dance costume; origins unknown. Some of the early seed beads were so tiny that they resemble petit point. Modern #10 beads are shown above the pouch. *Collection, Helen Irish.*

Fig. 313 This handsome tobacco pouch with Cayuse or Walla Walla (Washington) beadwork was collected in 1847. It belonged to Chief Taumaulish (Tamahas). The background is white, with figures and animals worked in green, red, and yellow. The pouch is lined with printed fabric. *Courtesy, The Oregon Historical Society.*

Fig. 314. The Paiutes specialize in fine loomed beading as well as netting, and even after they adopted white styles in clothing, they continued to add their own accessories. This charming photo of Lizzie and Emma Sue Penheimmer was taken in 1912 at Winnemucca, Nevada. *Courtesy, The Nevada State Historical Society.*

Fig. 315. Beadwork is still lavishly used on garments for Paiute tribal affairs. This is Dora Garcia, wearing a modern dance costume. *Courtesy, The Nevada State Historical Society.*

WOVEN BEADWORK

Bow looms were used for early bead weaving, as well as quill weaving. Strips of perforated bark or leather served to separate warps that were stretched taut between the ends of a flexible shaft. This uncomplicated tool is still a practical device for summer camps, since it can be supported between the knees, and does not require a table.

205

There are a number of other choices, however, that are better for more ambitious weaving. Small commercial looms are quite inexpensive, and can be used for belts, necklaces, and bands several inches wide. It is a simple matter to make a box loom that will accommodate larger pieces, even bags and miniature tapestries. The frame can be constructed from plywood or pine boards. Notched rulers, or hardware store "giveaway" yardsticks, make fine spacers for the warps.

Figs. 316–319. BEAD LOOMS

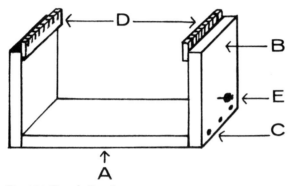

Fig. 316. Simple Box Loom
Looms of this type can be made almost any size, but a fairly large box, 14" to 18" long, will give you great flexibility. Use ½" or ¾" plywood for the frame. Cut base (A) to size, attach end pieces (B) with glue and screws (C). Cut a wooden ruler or yardstick to fit across end pieces, and notch on the ⅛" marks with a jigsaw or hand scroll saw. Attach with glue and screws inside the tops of the end pieces so that notched edges are elevated ⅛" to ¼" (D). Hammer a nail through a large wooden bead in the lower center of each end; they will serve as stays for the warps (E).

Fig. 317. This version requires more woodworking expertise, but is adjustable and less bulky. Build the basic structure as shown in Figure 316. Fasten right-angle metal braces (A) to the front and back edges of the end boards. Cut two segments of a 1" wooden dowel to fit between braces, and drill a hole through the center of each that will accommodate a ¼" threaded rod (B). Have this done at a cabinet shop if you do not have an electric drill and a long bit. Secure dowel between braces with wing nuts. They will control the tension on the rollers. Use thumbtacks (C) as warp stays.

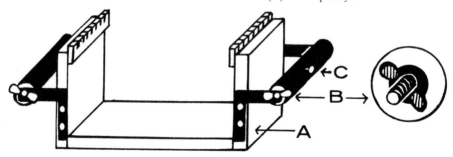

Fig. 318. This adjustable loom is 4″ high, 8″ wide, and 11″ long. Beaded sections can be wound on one dowel as they are completed.

Fig. 319. Commercial adjustable looms are constructed along the same principles. The selvedges of narrow beaded strips can be stitched together to make wide pieces.

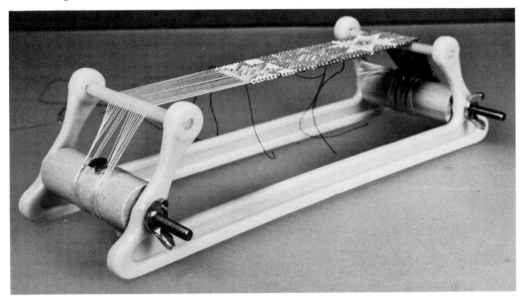

Warping a Simple Box Loom

Estimate the length of the finished project and add the extra inches needed for fringe, and for anchoring the ends to the loom. (Thirty-six inches is usually adequate for a long necklace.) Each bead will have a warp thread on each side. This means that there will be one warp more than the number of beads to a row. Double warps are used to strengthen the outer selvedge edges, adding two more strands. For example, if you have nine beads to a row, you must cut twelve warps.

Tie one end of the bundle in an overhand knot, and slip it under a warp stay (Figure 316 E). Separate the threads and draw them in parallel rows through the notches in the rulers. (Remember to double the outer edges.) Pull taut. Divide loose ends into two bundles and wind tightly from opposite directions around the remaining stay, then tie.

Warping Adjustable Looms

Tie a firm overhand knot in one end of the warp bundle, and a loose knot in the other. Secure knots to opposite rollers with thumb tacks, then wind extra thread smoothly around the firm knot, and tighten wing nuts. Untie knot in the other end and thread warps in parallel rows through the notches. Pull taut. Divide warps into two bundles, wrap around the thumbtack from opposite sides and tie. Tighten the wing nuts.

This may sound unnecessarily complex, but if you simply knot each end, fasten to the tacks and arrange threads in the notches, the center threads will be looser than those on the edges. The warps should not be fiddle string tight, but a firm, even tension is very essential for good work.

When you are ready to move a section of beading, loosen nuts at each end of the loom, and wind finished work on the empty roller. The beads on that end will then serve as spacers, as shown in Figure 319. If some of the warps in the unworked area are slack, untie the stay knot and readjust the tension.

For most work with seed beads, dental floss, beading thread, buttonhole thread, fine nylon fishing line (not monofilament), or fine carpet warp can be used for warps. In all cases, they should be waxed.

Designing the Weaving

The pattern in loomed beadwork is developed by counting, so designs should be carefully worked out on graph paper, with colored dots representing each bead. You need only to draw one segment of a repeat design, but you will have a better idea of how it will look if you draw at least two. Strong value contrasts are important. The beautiful bands in Figures 320–321 demonstrate the compatibility of basket designs with beadweaving.

Ordinary graph paper has a grid of perfect squares, and since beads are wider than they are thick, the woven design will be elongated. This is not really a problem, but bead graph paper will give you an accurate picture. (A mail order source is noted in the Appendix.) This paper is scored in small rectangles with the basic block made up of ten spaces across and six down. This closely approximates the proportions of an equivalent block of average-sized beads.

You can compare the graph paper pattern for the Humpbacked Flute Player in Figure 335 with the finished hanging to see how the character is altered by elongation. In this example, however, it is more exaggerated since extra rows of yarn were woven in between the beads.

Figs. 320–321. Influences of California/Nevada basket designs can be noted in this fine Plains beadwork, though some motifs resemble Southwestern pottery designs. *Photo, Jim Toms; courtesy, The Nevada State Museum.*

Fig. 322. The neckpiece at the top has a floral design and is trimmed with abalone pendants. The lower band with the beautifully conceived bird design is an exceptionally sensitive piece of work. *Photo, Jim Toms; courtesy, The Nevada State Museum.*

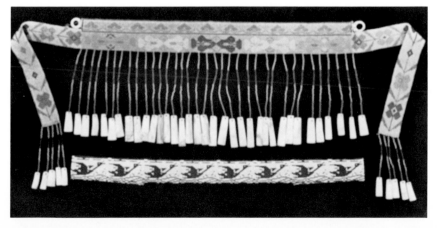

Fig. 323. Designs worked out on bead graph paper will closely approximate the proportions of average-sized seed beads. A sampler of different designs makes an unusual necklace, and is more interesting to work up than a single repeated unit. The central design in the necklace pattern on the left was adapted from the Sally bag in Chapter 4. Necklaces can also be made from straight bands by sewing the last two or three inches of the inner selvedges together before stringing the fringe.

Figs. 324–326. BAG DESIGN, ADAPTED FOR A NECKLACE

Fig. 324. This design for the front of a bag is drafted on ordinary graph paper.

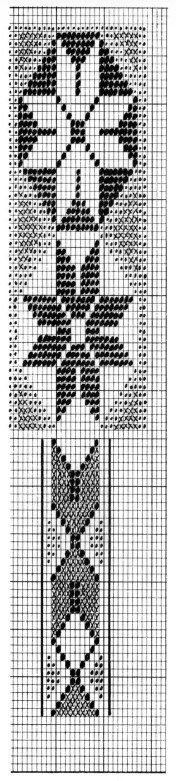

Fig. 325. Bead graph paper shows
more accurately how elements of the
same design will appear when they are
actually worked in beads.

Fig. 326. For extra versatility, two yardsticks were attached across the top edges of this large box loom. The outer one is scored on the ⅛″ marks for seed beads, and is secured only by screws so that it can be removed. The inner yardstick is permanently attached, and is scored on ¼″ marks for large wooden beads. The necklace in progress is in red, black, and yellow #12 beads.

Weaving the Beads

A simple armband, headband, or choker worked with #8 to #10 beads will acquaint you with the weaving process. After a little practice, you can move to smaller beads that permit more detail. Aside from beads, pattern, and warped loom, you will need long beading needles and strong waxed thread.

Pour beads in small piles on a piece of neutral colored felt, and slide it close to the loom where the beads can be easily picked up on the needle. When the weft thread gets short, pick them up from your left palm.

Beadweaving can be started in two ways. For unlined necklaces, tie a short length of yarn to the left selvedge and weave ends over/under warps to the right selvedge. Draw warps slightly together and tie in a single knot. This is a stay for the first row of beads. Tighten the knot after spacing is established, and remove the stay when the beading is completed.

For strips to be appliquéd to a foundation, form the stay with the weft thread itself. Weave four rows, then adjust the tension and tie after the first row of beads is in place. Turn this and selvedge under when the beadwork is stitched to the lining.

The length of the weaving thread (weft) is optional, though 30″ to 36″ is a good average. Tie it to the left selvedge with a Lark's Head knot and pull tight, leaving about 4″ on the short end. Following your graphed design, string on a row of beads with colors in the proper order. Bring them *under* the warps and push them up with your left hand so that they are positioned between the threads. Bring weft *over* the right selvedge, then go back through beads on *top* of the warps to lock the row in place. Draw them close together, evenly aligned against the end stay. Continue the sequence, taking care to reject irregular beads. If you accidentally string on too many beads, the extra one can be broken with sharp-nosed pliers. The hole should be between the jaws of the pliers. If it is crushed from side to side, it may cut the thread.

The needle will accommodate an entire row of six to ten beads. On wide pieces, go through a few beads at a time.

213

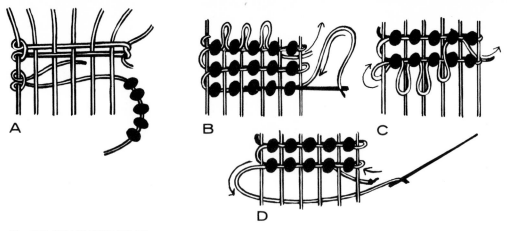

Fig. 327. BEAD WEAVING

A. Tie on a yarn stay to draw in the warps. Weave ends over/under to the opposite side and tie. Attach weaving thread to the left selvedge, leaving about 4″ on the short end. Following your pattern, string on a row of beads.

B. Bring thread under the warps and push beads up between them. Carry weaver over the right selvedge and go through beads again on top of the warps. After a few rows are completed, weave dangling end (shown at the top) through a few adjacent beads and leave hanging on the underside.

C. Always tie off an old thread inside a row, never on the selvedge where knots would show. Weave back through several beads, then pull thread to the underside.

D. Start new thread several beads back from where the old thread left off, and continue. When weaving is finished, clip off dangling threads on the underside.

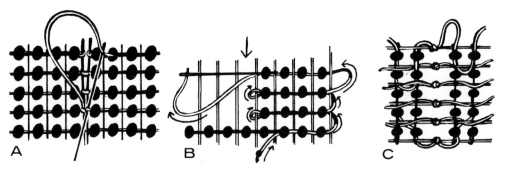

Fig. 328A. The easiest way to make a woven necklace is to weave a long strip, 1″ to 1¼″ wide, then invisibly stitch the last few inches together before stringing the fringe. Beads on opposite sides must be perfectly aligned.

B. If the necklace bib is no wider than 2″, the warps can be split in the center (indicated by arrow) to form straps to go around the neck. Turn the loom around to reverse the weaving order on the right side. You will need an odd number of beads and an even number of warps to the bib row for this style.

C. Unless the bead holes are too small, strap ends can be joined by tightly knotting opposite warps and weaving ends invisibly back into the work. Weave center warps over/under adjacent wefts, then conceal ends in beads. Weave outer warps through beads. If bead holes will not accommodate more thread, cut a 1″ long strip of leather or felt the width of the straps. Weave end selvedges as described for armbands, turn under, and stitch strap ends to the leather with opposite beads aligned.

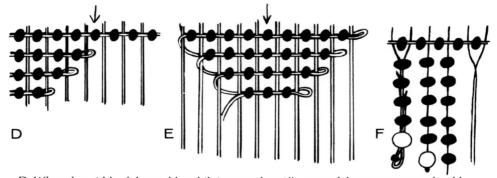

D   E   F

D. When the width of the necklace bib is more than 2″, some of the center warps should be eliminated to form a V; otherwise the straps will be too bulky. An odd number of beads to the row is needed. On each side of the center bead, weave one less bead to the row until an appropriate width remains. Ignore the central warps until the weaving is finished, then clip them from the loom one at a time and weave them invisibly back into the work.

E. Ends can be tapered the same way, leaving extra warps on one or both sides. Edges will look alike when superfluous warps are woven back through beads of the following row.

F. For a very full fringe, string beads on every warp thread at the bottom. For a flat fringe, periodically use two warps to a strand to compensate for the widths of the beads.

Making a Simple Armband

To determine the length of the beadwork, measure around the arm, and subtract ¾″ (½″ for extension of the foundation, and ¼″ for lacing to pull the band tight). Work up an accurate pattern on graph paper. If a repeat unit will not come out exactly even, fill in with several rows of the background color on each end.

The pattern in Figure 329 will make a 1½″ band in #8 beads. The outer rows can be increased to adjust it to smaller beads. A single unit of the repeat is indicated by the arrows.

Work the beading, weaving selvedges at each end of the strip as described earlier. Knot warp threads together before clipping them short. Bring outer threads slightly toward the center, cover selvedges with pieces of double-stick carpet tape, then fold to the underside.

Cut a strip of flexible leather slightly wider than the beadwork and ½″ longer. Center the beadwork on top of it, and fasten with long basting stitches down the middle. Use fine sewing thread to stitch them together as shown in Figure 331 A. The beaded strip must be slightly fuller than the lining or it will pucker when it is wrapped around the arm. Test it from time to time around a jar or bottle to make sure they fit smoothly together.

Lace ends with a narrow thong as shown in Figure 331 B.

Figs. 329–331. MAKING A SIMPLE ARMBAND

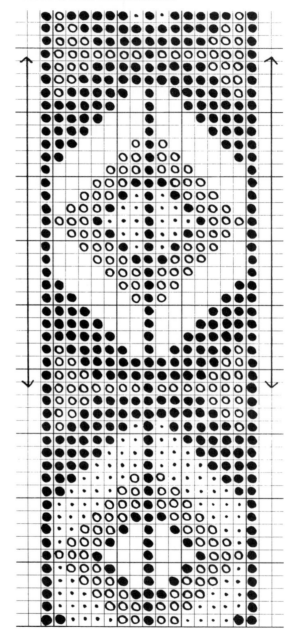

Fig. 329. Easy repeat pattern in four colors for a woven armband, choker, or headband.

Fig. 330. Stitch woven armbands and headbands to a thin leather or felt foundation. Headband ends can be attached to a strip of elastic, or a ribbon for tying under the hair. The armband shown here is to be laced through the holes in the end extensions of the foundation.

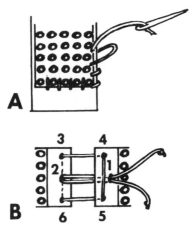

Fig. 331A. To attach a beaded strip to a lining, baste the two pieces together, then stitch around edges with fine waxed thread. On armbands, ease in the beadwork to make it slightly fuller than the lining.

B. Punch three holes in each end of the leather extensions. Bring ends together and thread a thin thong through hole #1. Go under the end, through hole #2, under leather, and come out at #3. Cross over and come out at #4, go down through #5. Cross over and go through #6, and out at #2. Cross over and come out at #1. Knot ends. After slipping over the arm, the band can be tightened by pulling on the thong ends. If the thongs fit snugly in the holes, the band will stay in place.

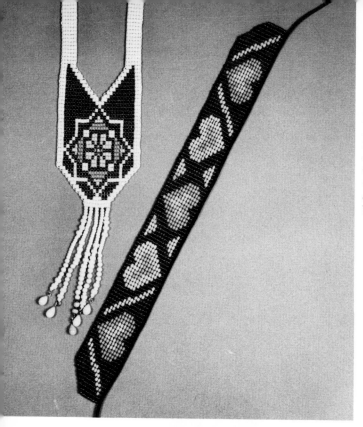

Fig. 332. Some warp threads were eliminated from the center of the necklace at the left to reduce the widths of the side straps. The choker on the right is unlined. The ends were tapered, then a length of silk cording was slip-stitched to the top edge for a tie. The ends of the warps could also be braided into a cord, or they could be knotted through a clasp.

Fig. 333. For bag fronts and wide pieces where bead rows are longer than the needle, go through only a few at a time. Be sure the needle does not skip a bead when it is reinserted.

Fig. 334. The bib on this necklace is 4″ wide, and the straps are ¾″. To make the flat fringe at the bottom, two warps were periodically used for a single strand to compensate for the widths of the beads. Large beads, teardrops, tin cones, and small shells make attractive finials for fringes. *By Mary Lou Stribling.*

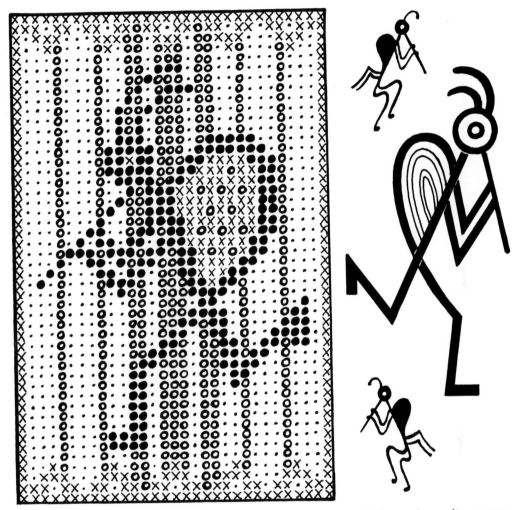

Fig. 335. The Humpbacked Flute Player is an ancient pueblo pottery design, and according to some accounts, originally symbolized a supernatural being who was an intermediary of the Fire God. Some modern potters say he is an ant, a creature they respect as they do all things in nature. The pattern on the left was drafted on 8-point graph paper, and could be duplicated exactly in embroidery or needlepoint. It will be elongated when used for loomed beadwork.

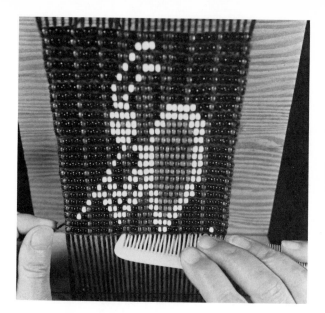

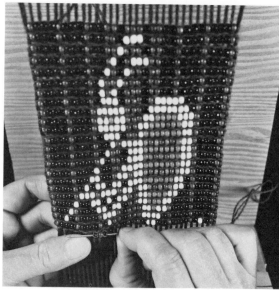

Fig. 336. Rows of woven threads between beads give them an embedded look. They must be made in multiples of two to return the weft to the left selvedge. Do not draw them too tightly. Use a comb to pack them firmly against the beads.

Fig 337. Tapestry yarn must be used with a long-eyed sewing needle instead of a beading needle. It will accommodate only three to five beads at a time, and they should be pushed up as high as possible so that warps are not split by the beading thread.

Fig. 338. The pattern for the Humpbacked Flute Player could be woven in seed beads and stitched to the front of a small bag. This hanging was made with ⅛″ beads that are close to the size of old Indian pony beads. Knitting worsted was used for warps; a single strand of tapestry wool for wefts. *By Mary Lou Stribling.*

8

THREAD EMBROIDERY

In some areas of the Americas, thread embroidery preceded foreign contacts by many years. It was highly developed in South America, especially in Peru. It also flourished among the pueblo tribes around the North American Rio Grande, where skirts, shirts, and blankets were decorated with paints, as well as with colored threads, often elaborately. Descriptions by early explorers indicate that designs of that period were very similar to those that were made later with commercial materials.

Early Southwestern needles were fashioned from thorns, or from slivers of bone or wood. Unique self-threaded needles were made by pulling spines from yucca and cactus plants so that long, thin strips of bark were peeled off with them. On dense foundations that the delicate needles could not penetrate, stitching holes were first perforated with an awl.

Hopi weavers invented a distinctive kind of embroidery for ceremonial sashes and kilts that is related to the technique of brocading. While the fabric was being woven, selected warp threads were encircled with fine colored weft threads, creating patterns that were somewhat corded in appearance, and slightly raised above the background.

The Nez Percé used a similar method, sometimes called "false embroidery," to work cornhusk patterns into their twined bags. False embroidery was also used by the Tlingits to weave colored designs into their baskets.

True embroidery is applied to fabrics that are already woven. Among many pueblo groups, the colored threads followed the grain of a coarse, cotton foundation material to create the effect of woven patterns. It was used profusely on sashes, kilts, robes, shawls, and mantas. When they were not being worn, these special garments were hung against the walls on wooden poles so that their glowing colors could brighten the dusky adobe interiors.

Fig. 339. Hopi kilt. The design of this dance kilt is traditional and was made by a form of false embroidery while the fabric was being woven. Unlike most textile arts, it was produced by men. To a limited extent, the art is still alive today. *Collection, The Millicent A. Rogers Memorial Museum.*

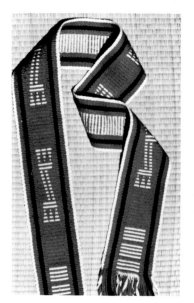

Fig. 340. Wool Hopi sash, 4″ × 5′. Warp-faced pick-up technique woven on an inkle loom. *Weaving and photo, Jacquetta Nisbet.*

Fig. 341. Southwestern embroidered runner or hanging. A different kind of pueblo embroidery was applied to already woven fabrics. By keeping the superimposed thread lines consistent with the grain of the foundation, the effect closely resembled patterned weaving. This example is in rich reds and blues. Its exact origin and age are unknown. *Photo, Jim Toms; courtesy, The Nevada State Museum.*

PUEBLO-STYLE EMBROIDERY

Characteristic Southwestern embroidery is somewhat like conventional satin stitching, but the threads run only vertically or horizontally, even though the design might have diagonal lines. The foundation fabric should have a fairly prominent, even grain. Homespun, monk's cloth, heavy linen, or almost any of the hand-loomed textiles that have straight warp and weft threads are suitable.

Pull lengthwise and crosswise threads to trim the fabric evenly, then machine-stitch the edges to prevent raveling.

On heavy materials, the embroidery can be made with knitting worsted, or tapestry and crewel yarns. Use cotton floss or single strands of wool yarn on fine materials. Stitches can be up to ½″ long, depending on the weight of the foundation, and they are drawn in between the foundation threads, without splitting them.

Measure the upright threads with a ruler to determine a scale for your pattern. On monk's cloth, for example, where two warp threads equal ¼'', stitches could be ⅛'' to ⅜'' long to enclose one, two, or three threads. If there were nine upright threads to the inch, stitches could go over one thread, or three, or six.

It is difficult to exactly follow the fabric grain if you transfer patterns with carbon. Instead, use ruler measurements as guides for marking the lines directly. It is also helpful to chalk a few horizontal lines 1'' to 2'' apart across the fabric. After the first row of stitches has been worked, it is easy to keep the lengths of stitches consistent on succeeding rows.

Figs. 342–344. PUEBLO-STYLE EMBROI-DERY

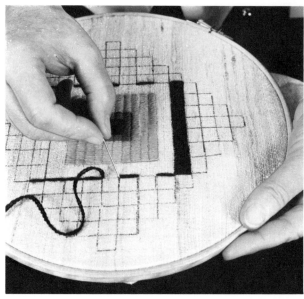

Fig. 342. Some of the simple terraced designs from Navajo weaving work up beautifully in pueblo-style embroidery. Loomed beadwork and baskets are good sources for other ideas. The thread should completely cover the foundation for an appearance of weaving. Use running stitches across every other block, then return to fill the spaces. Plunge needle from top to bottom in the same stitch holes.

Fig. 343. Even where the design lines are vertical or diagonal, keep stitch lines running consistently in one direction.

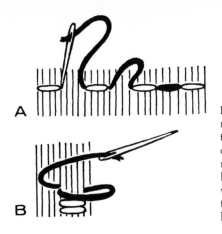

Fig. 344A. To work stripes, make a row of running stitches across every other block, drop the needle, and fill in the spaces with a second color threaded in another needle. Turn the fabric around and continue the sequence.

B. Some parts of the design will have to be worked vertically. Follow the foundation thread lines and keep the stitches the same lengths as on the horizontal rows.

BASKET-WEAVE EMBROIDERY

A different kind of woven embroidery is made by superimposing vertical threads on a fabric foundation, then weaving through them from the opposite direction. This has a certain relationship in principle to some of the sewn quillwork techniques that were described in Chapter 7.

Like pueblo-style embroidery, this is also worked on fabrics with an even grain, that is, where both warp and weft have the same thickness and same number of threads to the inch. The example in Figures 345 and 346 is being worked on chartreuse monk's cloth with lightweight wool yarn.

Transfer a design to the fabric, and secure the thread on the underside with several small stitches instead of a knot. Set in all vertical threads in one unit before starting the horizontal weaving.

Figs. 345–346. BASKET-WEAVE EMBROIDERY

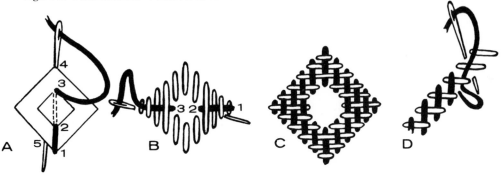

Fig. 345A. Warp threads can follow either the vertical or horizontal lines of the foundation fabric. For open squares, bring needle out at 1, go down at 2, and out at 3. Go down at 4, and back out at 5. Continue across the square, then come back to the center and work the other side with the same number of stitches. For a solid square, carry threads straight across without the central break.

B. To weave in the wefts, bring needle out at 1, carry thread over/under warps, then down at 2. Come out at 3 and continue.

C. Fill in one side, then come back to the center and fill the other side.

D. Narrow lines in the pattern are worked on the same basic principle. The stitch is similar to a herringbone stitch, except that the thread lines form +'s, instead of ×'s.

Fig. 346. Unusual effects can be obtained by using one color for the vertical warps, and another for the horizontal wefts. This design was adapted from the Wasco Sally bag in Chapter 4.

FLORAL EMBROIDERY

Moosehair embroidery is prehistoric. It was made by dyeing the long cheek hairs and twisting them into soft threads. They were spun too loosely to withstand the wear of passing in and out of a foundation, so they were laid on the surface and secured with a second thread of sinew.[1]

Moosehair embroidery was well suited to flowing lines, and was a forerunner of realistic thread embroidery. They have certain stylistic similarities, but hair embroidery was an indigenous art, whereas floral embroidery evolved from materials, designs, and techniques that were brought to America by colonists. Like many other arts that were not native in origin, however, it gained something in the translation that deserves our attention.

There was more exposure to colonial training and tastes in some areas than in others, and really fine floral embroidery was largely confined to tribes of the northern Plains, Canadian Subarctic, and Northeastern Woodlands. It is not pure coincidence that these peoples also produced fine floral beadwork, and sometimes the two were combined.

Scrolling lines and vaguely petal-like shapes that resemble distorted hearts or arrows with rounded points are often included in floral designs, and may have come from aboriginal sources. Attempts have been made to trace an orderly historical progression from these abstractions to eighteenth-century realism, but deductions are pretty arbitrary at best. We know that embroidery techniques were taught to young Indian girls in Canadian French convents in the early 1600s. Realistic art was popular in Europe at that time, particularly in the religious arts, and there is little doubt that the nuns also passed on the favorite patterns of their homelands.

[1] This couching technique was also used for spot-stitched beadwork.

This influence appeared first in the Northeastern regions around the Great Lakes, and gradually spread across the continent, eventually even reaching the Northwest Coast.

By the mid 1800s, these realistic patterns were greatly in demand by tourists, and were made in increasing quantities. Moosehair embroidery did not die out completely. The Quebec Hurons were especially adept at the work, and produced it for commercial trade into the early 1900s. Interestingly enough, the technique was picked up by non-Indians in the same area, who probably sold most of it as genuine "Indian" goods.

Figs. 347–349. WOODLAND CREE EMBROIDERY

Fig. 347–348. The Woodland Cree lived primarily by trapping and hunting, and were prominent in northern fur trade. Dog teams were their main means of transportation and were essential for operating winter traplines. These beautiful blankets were embroidered about fifty years ago, and no doubt were designed for use on special festive occasions. *Collection, Glenbow–Alberta Institute.*

Fig. 349. Cree jacket embroidered with silk thread. This is an exceptionally fine example of Cree floral silk embroidery. The jacket is made of moosehide, and is trimmed with mink or martin fur. *Collection, Glenbow–Alberta Institute.*

Fig. 350. FLORAL EMBROIDERY DESIGNS

CONTEMPORARY ADAPTATIONS OF FLORAL EMBROIDERY

The handle, front, and back of the bag in Figure 351 were cut in one piece so that seams would not detract from the embroidered design. This creates certain problems for machine-stitching that may not be apparent until you have tried it. Unless you want to cut the handle separately, and adjust your embroidery design accordingly, it is best to assemble the bag the way the Indians would—by hand. This actually takes very little more time, especially if you use a flexible braid with a bias weave to "box" the front and back together, and to bind the edges of the handle and top opening.

Like the fabric bags in Chapter 6, the outline should be marked on the fabric and the embroidery completed before cutting it out.

Figs. 351–353. CONTEMPORARY ADAPTATIONS OF FLORAL EMBROIDERY

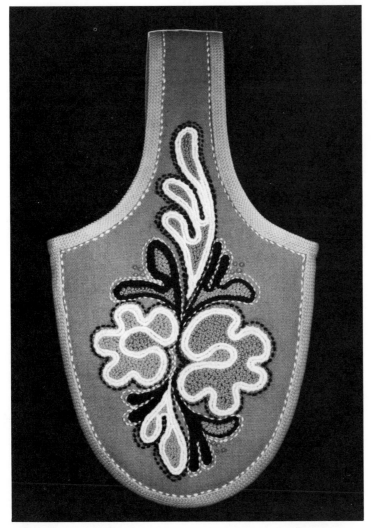

Fig. 351. The technique and materials for moosehair embroidery were not appropriate for detailed realistic designs. Typical designs were made up of scalloped borders and flowing, stylized flowers. This contemporary adaptation is a composite of elements of nineteenth-century Huron work. It was embroidered with knitting worsted on lightweight wool fabric.

Fig. 352. To work similar pieces, transfer the design to fabric, and attach outline threads first by couching (A). Use two rows in appropriate areas to vary the widths of the lines. Fill enclosed areas with closely compacted French knots (B), for the textural effect of beads. Add tiny running stitches and isolated French knots last.

Fig. 353. BAG CONSTRUCTION

The bag in Fig. 351 measures 8″ across the widest part, and is 15″ long. The handle is 2″ wide at the top.
A. Use 1¼″ wide woven braid for boxing front and back together, and for binding edges of the top and handle.
B. Fold fabric lengthwise and arrange pattern with the top of the handle on the fold. Cut out fabric and matching lining pieces.
C. Stitch across the end of the woven braid to keep it from raveling. Pin along the front seam line, easing in fullness smoothly around the curve. Baste and slip stitch invisibly. Stitch across the braid before cutting it off. Pin other edge of braid to the back of the bag and repeat. Make lining the same way, using larger seams and a 1½″ bias strip of lining material instead of the braid. (If it is carefully basted, it can be machine-stitched.)
D. Slip lining inside bag and baste edges together. Baste and blindstitch braid around seam lines on the top side. Fold braid to inside and blindstitch.

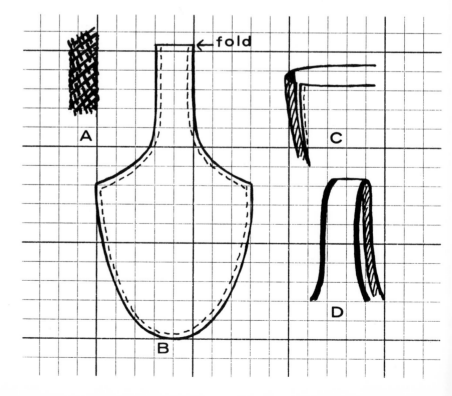

EMBROIDERY FROM BEADWORK

A beadlike texture can be obtained by working small loops on needlepoint canvas along the principle of punch-needle tufting. Geometric designs are appropriate, and samplers of simple beadwork patterns make handsome handbags.

Use knitting worsted and 10-hole-to-the-inch (or smaller) double mesh canvas. The stitch is basically a running stitch, except that it is not drawn down flat against the canvas on the top side, so that small loops are formed. Hold back the loop with your left thumb when you make the next stitch to keep from pulling it out. When you get the feel of the rhythm, you can easily keep the loops even, but a bit of irregularity will not be noticeable when they are compacted. Coat the back side with diluted rug adhesive or rabbitskin glue when the work is finished.

Figs. 354–355. EMBROIDERY FROM BEADWORK

Fig. 354. Tiny wool loops worked on needlepoint canvas have the appearance of small beads.

Fig. 355. Work loops in vertical rows. Secure thread and bring needle up through a hole. Go over a canvas thread and down through the adjacent hole. Pull thread down, leaving a loop from 1/16″ to ⅛″ on the top side. Hold the loop back with your left thumb, go under the next thread and continue. Worsted is "fat" enough to be well secured by the small mesh.

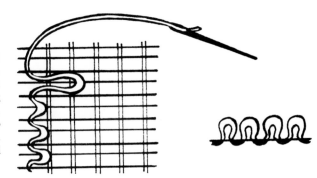

CONTEMPORARY EMBROIDERY FROM SOUTHWESTERN DESIGNS

Indian representational embroidery was largely restricted to flowers, but many painted figures on Southwestern pottery are well suited for embroidery techniques. The bird on the right in Figure 356 is from an Acoma pot in the next chapter. On the left, it has been adapted to a design for an embroidered pendant. Use dressmaker's carbon to transfer it to a firm, black cotton fabric, such as poplin, denim, or linen, and stretch in an embroidery hoop.

Work embroidery with three strands of cotton floss. Fill in the borders and the bird's legs, beak, and body with long-short stitches. Use satin stitches for details on the plume, eye, tail, wing, and branch. Add running stitches in the background as indicated on the pattern.

After the design is embroidered, brush flexible fabric glue around the outside edges of the stitchery on the wrong side, to keep fabric from raveling. When it is dry, cut around outline, leaving a ⅛" margin all around. Attach with spray adhesive to a matching piece of leather, then carefully trim away excess fabric and leather close to the stitching.

Perforate holes at the top of the pendant with a large needle, and suspend from a chain of beads. Make a 1¾" beaded fringe at the bottom, using thread covered beads on the ends of every two or three strands.

The pattern for an appliquéd and embroidered pillow top in Figure 361 is closer to the Acoma bird than the two pendants. The pillow was made from scraps of white, olive, and rust-colored blankets, and was embroidered with single strands of tapestry yarn. Other color combinations of felt or flannels that do not ravel excessively would be equally suitable.

Fig. 356. The bird at the right from an old Acoma pot was adapted for the pendant design at the left. On a larger scale, the circle could be used for an embroidered pillow.

Draw pattern full size, and cut out paper patterns for the appliqué patches. Trace around appliqué patterns on appropriate fabrics. Machine-stitch outlines with matching thread, then cut out close to the stitching. (Stitching can be eliminated for felt.) Repeat to make a 10½" white circle.

Trace a 12½" olive circle on fabric, allowing enough material around it to accommodate a large embroidery hoop.

If you are working with soft fabrics that cannot be marked with dressmaker's carbon, use a perforated pattern as described in Chapter 10 to transfer the drawing to the white circle. Center it on the olive circle and baste. Stretch in an embroidery hoop and stitch around the white circle as shown in Figure 360 A. Repeat for other appliqués, using short stitches and matching thread on all pieces.

Work embroidered details as shown in the pattern.

Fig. 357. The embroidery was worked on black cotton fabric with cotton floss, in shades of brown, terracotta, and bone. (See color plates.) It was mounted on a matching piece of leather.

Fig. 358. With minor alterations, the same design could be used for needlepoint of any scale. For a petit-point pendant, use canvas with 17 holes to the inch, and a single strand of tapestry yarn. Cut out embroidery, leaving a ⅛" margin. Cut out a leather disk ½" wider than the embroidery. Attach a twisted cord or chain, and glue embroidery in the center. From a plastic can top, cut a frame ¼" wide to fit the leather disk. Wrap with black yarn, concealing ends on the back side.

Fig. 359. Glue frame over embroidery, weight lightly until dry, then glue a row of yarn between frame and leather to fill the shallow crevice.

234

Fig. 360. The Acoma bird can also be modified for an appliquéd and embroidered pillow top. After appliqués are attached (A), embroider the lower branch and bird's legs with closely spaced long-short stitches (B). Use radiating straight stitches for details on the bird's eye, plume, and wing (C). Work dots with tiny seed stitches drawn firmly through all three layers of fabric to greate a dimpled texture (D). Add running stitches as indicated.

Fig. 361. Cut a 12½″ circle for the pillow back, and a 2½″ boxing strip. Assemble parts to snugly fit a 14″ pillow form.

Fig. 362. Embroidered pillows by Jackie Curry. Rows of rug yarn were used for these Southwestern designs, and they were attached with flexible fabric glue instead of a second couching thread. *Courtesy*, Family Circle.

Fig. 363. Appliquéd and embroidered felt mask. Gold felt was bonded with fusible webbing to one half of the basic shape; turquoise felt to the other half. Cobalt, rust, and black felt cutouts were bonded on next, then embroidery details were worked with tapestry yarn. The mask was glued to a matching form cut from mat board, and black cotton fringe was glued around it. Two rows of rug yarn finished the inner edges of the fringe. The design was based on a Zuñi Kachina mask of the Earth and Sky Being.

Fig. 364. The Continental stitch was used on this needlepoint bag front with a South-western feather design. *Worked by Lu Lundstrum.*

EMBROIDERED SHELL AND METAL INLAYS

Abalone shells were avidly traded along the entire western coast of North and South America. As described in Chapter 2, these shells can easily be perforated with the tip of a sharp knife to make holes for suspension or stitching. Broken fragments can also be attached to fabric in thread "pockets," and they are compatible accents for embroidered designs. The shape of the pocket is determined by the outside stitching line, though the central opening that exposes the shell will be rounded.

The technique diagrammed in Figure 365 is similar to Oriental mirror embroidery; however, the stitch for surrounding the inlays with a solid thread border is entirely different. It produces a more closely compacted frame that is as much a part of the design as the inlay itself. The technique is also suitable for fragments of colored glass or plastic, coins, and pieces of tin.

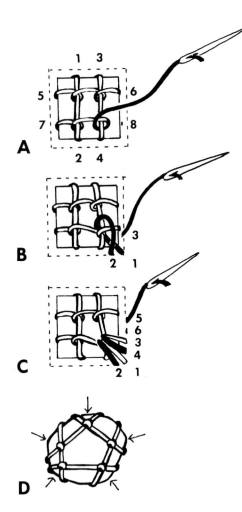

Fig. 365. EMBROIDERED SHELL AND METAL INLAYS

A. Cut squares, circles, or hexagons from tin cans and file burrs from the edges. Hold the tin in the center of the stitching area with the left hand, and bring needle out at 1. Go over tin and down at 2. Pull thread taut and take a tiny catch stitch on the underside. Bring needle out at 3, go over tin and down at 4. Make a catch stitch on the underside and come out at 5. Follow thread lines and numbered order as shown to fasten the tin in a snug tic-tac-toe frame.

B. Bring needle out on the stitching line opposite one of the corners of the framework (1). Go under threads of the framework, bring needle over them and down through the fabric at 2. Pull gently to tighten the stitch, and bring needle out at 3.

C. Bring needle under framework, swing thread over and down at 4. Come out at 5, and continue the forward/backward sequence all around the inlay.

D. Pockets for shell fragments and other irregular shapes can be made the same way by adding extra lines to the basic framework. Be sure the corners of the frame, indicated here by arrows, are well inside the outline of the shell, or edges may be exposed by the drawing action of the stitchery.

Circles for the owl's eyes in Fig. 367 were cut from the lacquered gold lining of tin can lids. The design was embroidered with cotton floss on heavy cotton fabric.

Transfer the design with dressmaker's carbon. Cut circles from can lids and attach as described in Figure 365. Embroider the face, then trim around edges, leaving a 1″ margin all around. Cover the embroidery with tracing paper and draw around the outline to make a pattern for a backing of very thin board or balsa. Spray one side of the backing and the back side of the embroidery with adhesive, and carefully position the two together, making sure that the pattern is properly aligned with the backing. Cover with several sheets of tissue and weight with heavy books until it is dry. Spread a border of fabric glue on the back side of the backing. Bring the fabric margins over the edges and into it. Distribute gathers evenly and press them down flat. Use pins or small tacks to temporarily hold the fabric in place until the glue dries. Remove pins, then coat the entire back with glue, and cover with a matching piece of black felt.

For thread-covered beads, use wooden beads with fairly large holes, and three strands of embroidery floss in a small needle. Bring thread through a hole, tie tightly, and pull knot to the inside. Continue around bead, leaving small spaces between each row so that thread does not pile up. When you return to the starting point, go back around bead again to smoothly fill in the gaps. Fasten thread by drawing it through several strands inside the hole.

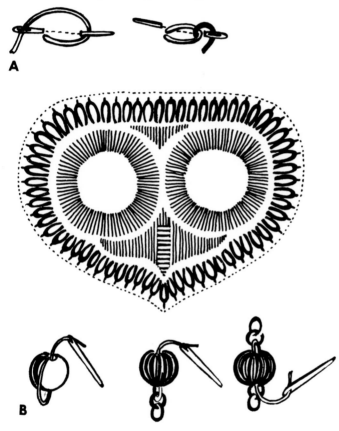

Fig. 366. Inlay gold colored tin for the eyes, as shown in Figure 365. Work embroidery with satin and daisy stitches (A). Cover six wooden beads with thread (B), and attach four to short lengths of chain.

Fig. 367. Shorten one chain by several links and join with another to a jump ring. Stitch ring to bottom of pendant. Join other two chains to thread-covered beads and jump rings, and stitch to each side at the top. Add chain to go around the neck.

Fig. 368. Metal inlays that reflect the light like bits of stained glass, can be cut from the colored sections of aluminum soft drink cans. The inlays on the body of this fish are emerald green; the eye and tail are gold. The embroidery was worked in luminous shades of green, lime, avocado, blue, purple, rose, and coral. It was mounted with spray adhesive on a circle of plywood cut to fit inside a wooden embroidery hoop:

Fig. 369. The design was adapted from a painted ceramic bowl made by the ancient inhabitants of Mimbres Valley, New Mexico. They produced some of the finest pottery of the early pueblo cultures, and though geometric designs were popular, their stylized fish, birds, and animals were outstanding. This adaptation could be used for appliqué or conventional embroidery. For metal inlays, the triangles on the back were changed to squares.

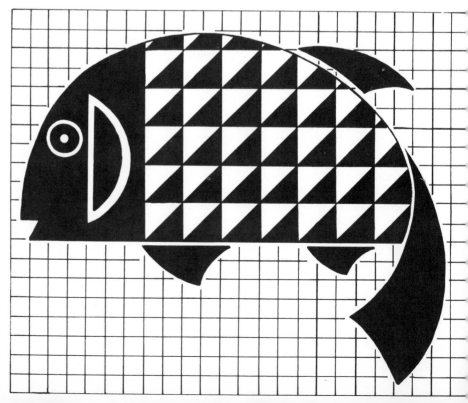

9

GOURDS AND CLAY WORK

The gourd family is very large and includes melons, cucumbers, pumpkins, and squashes. The bitter fruit of the branch familiarly known as gourds cannot be eaten, but they were valuable household commodities in many tribes, especially during prepottery periods. Their tough, hollow shells were natural bowls, bottles, pots, and jars, and they were easy to carve into ladles, tools, ornaments, music makers, and masks.

They are not as essential in our culture today, but they are still fascinating to grow and work with. Nearly every rural garden in regions with a few sunny months and a reasonable amount of rainfall has a section set aside for gourds. They are harvested in the fall when the connecting stems shrivel and turn brown, then the shells are cured in a dry spot indoors.[1]

GOURD POTS

The bottom of the gourd should be leveled before cutting the opening for a standing pot. Sometimes this is a simple matter of rubbing it on sandpaper, or gluing on disks of cork for feet. But if they are fully rounded, or one side is considerably more bulbous than the other, it is best to use them for hanging pots.

Stand the gourd upright, using floral clay under rounded or uneven forms, then establish a level cut line for the top opening with calipers or a ruler. Score the line carefully and gradually incise it deeper with a knife or hacksaw until the

[1] Mail order sources for gourd seeds are listed in the Appendix.

241

Fig. 370. Old Zuñi gourd dance rattles. *Collection, The Nevada State Historical Society.*

wall is penetrated. This can be done quickly with an electric carving knife if you do not apply much pressure.

Use a spoon to scrape out the seeds and pulpy lining of open pots. Clean bottles and vase shapes that have narrow necks with a long chisel or stiff wire. Loosen and shake out as much of the pulp as possible, then drop in a handful of crushed rocks and shake them vigorously to remove the rest. Refine and round the cut edge with fine sandpaper.

For protection against moisture, coat the inside with paraffin. Melt the wax in a can set in a pan of water. When it is fluid, not smoking hot, pour it into the gourd and roll it around until the inside is covered, then set the gourd upright and allow remaining wax to pool in the bottom. This will provide extra weight to stabilize both hanging and standing pots.

Fill finished pots about halfway with fine gravel or sand to support dried flowers or seed heads. A glass or metal liner will be needed for water or potting soil.

Hanging pots can be suspended on decorative cords through three equidistant holes drilled three to four inches down from the top. If their contents are heavy, use a net instead to eliminate the strain on suspension holes.

Fig. 371. Only simple alterations were needed to make these pots stand straight. A single concave patty of wood putty formed the foot for the pot on the left. On the right, three flattened putty pellets were attached on one side.

DECORATING GOURDS

Gourds can be decorated with any paints that are suitable for wood, but paints made from colored earths have the character of pottery and are opaque enough to cover mottled surfaces.

Indians mixed earth colors with water to make body paints and temporary decorations. Blood, animal fat, and eggs were more permanent vehicles, and some Southwestern murals painted with these mixtures have survived for centuries.

Soil with a high clay content is best, though any kind of earth that can be pulverized will work as long as it is not too sandy. Place clods and hardened materials in a cardboard box and crush them with a hammer or wooden mallet. Sift through a fine strainer to remove pebbles and foreign matter, then grind small amounts at a time with a mortar and pestle until they are reduced to a smooth powder.

Whole milk can be used as an experimental binder, but clear matt acrylic medium makes a more paintable consistency. Its white color will temporarily lighten the earth tones. They will become dark again as they dry.

Other earthy paints can be made very inexpensively from compounds of gesso, matt acrylic medium, and dry cement colors. They have the velvety texture of clay, and a wide range of intermediate shades can be obtained by intermixing basic batches.

Cheaper grades of cement colors may be slightly gritty, and they can be improved by pulverizing them further with a mortar and pestle. It is easier to distribute the colors evenly if they are slightly moistened with water before adding other ingredients.

The colors can be obtained where masonry supplies are sold, and are most commonly available in brown, black, brick red, and yellow ochre. Acrylic medium is used as a binder; gesso as an opacifier. Gesso also makes a very hard finish, and has enough body to help smooth out eroded or scaly surfaces.

Earth Paints

The following recipes can be varied by changing the proportions of the pigments, and they can be thinned if necessary with a few drops of water or additional medium. Use a ½ teaspoon measure for small amounts, and store paints in glass jars with tight lids.

Gesso is not used in the darkest, most intense shades. They are, therefore, more transparent, and several coats may be required for even coverage.

COLOR	DRY CEMENT COLORS	ACRYLIC MEDIUM	GESSO
Black	1 black	1	0
Dark red brown	1 red brown	1	0
Rich gold	1 yellow ochre	1	0
Dark brown	1 brown	1	0
Med. cool brown	4 brown	1	1
Med. warm brown	2 brown; 2 red brown	1	1
Lt. golden brown	4 ochre; 2 red brown	2	2
Terra cotta	2 ochre; 5 red brown	3	2
Charcoal grey	3 brown; 1 black	1	1
Ivory	2 ochre	1	2
Pale gold	2 ochre	1	1
Med. gold	4 ochre	1	1

These paints have a thick, creamy consistency, and are most useful for coloring large areas. Acrylic paints are better for fine details. Moist acrylics can also be mixed with gesso instead of the dry cement colors, though hues are a bit harsher and darker shades will be less opaque.

Start with a small amount of gesso, stir in several drops of acrylic color, and mix well. Continue adding the acrylic until the desired depth of color is obtained. The paint can be thinned with a few drops of water or matt acrylic medium.

Gourds are never perfectly symmetrical, and their organic irregularity is a part of their charm. But it also means that you will have to make some adjustments on the spacing of repeat designs, as the Indians did on baskets, beaded bottles, and clay pots. The variation is actually more interesting than mathematical precision, and is better suited to the natural form.

The inside and outside surfaces of the gourd pot in Figure 373 were coated with two applications of medium terra-cotta earth paint. The upper half was divided into six parts for a repeat pattern. The back side of one unit of the paper pattern was heavily coated with chalk and fastened to the pot with masking tape. The drawing was then transferred by going over the lines with a pencil.

Solid bands and large areas of the pattern were painted with brick red acrylic. Fine black details are also acrylic. The pot was finished with two coats of clear matt acrylic medium.

Figs. 372–374. GOURD POT

Fig. 372. Transfer repeat designs a unit at a time. Coat the back side of the paper pattern with chalk, tape it to the pot, and go over the lines with a pencil. Any remaining chalk residue can be wiped away with a soft damp cloth after the design is painted.

Fig. 373. Gourds might have been partly responsible for the concept of hollow clay vessels, and it is easy to see why they have remained a source of inspiration for pottery shapes. This gourd pot was painted with medium terra-cotta earth paint. Brick red and black details were made with acrylics.

Fig. 374. The design was inspired by old Hopi pottery. Vertical lines indicate the edges of one unit.

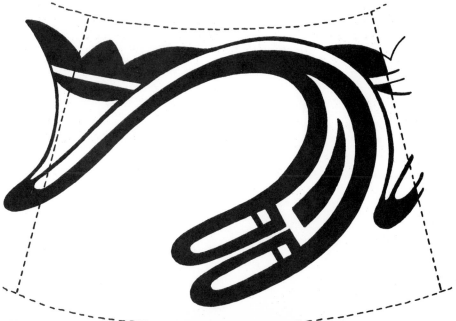

Fig. 375. The idea of charcoal grey and black designs on these nest egg gourds was borrowed from Santa Clara black-on-black ware, but the motifs were adapted from other tribes. The butterfly design on the left is from old Sityatki (Hopi) pottery. The rosette and scroll design on the right is a combination of Zuñi elements. *By Mary Lou Stribling.*

Figs. 376, 377. Gourds, cut on lines of the designs to make lidded containers. The character of the acrylic designs was inspired by Southwestern pottery. *Gourds and photo, Jacquetta Nisbet.*

POTTERY

The earliest excavated North American pottery was made about 2000–1200 B.C. in the regions that are now Georgia, Florida, and South Carolina. By 1000 B.C., Southeastern pottery had evolved from crude forms to refined wares decorated with stamped designs from wooden paddles. Two thousand years later potters in these areas were producing shapely well-tempered forms that had a certain kinship to pottery in Central America.

Trade along the eastern coast from north to south was lively, though participation in bargaining sessions was not always voluntary, and it was understood from the beginning that the weaker party would get the worst of the deal. But raiding was an accepted practice for acquiring arts, as well as more practical goods, and it contributed to the spread of ideas and materials for pottery making from one tribe to the other.

Deserts and high mountains kept the Southwestern peoples more isolated, and their ceramic arts were developed independently. The Pueblo culture began about A.D. 400–800, and fine pottery was made toward the latter part of that period. It was fully mature when the Spaniards arrived in the late 1500s, and is the only area where traditional pottery is still produced in quantity today.

Fig. 378. Painted pottery bowl from Arizona, made around A.D. 1050–1300. *Courtesy, The M. H. De Young Memorial Museum.*

Fig. 379. Wilford polychrome pot made by an unknown tribe around A.D. 1500. Found in Coahoma County, Mississippi. *Courtesy, The Mississippi Department of Archives and History.*

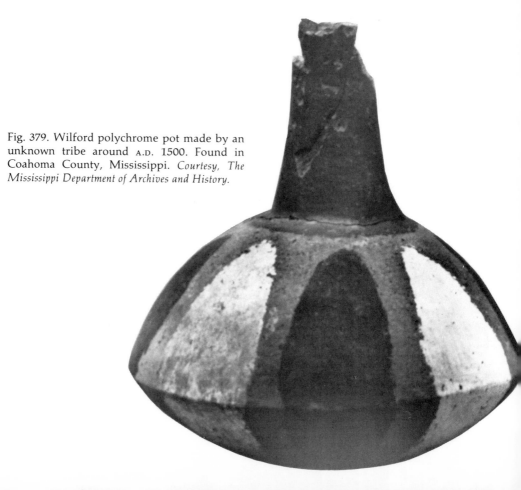

The Spaniards influenced many aspects of Southwestern culture, even to the extent of causing some ancient traditions to be completely abandoned, but they had little if any effect on the Indian style of pottery. Nor up until the last century has any other non-Indian culture. The white influence did have an effect on production, since the availability of commercial wares eliminated the necessity of producing pottery by hand. The art was kept alive, however, by a diminishing number of artists who enjoyed making and using containers with forms and designs that were rooted in tribal histories.

Sadly, although these potters resisted the destructive force of invasion, conquest, and expatriation, most could not resist the equally destructive power of the white economy. Once their pots were discovered by tourists and collectors, the art degenerated. Forms were hastily constructed with little attention to balance, symmetry, or surface refinement. Designs became weak and indifferent, were poorly adapted to the basic shapes, and often derived from what the potter considered salable rather than personal taste. Garish poster paints and glossy varnishes were substituted for subtle earth pigments and hand polishing. Pots were cracked and warped by hurried, uneven firing, and in many cases were not fired at all.

A revival of fine pueblo pottery began early in this century, though it should be credited to the vision of a few talented individuals rather than the impact of a broad cultural movement. The Hopi potter Nampeyo of Hano (Arizona) was a major force. In 1895 archeologists excavated near her home the ancient village of Sikyatki (See-kat'-kee), which had been inhabited some 600 years earlier. The vitality of the designs on the old bowls and shards inspired the flowing rhythmic patterns that became her trademark.

When Nampeyo's eyes began to fail, her husband painted the designs. Then her three daughters, Annie, Fannie, and Nellie, carried on their mother's work. Now the names of granddaughters Daisy Hooie,[2] Rachel, Elva, and Leah have been added to this distinguished line of potters, as well as great-granddaughters Dextra, Priscilla, and Lillian.

Maria Martinez of San Ildefonso also figured prominently in the revival of Southwestern pottery. She was essentially a modeler, and left the decoration of her exquisitely shaped forms to her husband, Julian. About 1919 they introduced a distinctive pottery style of polished black designs on a matt black background.[3] It was adopted by potters in the neighboring Santa Clara Pueblo, and its influence was soon felt throughout the Southwest.

The effect was obtained by burnishing the entire piece with a smooth stone, then painting either the background or design with an unpolished coat of slip (liquid clay). The black color was created by a reaction of the clay when oxygen was smothered from the area around the pot during the final stages of firing.

[2] Daisy (Nampeyo) Hooie provided some of the information in this section on pueblo pottery making.

[3] This technique had been used by Tewa potters a hundred years earlier, but had disappeared.

Fig. 380. This photo of Maria Martinez was taken at the peak of her production period. She continued to model, even after her eyes failed, but is now past 88 years old and no longer makes pottery. She started her beautifully shaped forms in clay saucers. Although she is especially famous for black-on-black ware, she also made polychromes and redware. Her son, Popovi Da, perfected a clay body with subtle sienna tones, and her grandson, Tony Da, has introduced such innovations as silver and turquoise inlays on pottery. *Courtesy, Bureau of Indian Affairs.*

Following Julian's death about 1943, other members of the Martinez family decorated Maria's pots. Her son, Popovi Da, followed some of the trends that were popularized by Julian, but added innovations in both colors and designs. Her grandson, Tony Da, has become a major figure on the Southwestern scene in a comparitively short period of time. His pottery reflects certain stylistic family traditions, but they are also highly individual statements that are likely to become traditions of their own.

The teamwork that is involved in much Southwestern pottery is practically unique in the modern world, where art is generally a solitary undertaking. Each member of an entire family often has some part in the production of a pot—gathering fuel, preparing clay, polishing, painting, or firing. Only one might be a true artist, and this fact is recognized, but the contributions of the others are equally important, and the finished pot belongs to them all. For this reason, pots were never signed until Maria reluctantly started the practice at the urging of the American School of Research.

Fig. 381. Other distinguished families of Southwestern potters include the Tafoyas (Santa Clara), to which Grace Medicineflower and Joseph Lonewolf belong, Chinos (Acoma), the Gutierrez (Santa Clara), and the Naranjos (Santa Clara). There are also many family teams who work together, each member contributing what she or he does best. This miniature black-on-black bowl was made by Geraldine Naranjo when she was sixteen years old. *Collection, Mary Lou Stribling.*

Fig. 382. Daisy Hooie's kiln is an old stove top propped up on iron bars, and is fueled by sheep manure. Her polishing rocks were handed down from her grandmother, Nampeyo, as was her paint mortar from Sikyatki—a flat stone with a shallow depression worn smooth by generations of potters. This large coil-formed pot was painted with colored clays and beeweed, using a yucca brush.

Fig. 383. Platter by Nevlyn Marie Eckerman. The design of a spirit-figure with an onion-shaped head came from a Zuñi bowl made at Hawikuh Pueblo in the sixteenth century. *Collection, Mr. and Mrs. J. T. Michelson.*

PUEBLO TECHNIQUES FOR POTTERY MAKING

Up until modern times Indian pottery was generally the work of women, and they discovered early that certain additives reduced the shrinkage of clay and made it less likely to crack and warp. Vegetable fibers were used first, though they made a very porous body, and Southeastern potters eventually substituted pulverized shells. In the Southwest, waterworn sand and crushed basalt preceded the use of finely ground pot fragments. This later material, called grog, is a standard additive today.

Grogged clay is especially recommended for open firing, since it makes the body more resistant to thermal shock from uneven temperature changes. It can be purchased from most ceramic shops, but you can easily prepare your own by mixing 10 percent to 30 percent grog with plain clay. Measurements need not be precise, and Indian potters do not use a recipe. Too much grog will reduce plasticity. The mix should be pleasantly granular, not harsh and gritty. As a test, roll out a coil and shape it into a small circle. If it cracks, add more clay.

For the projects shown here, 1 heaping tablespoon of grog was mixed into a 4" cube of clay.

Cover your worktable with a sheet of oilcloth, fabric side up, and moisten the grog with water until it feels like damp meal. Pound a large lump of clay into a pancake about ½" thick, sprinkle the grog over it and punch it into the clay with your thumbs. Roll up the pancake and knead it on the oilcloth until the particles are evenly distributed.

Mix large amounts in small batches, then wedge together a slice from each to make sure the texture is consistent throughout.

Even commercially prepared clay contains a certain amount of air that must be eliminated, or it can cause a pot to crack when it expands during firing. Place an old towel or sheet of oilcloth on the floor, and set a chair beside it. Stand on the chair and drop the clay several times until a cut through the middle reveals no bubbles.

Forming

Some very old and crude clay objects were apparently unrelated to shapes that were already in existence,[4] but it is generally believed that the first clay pots were made inside another container, usually a basket or net.

Surprisingly enough, though Indians made many round objects, they never discovered the wheel. Nearly all pueblo pots were hand formed with spirals of clay coils, but there were regional preferences in techniques for shaping and smoothing the basic structure. Some of the desert potters slipped a support of some kind inside the roughly built pot—a rounded stone, bone, or gourd shard—and pounded against it on the outside with a paddle. The most popular method, however, was to start the pot in a shallow mold and finger-shape the coils as the work progressed. When the clay was stiff enough to handle without damage, the edge was trimmed and the walls were refined by paddling and scraping.

Imprinted shards excavated from nearly every region of the United States indicate that baskets were widely used for early molds,[5] and to a lesser extent, so were gourds and other natural objects. Later, potters made soft-fired clay saucers for supporting the base of the pot, and many continue to do so today for very practical reasons. The potter can work outside with the pot either on the ground, a box, or in her lap, without danger of collapsing the bottom or

[4] Franz Boaz describes Eskimo clay lamps that were unlike any other technical form.
   Franz Boaz, *Primitive Art* (New York: Dover Publications, Inc., 1955), p. 151.

[5] George Wharton James, *Indian Basketry* (Glorieta, New Mexico: The Rio Grande Press, Inc., 1970), p. 18.

deforming the sides. Since every inch or so the clay must be allowed to stiffen before adding new coils, the protective shell enables her to set pieces aside at various stages of development, and work on several at a time. (See Figure 380.)

Pottery molds must be porous enough to absorb water from the clay so that the form can be removed. You can make a shallow plaster mold from the bottom of any object that does not have undercuts, but it is easier to use unglazed saucers or bowls that are available at low cost from most nurseries. Excellent Mexican products are fired to such low temperatures that they are almost as absorptive as plaster.

You can also start the pot inside wooden, plastic, glass, or glazed ceramic bowls if they are lined with paper towels or a soft fabric, such as cotton jersey. A more efficient lining can be made from surgical plaster bandage. Cut the bandage into tapering strips, dip them one at a time in water, and arrange them in overlapping spirals inside the bowl. When the plaster has begun to set, add a second layer with seams in between the seams of the first. Let the plaster harden one to two hours, then mix a small amount of thick plaster of Paris and spread it over the bandage with your fingers to make a coating about ⅛″ thick. Most ridges and depressions can be smoothed out, and any remaining irregularities can be removed from the clay form. Wait several days for the plaster to become completely dry before using the mold.

Baskets for molds should be fairly closely woven, preferably of rounded materials that will not cut too deeply into the clay. Cover the bottom with a piece of paper or aluminum foil to avoid undercuts that might lock in the pot.

Line the basket with a single sheet of clay ⅜″ to ½″ thick if you plan to leave the imprinted texture as surface decoration. If you build with coils or flattened clay pellets, tiny lines will mark each new addition of clay. They can be obliterated, along with the basket imprint, by rubbing soft clay over the surface and paddling the pot until it is smooth.

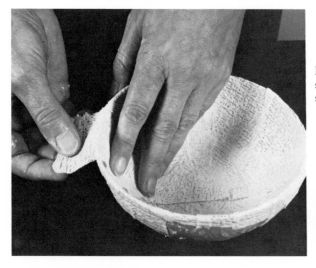

Fig. 385. Many early Indian pots were formed inside baskets. Oval shapes can be modified for effigy pots, and the texture obliterated by paddling.

Fig. 384. Nonabsorbent bowls can be lined with surgical plaster bandage and used as molds for starting clay pots.

Figs. 386–390. EFFIGY BOWLS

Fig. 386. The base of this bowl was formed in an oval basket, then coils were added on each end to raise them higher than the sides. The front end is higher than the back. The owl design was borrowed from a Columbia River carved stone bowl in the collection of Maryhill Museum.

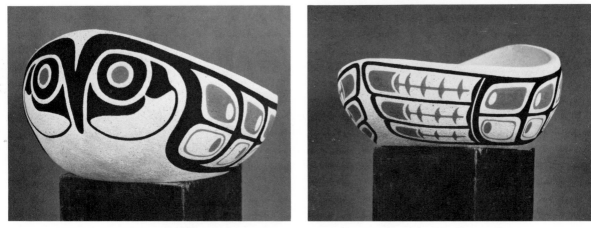

Figs. 387, 388. The same form was used for an owl design inspired by Northwest Coast carvings.

Fig. 389. In that area, feather and wing patterns were generally standardized. Special characteristic details set different species apart.

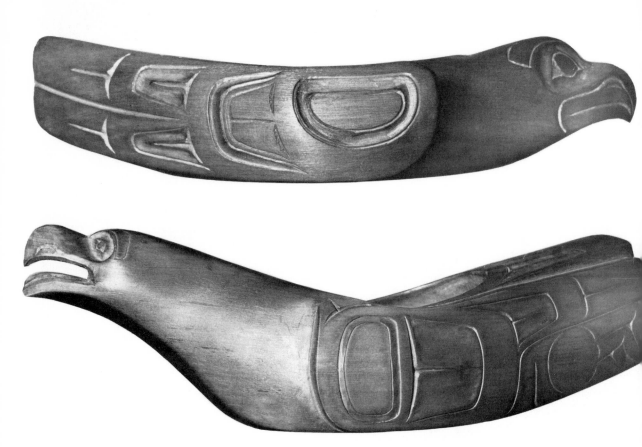

Fig. 390. Carved eagle bowls from Ksan Village, British Columbia, are typical of Haida and Tlingit food dishes.

Forming a Pot in a Pot

Before using a low-fired Mexican bowl as a mold, run water over both sides to remove dust and reduce porosity. Prepare a batch of slip by mixing clay with water until it is the consistency of thick cream. This will be used as "glue" between each new addition of clay.

Roll out a number of clay coils, slightly flatten them with your palms until they are about ½″ thick, and set them aside in a damp towel. Follow the instructions in Figures 391–397 for building the pot, and finish it by one of the methods described in the following sections.

The mold itself can also be decorated. Smooth the surface with sandpaper, apply a sealer coat of acrylic medium, and use the natural clay color as a background for a painted design. If the surface is badly pitted, fill the depressions with wood putty, sand smooth, and cover with one of the opaque paints described in the section on gourds.

256

Fig. 391. Start the pot with a clay pancake about ½''
thick, and smooth it firmly against the dampened
pottery mold. Paint the edge with slip and attach a
coil around it. Coils should overlap, not be placed
edge to edge.

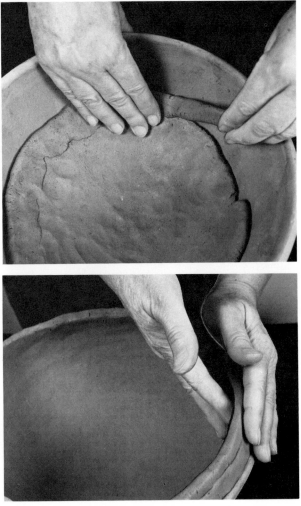

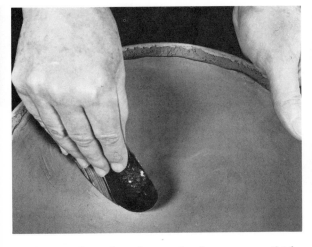

Fig. 392. Smooth each row of coils to an even thickness as you continue to build. When you reach the
rim of the mold, trim the clay level.

Fig. 393. After adding two or three
coils above the mold, use a ruler or
calipers as a guide for trimming the
pot to an even height. Let the clay
stiffen slightly before building further.

Fig. 394. Fill depressions between
coils with soft clay, and paddle the
surface smooth.

Fig. 395. When the clay starts to shrink from the mold and the upper part is firm enough to handle without damage, pad a tall can with a soft cloth, turn the pot upside down over it, and lift off the mold (shown at the top). Scrape away the ledge left by the rim of the mold and smooth the surface.

Fig. 396. If you wish to build higher, score the edge with a dull knife and coat it liberally with slip before adding new coils. Trim the top even and when the clay is leather hard, polish it with the back of a spoon or a wooden tool.

Fig. 397. A feather design was painted with ceramic underglaze colors on the pot at the lower left. After kiln firing, it was coated with a clear matt glaze. The Mexican planter on the left that served as a mold was painted with charcoal and black earth paints, and sealed with matt acrylic medium. *Large pots, Mary Lou Stribling. Hanging pot, Ann Jack.*

Decorating

Although their equipment was simple, Indian potters knew the fundamentals of nearly every modern ceramic decorating technique. Baskets, cords, textiles, nets, and carved paddles were pressed into soft clay to make imprinted designs. Stenciled and resist patterns were created with resinous substances that protected parts of the basic clay body from coatings of contrasting colors. Pots that were strictly utilitarian were sometimes left plain, though often they were embellished with a pinched rim, or were corrugated with the end of a stick.

The choicest pots were usually painted, either before or after firing. Brushes were made from tufts of fur, shredded fibers, or porous bones that held liquid colors in much the same way as felt-tipped pens. Southwestern potters made markers from yucca fronds split into strips of varying widths. They were chewed gently to remove the pulp, then were dipped in paint and drawn freely across the pot.

Paints were extracted from plants or dug from the earth. Beeweed (genus *Cleome*) provided the black color on many old pueblo pots, and is still used by Daisy Hooie, Blue Corn, and other Southwestern potters. (Sprouts of this common weed are also cooked like spinach, and eaten.) The beeweed is boiled for a long time in a big pot, then is drained and allowed to dry out slowly. When it becomes stringy, it is boiled again, sometimes with a bit of sugar, until it has the color and consistency of molten tar. It is then poured out on a layer of cornhusks and allowed to harden. Small pieces are broken off and rubbed with a little water on a stone mortar to make a strong ink. It does not change color when it is fired.

Fig. 398. Zia pot. *Courtesy of the collector, Jacquetta Nisbet.*

Other paints are made from dried sticks of colored clays, ground on mortars and mixed with water.

At Jemez and Tesuque, pottery is usually painted after firing, or the clay may only be dried in the sun. Tourist wares are decorated with poster paints, though better artists, including Sophia and Rafael Medina, use more permanent acrylics. The well-known Papago potter, Laura Kerman, also paints her vignettes of Papago life with acrylics.

This blend of ancient and modern techniques can be observed throughout the Southwest. A pot shaped in a clay saucer several generations old may be polished with a Popsicle stick and dried in an electric oven before it is fired outdoors with dried dung. The potter may laboriously dig her clay from pits that have been worked by her people for centuries, then decorate it with commercial pigments and fire it in a kiln. The decisions are as individual as the people who make them.

Figs. 399–400. Old Acoma polychrome pots. *Collection, The Millicent A. Rogers Memorial Museum.*

Fig. 400

The dry cement colors described in the section on gourds are unexpected sources for inexpensive clay paints, and can be used either before or after firing. Heat causes surprising changes in certain colors. Yellow ochre, black, and red derive from iron oxides, and will all turn various ruddy shades, but you can get a beautiful range of purplish tones, rusty reds, and browns that have the soft worn quality of antique bricks. They are quite unlike anything that can be obtained with commercial paints, and compare favorably with colors on old Indian pots.

For fired decorations, thin slip must be used as a binder instead of gesso and acrylic medium. Do not make colors too concentrated, or there will not be enough binder to keep them from dusting off. Start with ½ part color to 1 to 3 parts slip, and keep a log of your tests, including the brand of cement colors used. Pigments may vary with different manufacturers.

A final sealer of spray matt varnish after firing is recommended.

Indians never developed glass glazes, probably because they never developed a true kiln that would reach the high temperatures required to melt them. They obtained some satiny finishes with various organic coatings after the ware was fired, but more often they relied on hand polishing before firing.

New pots were sometimes rubbed with tallow, and cooking pots gradually became watertight from continued use, during which animal fats and vegetable juices were absorbed into the pores. If they were not intended for cooking, the inside surfaces might be coated with pitch.

All-purpose wax, dull sheen varnishes, acrylic mediums, and plastic sprays will make the surface of soft pots washable and stain resistant, but they will not make them waterproof. Use glass, plastic, or metal liners inside widemouthed pots, and reserve narrow-necked pieces for dried materials.

Milk is the source of casein, a base for many glues and paints, and milk was used as a sealer and glaze for low-fired pottery long before the invention of modern plastics.

As an interesting experiment, brush a coating of sweetened condensed milk over the outside of the pot. Brush marks will smooth out, but keep it as even as possible, and be sure there are no bare spots. Cover the bottom of a pie tin with foil, set the pot on it, and paint the inside. Let it dry for several hours, preferably overnight, or the milk may blister when it is heated. Place in the oven with temperature set on warm, then gradually raise the temperature 50° every fifteen minutes up to 500°. Leave for an hour, turn off the heat, and allow pot to become cold before removing.

This glaze forms a very hard satiny black finish that can be washed. If there are any thin brownish spots, repeat the treatment.

Open Firing

The discovery that sundried clay linings became self-supporting when they were cooked in a fire was probably accidental. We can imagine that this might have been revealed when a house burned, or perhaps the Indians observed that the earth beneath their campfires became hard after a period of time. However it came about, firing was the essential key to the development of true pottery.

Low-fired clay is not as durable as clay that has been fired to full maturity, but primitive pottery has its own personality, and should not be judged by standards for contemporary stoneware. Indian pots that were hardened in an open fire have survived for hundreds of years, though many pieces must have cracked in the firing process. The heat rise could not be completely controlled, nor could the pots be fully protected against sudden drafts and abrupt changes of temperature. There is abundant evidence of a high percentage of success, however.

Many modern traditional potters follow the same basic procedure that was used in early periods, though they have added a few refinements. Instead of supporting the pots on stones, they may prop grids from old stoves or automobile radiators on bricks or cans, and cover them with a layer of pottery shards as insulation. The pottery is stacked on the shards open side down, then is covered with another layer of shards for protection. A slow fire of dried sheep or cow dung is started under the grid, and salvaged sheets of metal, often from junked automobiles or wrecked buildings, are propped around the firing area to hold in the heat.

Fuel is added gradually until the tops and sides of the pots are completely covered with hot coals. The fire may be kept burning from three hours to all day. It is terminated when the glowing colors of the shards or the potter's instincts tell her it has reached the proper temperature.

According to Daisy Hooie, Nampeyo sometimes added coal, bones, and different kinds of animal dung to the basic fuel to produce certain red and purple tints in the clay.

For black ware, about halfway through the firing period, pots are covered with a thick layer of dried manure mixed with bark, leaves, or straw. They are left to smolder under the smoky blanket for several more hours, during which the lack of oxygen causes minerals in the clay to turn black.

It has been estimated that pots fired in this manner reach temperatures between 1200° and 1400° F. Daisy Hooie has placed pyrometric cones in her fires and they indicate an average of 1400°–1500° F. She evaluates the hardness of a fired pot by the way it sounds when it is struck with a stick.

Fireplace Firing

Indian procedures can be duplicated in any safe outdoor location, but for small decorative pieces, the concept can be adapted for a fireplace. It is important that the clay be protected from rapid temperature changes of the metal grate. You can use broken clay flowerpots for insulation, just as Indians use pottery shards. (Small flower pots are also useful for holding clay beads.)

Be sure your clay pieces are thoroughly dry, and arrange them open sides down over the broken pots. Cover with another layer of fragments. Shape strips of roofing tin into a tent with an opening at the top around the back and sides of the grate to help hold in the heat.

Start a small fire with kindling, and keep it low until the clay has warmed. Fuel can then be added gradually around and on top of the pottery.

There is really no better fuel than well-dried chips of cow or sheep dung, and perhaps a word should be added here for the squeamish. This material is vegetable, and the odor is not unpleasant. It makes a slow-burning hot fire that is less likely to create smoky discolorations on the pot than other fuels. You can, however, use charcoal, scrap boards, and other wood cut into small pieces. Keep the fire burning consistently for several hours.

There is no way to set an accurate time schedule for this kind of firing. The surface of decorative pieces can be further hardened with finishes described for gourds.

DESIGNS

Certain kinds of Indian pots were used in ceremonial rites, and they were treated with the same respect and affection all other peoples regard objects that are closely related to their spiritual lives. However, many potters painted prehistorical motifs over and over without ever knowing or wondering about who used them first, or why.

It is doubtful that anyone today can positively interpret the symbolism of many old designs, but the puzzle has tantalized countless historians. Some Indian artists are reluctant to discuss them at all and will avoid giving a direct answer to what they may consider an impertinent question.

Generally, in these arid lands, anything relating to water is considered a "life" symbol. This includes dragonflies, frogs, tadpoles, water serpents, and surprisingly, bear tracks.

According to a legend, the Santa Clara bear track design goes back some four hundred years to a time when there was no snow or rain for a long time. The rivers dried up, the corn died, and the people were starving. An old Medicine Man went into the mountains to pray for water. He prayed three days and nights, and the next morning saw bear tracks. Knowing they were a sign from the gods, he followed them and found a little spring. It saved the tribe, and after that they put the tracks on their pottery to show they were thankful.

Fig. 401. Old Zuñi pot. A "lifeline" is drawn on many Zuñi fetishes and animal designs, and is said to help ensure success in hunting. The deer motif on this pot is popularly associated with this tribe, but there is no evidence that they used it before the middle of the nineteenth century. Similar designs were painted on Kiva walls in the mid-1600s, and on ancient Mimbres pots. *Collection, The Millicent A. Rogers Memorial Museum.*

Fig. 402. Pot with a water serpent design, by Margaret and Luther Gutierrez, Santa Clara Pueblo. *Collection, Mary Lou Stribling.*

Fig. 403. Motifs adapted from Indian pottery. The sun design at the upper right is from the Southeastern region. Others are from the Southwest.

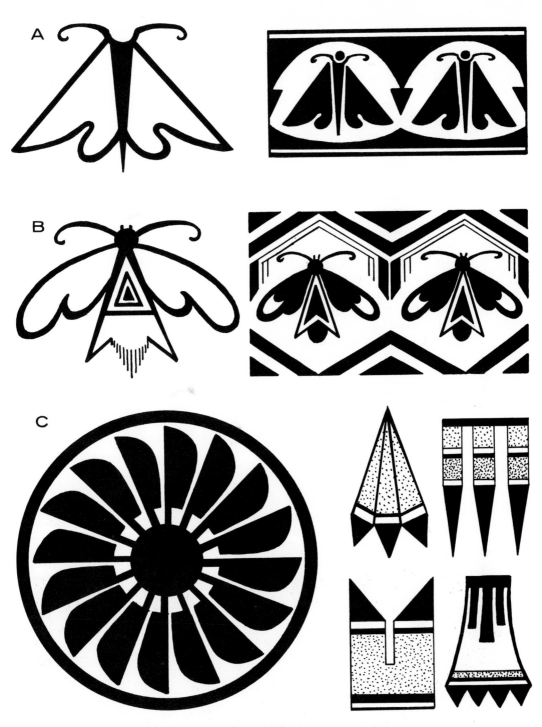

Fig. 404A and B. Butterfly designs from old Hopi pots.
C. Southwestern and Plains feather symbols.

FETISHES AND EFFIGIES

A fetish is an object that is believed to possess a supernatural spirit that can be beneficial to the owner. It is usually fairly small, and may resemble something real, or something unreal. An effigy is simply a likeness of something.

Indian fetishes date far back into prehistory, but their use has continued into the present. In our own culture, the lucky rabbit's foot, ornament, coin, or religious talisman may not receive the same reverential treatment that Indians give their small figures, polished stones, and carved sticks, but they represent the same human need for a private source of magic.

The most valuable fetishes in the Southwest are natural objects that suggest the shape of an animal, bird, fish, or reptile, since they have been created by unknown forces. Next in order of desirability are very old fetishes that have been handed down through several generations, presumably becoming more potent from the good treatment that they have received through the years.

Fetish making is a specialty of the Zuñis, who produce them for other tribes as well as their own. Hunting and gambling fetishes might be unusual pebbles, or pieces of horn dressed with feathers, beads, and shells. The Navajos are fond of figures of sheep, cattle, or horses to protect their flocks and encourage their fertility.

These figures are regarded as sacred possessions, and are housed in special pottery fetish jars, where they are ceremonially fed with cornmeal and pollen from time to time. Gifts of feathers, arrowheads, bits of turquoise, or shell beads are sometimes tied on their backs to promote their goodwill. Unless they are properly tended and respected, the spirits might leave, or even turn against the owner and do him harm.

Fig. 405. Pueblo carved stone bear fetish, 1½″ × 3″. There were two kinds of animal fetishes in the Southwest: food animals, and prey animals who were a menace to both food animals and humans. The Zuñis are the best-known fetish carvers today. *Courtesy, The M. H. De Young Memorial Museum.*

The popular Zuñi "fetish" necklaces with carved shell birds are not true amulets or charms, and are more accurately classed as effigies. Their best-known ceramic effigies are small owls, distinguished by scalloped feather patterns, fin-shaped wings and tails, and droll snoutlike beaks. Some owls have baby owls perched on their shoulders. These designs are prehistorical, but have been produced for sale only some hundred and twenty-five years.

Several other pueblo tribes produce a variety of ceramic birds, animals, frogs, turtles, bears, and chickens, some of which are delightfully humorous.

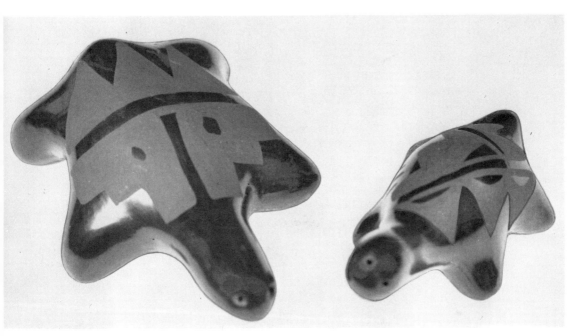

Fig. 406. Black-on-black ceramic turtles, made by Ervin Naranjo (Santa Clara) when he was twelve years old. *Collection, Mary Lou Stribling.*

Figs. 407–408. Zuñi ceramic effigy. Owls were surrounded by superstition in many Indian tribes, and were not portrayed in commercial Zuñi products until the mid-1800s.

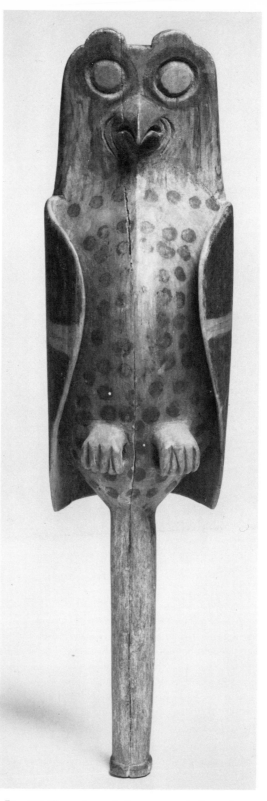

Fig. 409. Carved wood charm or rattle from the
Northwestern Coast of Alaska. *Courtesy, The M.
H. De Young Memorial Museum.*

MODELING CLAY ANIMALS

Blunt knives, wooden paddles, cuticle sticks, and many other common implements are useful for clay modeling, but wire-ended tools cost very little and are almost indispensable for hollowing out forms.

Most animals and birds can be started with an egg shape. Add small balls, rolls, or pellets to suggest heads, legs, or wings. Long thin legs would not support the weight of the clay body and should be eliminated, or suggested by a base, as shown in Figure 410.

When the basic form is roughed out, build up ears, beaks, and tails, and refine the surface. At this stage, there is always the temptation to simply rub the surface smooth, or count on sanding it after it is dry. Instead, fill surface depressions with small bits of clay on the tip of a modeling tool, and build up rounded contours rather than try to scrape them into shape.

Minor details, such as eyes, feathers, and fur, can be incised or painted on after the clay has hardened.

The Alaskan owl in Figure 409 is a good example of simplified structure, and would not be hard to duplicate in clay. The body is an egg shape positioned with the small end up. The head is a half ball. The wings can be cut from a sheet of clay and wrapped around the body. With the handle eliminated and the feet set lower, the figure would be freestanding.

Unless they are to be simply sun dried, clay forms must be hollow with a vent to the outside to permit escape of steam and gases. If the figure has a flat bottom, it will save time to build it around a core of crumpled newspapers or paper towels. When the clay is stiff enough to handle without damage, cut a hole in the bottom and pull out the paper with tweezers or sharp nosed pliers. Use a wire-end tool to finish hollowing out the inside until the walls are less than an inch thick.

A small round inflated balloon can be used as a core instead of paper. Prick it with a pin to draw it through the bottom opening after the figure is finished.

The modeling technique shown in Figures 411–416 is applicable to papier-mâché as well as clay, and with this material the inner core would not have to be removed.

It is probably better to build footed figures solid, then hollow them out through long incisions cut in the back or sides while the form is still rough. Mend the incisions by packing small pellets of clay firmly against the cut edges. When the seam is solid, refine the surface and drill vent holes through the legs into the hollow chamber.

Cover finished figures with dry towels and leave them in a cool spot until the clay is completely hard. If they dry too fast, they may crack.

Small decorative figures can be sundried after the clay is completely hard, as were many made by Indians. They will be quite durable if they are well sealed with several coats of gesso, followed by earth paints and a final sealer of clear shellac, varnish, or acrylic medium.

Fig. 410. Simple animal and bird figures can be based on an egg-shaped foundation. Either eliminate legs, or suggest them by a base that is large enough to support the figure. These shapes are from Southwestern, Northwestern, and Southeastern effigies and fetishes.

Figs. 411–416. MODELING FIGURES OVER A PAPER CORE

Fig. 411. Build up a ball with small sheets of slightly dampened newspaper or paper towels.

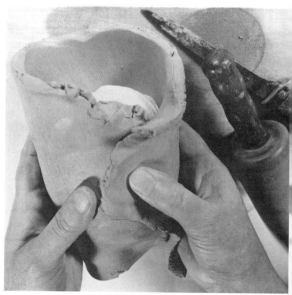

Fig. 412. Roll out a clay pancake ½″ thick, and wrap it around the paper core. Wedge seams firmly together, trimming as necessary to keep the clay fairly even in thickness.

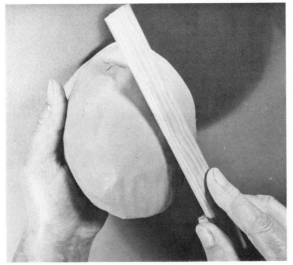

Fig. 413. Paddle the entire surface to remove air bubbles.

Fig. 414. Use small pellets of clay to build up wings, tail, beak, and ear tufts. When proportions are established and the pose looks comfortable, let the clay stiffen slightly before cutting a hole in the bottom. Pull out the paper in small pieces. Use a wire-end modeling tool to scrape out extra clay in the head and tail. Refine the surface.

Fig. 415. The dry form can be painted with underglaze colors and kiln fired, but since these pieces are decorative, not functional, they can also be sundried, painted with acrylics, and coated with sealers to make them more durable.

Fig. 416. This example was fired in the fireplace, coated with gesso, then decorated with earth paints. Fine line details were made with acrylics.

Figs. 417, 418. MODELING SOLID FIGURES

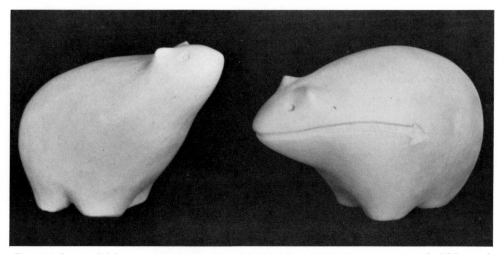

Fig. 417. Start solid forms with an egg-shaped ball of clay. Paddle it to remove air bubbles and follow the modeling procedure described for the owl. The bodies of these two bears are almost identical, but their poses give them the character of different species. The small upraised head on the left is typical of a polar bear, while the figure on the right resembles a grizzly. A lifeline has been incised to accommodate an inlay.

Fig. 418. Some Indian animal figures were inlaid with abalone shell, coral, or chips of turquoise. This figure was polished, glazed black, and fired. The lifeline was then inlaid with turquoise eggshells as described for the mosaicked jewelry in Chapter 2.

10

DRYPAINTING

In the development of art skills, the Navajos were late bloomers, yet within a short span of three or four hundred years, they became recognized masters of weaving, silversmithing, and drypainting.[1]

The sand pictures produced in the Southwest today for commercial purposes are related to original Navajo drypaintings only in that certain attractive traditional designs are sometimes reproduced. The authentic paintings might have aesthetic appeal, but this was incidental. Their purpose was religious. Designs were profoundly symbolic, and their creation involved sacred, formal ceremonies that could be executed only by medicine men, or priests, and their helpers.

There is some disagreement on exactly where and when the Navajos might have first been exposed to the idea. It was unknown among their northern Athabaskan ancestors, and it is possible that they might have seen a few crude examples on their long migration south. If so, they were evidently unimpressed, for it was not until they established themselves close to the pueblos, who used drypaintings in certain rituals, that they took up the practice themselves. Eventually, they perfected it into one of the most impressive ceremonial arts of the Indian peoples.

[1] Pictures made with colored earths and sands are popularly called "sandpaintings," but since Indians used many other kinds of materials for ceremonial drawings—cornmeal, pollen, crushed flowers, pulverized bark, charcoal, and the like—the term "drypainting" is more appropriate. Simple drypaintings were made by several California, Plains, and Pueblo tribes long before the Navajos reached the Southwest.

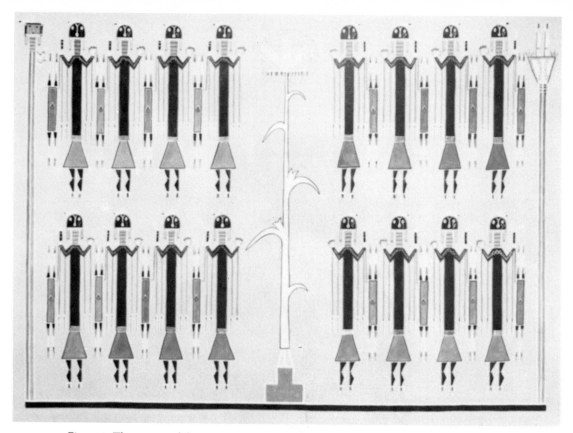

Fig. 419. The principal figures in this magnificent sand painting from the Navajo Night Chant are sixteen Black Fire Gods, arranged in symmetrical order on each side of a cornstalk. They carry fire-making wands in one hand; corn cakes in the other. Life-giving water is represented by the black line at the bottom. A Rainbow Girl guardian similar to the incompleted figure on the Navajo rug in Figure 215, Chapter 5, encircles three sides of the painting. *Courtesy, The Museum of Navajo Ceremonial Arts.*

In order to understand the drypainting ritual, it is necessary to understand something about Navajo beliefs. They do not have a clearly defined set of gods that they envision as being consistently good or evil. They recognize the existence of two classes of beings: humans, or Earth People, and supernatural dieties, or Holy People who dwell in the sky.[2] The Holy People have great power over various forces that can affect the fates of humans, and harmony between the two is maintained by the strict observance of established rules. If these rules are broken by a human, either accidentally or deliberately, the Holy People will send some punishment in the form of illness or other disaster in proportion to his misdemeanor.[3]

It is beyond the capacity of an ordinary individual to fully comprehend and interpret the complex laws that govern the universe. This wisdom is acquired by

[2] C. I. Alexander, *An Introduction to Navajo Sand Paintings* (Santa Fe: Museum of Navajo Ceremonial Art, Inc., 1967), p. 13.

[3] These general concepts of the status of human and supernatural forces were almost universally shared by all tribes, but there were great differences in their rules for maintaining harmony, and penances for disobedience.

priests after many years of dedication and apprenticeship. From the knowledge that has been handed down from generations of other priests, they are able to diagnose the human transgression that has brought on some affliction, and prescribe a ceremonial treatment to pacify the deity who has been displeased. During chants, prayers, and dances, they summon the gods and their mediators, and petition their forgiveness. By participating in the ritual, the guilty human demonstrates his penitence, and if the diagnosis has been accurate, is cleansed and reprieved from his sentence. If not, the need for more potent medicine is indicated, and it might include the creation of symbolic pictures with colored powders.

Descriptions of drypainting healing ceremonials vary, as do the ceremonies themselves, for both procedures and designs are selected to fit specific situations. It has been estimated that there are probably a thousand different drypainting designs, and even a very learned priest can duplicate only three or four hundred. But if he has need for one that is unfamiliar, he will call on another priest for assistance. He never improvises, for the slightest variation of the linear pattern would be considered an impertinence, and might even direct the gods' displeasure to himself.

Navajo legends relate that the designs were created by the Holy People,[4] who drew them on black clouds and ordered the medicine men to commit them to memory so that they could be duplicated. Although some symbols for rain, lightning, and rainbows are suspiciously similar to painted motifs found in murals on the Kiva walls in ancient pueblo ruins, the Navajos added many mystical images that have parallels in no other art.

The creation of a painting is but one kind of healing ritual, and may be used only if less complex and expensive rites fail to bring relief. They are usually made in the medicine lodge and are accompanied by chants, rattles, and other music makers. An assortment of healing devices is included—medicines, herbal drinks, aromatics, and fetishes. The painting can be small, or very large, but every detail is formalized and performed according to a designated sequence.

With the assistance of one or more apprentices, the ground (or a large skin) is first smoothed and neutral background color is sifted on it. Without reference to any drawing but the one in his mind, the priest meticulously builds up the design with thin trickles of powder from his closed fist. The widths of the lines are regulated by his thumb. Some of the pictures are extremely elaborate, and he must not add nor subtract any detail from the prescribed pattern.

When it is finished, the patient is brought into direct contact with the spirits the symbols have summoned by having some of the sacred pigments rubbed on various parts of his body.

The ritual must be completed within a designated period of time that is based on the rhythm of the sun. The painting is then destroyed from the center out, following the order of its creation. The powders, which are considered con-

---

[4] Erwin O. Christensen, *Primitive Art* (New York: Bonanza Books, n.d.), p. 126.

taminated by the infections they have absorbed, are carefully gathered up, placed in a container, and carried out to the northern side of the lodge. The container is moved farther away day by day, taking along with it the evil pestilence it has drawn from the patient's body.

It is understandable that anything so intimately associated with life and death is regarded with the utmost reverence, and it was not until modern times that the Navajos allowed drypainting designs to be recorded and executed in permanent materials. Very beautiful and complex paintings from glue and natural sands are made in the Southwest today by a few talented individuals. Unfortunately, a great many more have trite, sentimental subject matter that is poorly executed in unimaginative colors.

The imagery and crisp, clean lines of the old drypaintings and Kiva murals have greatly influenced a new school of Southwestern painters who work with modern watercolors, oils, and acrylics. Although they do not use traditional designs, the inspiration for certain symbolic elements is clearly definable.

Fig. 420. "Yei," by Navajo artist A. Joe. The elongated figures that represent various Holy People are pictured wearing masks, for no deity or supernatural mediator would reveal his face to a mortal. Round masks are male; square masks are female. *Collection, Mary Lou Stribling.*

Fig. 421. Modern Navajo sand painting with elements from traditional healing rituals. *Collection, Charles and Charlotte Patera.*

CONTEMPORARY DRYPAINTING

Drypaintings differ from conventional paintings in that pigments are not combined with a liquefying vehicle, or binder, for application with a brush. Instead, the binder alone is applied to a prepared backing and dry colors are sprinkled into it.

Colored sands are the most common materials used for drypaintings, but there are many other choices. Some can be collected and used almost in the form in which they are found. Others may require refining or additional preparation, and still others can be purchased. In any case, the financial investment is very small.

There are a few requirements to consider when making a selection. The materials should be reasonably permanent, ruling out such things as pollen and crushed flowers that were sometimes used by Indians in healing ceremonies. It does not, however, eliminate cornmeal, ground coffee, and certain granular spices. Although these are more fragile than sand, colors can be very rich and they will not deteriorate after they have been thoroughly permeated with glue and sealer.

Materials should also be nontoxic, for obvious reasons, and they should not be soluble in water. Salt and sugar, for example, would simply liquefy if they were sifted into wet glue.

Unpulverized materials should be soft enough to be reduced to the consistency of fine sand. For small accents of a very special color, it might be worth the trouble of crushing a hard rock, but you can nearly always find a substitute that is less laborious. And finally, materials should not be so powdery that they will leave a chalky residue on adjacent areas. As a test, rub a pinch between your fingers, or drop a small amount on a sheet of sandpaper and shake it off. If a smear of color remains, even after dusting the paper with a brush, you can save it for the earth paints described in Chapter 9, or you can pretreat it by one of the methods explained later.

Certain effects can be obtained with fairly coarse grits, but for detailed work, a fine, consistent texture is necessary. Pulverize hard materials with a hammer or wooden mallet, sift through a strainer, then grind with a mortar and pestle until they will pass through a fine sieve. (The grid of a coarse sieve can be reduced by stretching a nylon mesh stocking over it.)

To make an excellent strainer for large batches, remove both ends of a one pound coffee can, then stretch a layer of organdy, nylon mesh hose, or several thicknesses of fine netting over one end. Secure tightly with a rubber band and bind the top edges with masking tape. The screen should be very taut. Drop in a few tablespoonfuls of pulverized material, replace the lid on the open end, and shake into a three-pound can. This will greatly reduce the dust that is produced with an open sieve. Return the coarser particles that will not pass through the sieve to the mortar and pestle, and grind again.

Small individual strainers are very handy for sifting prepared materials into the wet adhesive, and they can be purchased where copper enamels are sold. Empty spice jars or pepper shakers can be used if the perforations are fine, or they can be covered with the screens noted earlier. Scraps of 17-hole, or smaller, petit-point canvas make especially durable sieves. Wet the canvas, shape it tightly over the jar top, and secure with a rubber band. After it is hard and dry, you can remove and replace it when it is necessary to refill the container.

Chunky materials can be wrapped in a firm cloth and crushed on a sidewalk or other hard surface. If they are quite hard, the fabric will soon become shredded. It is better to crush these in an old iron skillet, shallow pot, or other piece of flat metal, placed in a large cardboard carton. One flap of the carton can be folded down to cover half the top and will help confine flying particles.

Always wear glasses when pulverizing hard materials, and note their sources on storage containers.

Preparing Special Materials

Sands: Fine builders' sand can be purchased from suppliers of masonry materials. Like river and lake sands, it needs only to be sieved. Seashore sand usually contains a great deal of salt that can be incompatible with glues and pigments. Stir small batches in a large bucket of water. Drain, and repeat several times. Spread the sand on newspapers until it is dry.

Cement colors can be added to any kind of sand to make a varied palette that would be difficult to obtain with natural materials. The colors are strong, and should be used sparingly. For example, 14 parts sand and 1 part brown color make a rich medium brown. A darker brown can be made with 1 part brown color, ¼ part black, and 14 parts sand. One part yellow ochre and 10 parts sand make a beautiful soft yellow.

The pigments are clinging and chalky, however, and may smear unless they are treated. Method #1 noted below requires a longer drying period than #2, and a little extra grinding. However, the glue base makes the colors easier to recoat and build up in successive layers.

Powdery Colors: Method #1. Mix sieved sand and dry pigments to the desired shade. Pour into a disposable container and sprinkle with 1 part white glue diluted with 2 parts water. Continue stirring and sprinkling until every particle is dampened, then spread out on a sheet of plastic or aluminum foil to dry. The sand will feel very hard, but it takes very little hammering to return it to a granular state. Resieve before using.

Powdery colors: Method #2. Spread a layer of prepared material on a sheet of plastic or aluminum foil and spray heavily with a clear plastic finish. Stir and spray until completely dampened. Allow to dry and resieve.

Clay: Crush dry lumps with a hammer, and pulverize until particles will pass through a fine sieve. Convert into grog by placing in an unglazed pottery bowl and hardening in a kiln or open fire. To use raw and unfired, treat as described for powdery colors. Clay powders are especially effective for building up three-dimensional designs on painted wood backgrounds. (Use acrylic paints, not varnishes that will resist water-based glues.)

Charcoal briquets: Crush, grind, and sieve as described for clay. Pretreat as described for powdery colors.

Shale, limestone, old bricks, clay flowerpots, low fired pottery, and other hard materials: Crush, grind, and sieve as described for clay.

Eggshells: Wash fresh shells and peel away inner membrane. When dry, place in a mortar, tap lightly with the pestle to reduce to small chips, then grind into fine particles and sieve.

Coffee, cornmeal, nutmeg, paprika, pepper, and other granular spices: Press with a spoon through a fine sieve. Use on painted backgrounds or fine sandpaper blocks. Coat the finished piece with a solution of 1 part white glue to 3 parts water.

Ground copper enamels: These materials can be purchased from most ceramic supply companies and are ready to use. Many are available in containers with sifter tops, or you can stretch nylon hose over the open end. Although a large painting involving a number of colors might be fairly expensive to make with enamels, the colors are beautiful and quite practical for jewelry and small hangings. They are also a source for colors that cannot be obtained elsewhere.

BACKINGS

Plywood or pressed boards are generally preferred for drypaintings, and the small plaques manufactured for decoupages are excellent for initial experiments. The surface should not be coated with varnish or oil paints, since they are inclined to repel the binder used to make the designs. Fill any depressions with wood putty; sand top and edges smooth.

No sealer is required for small pieces, but for paintings larger than 10″ square, size the backing with a thin, even coat of 2 parts glue mixed with 1 part water. This will reduce porosity that can cause the first application of binder to dry too quickly, resulting in a spotty layer of powdered materials.

Fine to medium grades of sandpaper and emery cloth can be mounted on plywood or heavy mat board to serve as backgrounds, instead of layers of grit. Since some sandpapers will buckle from the wet glue, preliminary tests should always be made.

Attach the sandpaper to the board with a pressure-sensitive adhesive, cover with a sheet of heavy cardboard, and weight overnight with bricks. For blocks smaller than a full sheet of sandpaper, mount the entire sheet, then cut it to size after the cement has set. Scraps can be used for tests or as spacers between decorated blocks on composite arrangements.

Rounded surfaces, such as gourds or wooden bowls, are more difficult to handle since the binder has a tendency to flow downhill and puddle along the lower edges. However, handsome effects can be obtained by leaving the background plain and building up only small areas of the design at a time, using a fairly thick mixture of glue.

Leather and chamois stretched in frames are other unusual backing possibilities.

BINDERS

Clear matt acrylic medium is a good binder for drypaintings, especially for very fine grits. Usually, it requires no dilution unless it has become thickened with age. In this case, add a few drops of water until it can be applied without spreading or piling up.

White glue thinned with water is more often used, and the consistency can best be determined by experimentation. As a rule of thumb, use 2 parts glue and 1 part water for background coats. A richer mix is needed for the design areas or the lines may spread. This will range from 4 to 5 parts glue to 1 part water. Mix the solution in a jar and pour out small amounts at a time in a foil-lined jar lid. Since it will thicken from exposure to air, it may be necessary to add a few drops of water occasionally.

DESIGNS

The sandpaintings in Figures 419–421 have delicate details that can be obtained only with materials that have been pulverized almost to the consistency of flour. It also takes practice and patience to handle designs of this complexity. It is better to start with simple patterns in two or three colors. Pueblo pottery and Northwest Coast arts are good sources for ideas, especially where lines are curving rather than angular, and color areas are not too large. Positive/negative images in two colors alone can be quite dramatic, and are more effective when many layers are used to build up high reliefs. By using a sandpaper or emery cloth block as a foundation, only a single contrasting color would be needed.

When straight, even lines are required, use a ruling pen filled with a solution of 2 parts glue and 1 part water. Subsequent layers can be built up with a brush.

Designs can be transferred to the block in several ways and your choice will depend on the color and texture of the background. White dressmaker's carbon works well on black emery paper and very dark fine sands. Red dressmaker's carbon will show up on light backgrounds but is difficult to see on medium shades. For these and for coarser grits, make a pricked pattern for a chalk transfer. This is an old technique that is often used on textured fabrics.

Tailor's chalk, conté crayon, or mason's powder tied in a scrap of porous cotton fabric to make a pounce can be used with pricked patterns, but do not use ordinary blackboard chalk. It will not adhere properly to the block.[5]

MAKING A DRYPAINTING

Drypaintings are interrupted by stages when you can go no further until the binder has hardened. This may take only about fifteen minutes in a warm dry climate, but several hours may be required where it is damp and cold. The waiting period can be reduced by placing the block in the sun. If you prepare three or more blocks at a time and move from one to the next, step by step, color by color, by the time you have finished all that can be done on the third block, the first will be dry enough for the next step.

The procedure is simple but orderly, and there are really no shortcuts for good work.

Draft full-sized accurate patterns, preferably in colors that are close to the dry materials you plan to use. If the backing is dark and the background color is light, paint the backing with white acrylic paint before starting the decoration.

Use a soft, flat brush to coat the backing evenly with a solution of 2 parts glue and 1 part water. The coating should be thin, without puddles, especially around the edges. Immediately sprinkle it with the background grit from a small sifter until no wet spots are visible. Tilt the board on edge over a sheet of clean paper and tap it lightly to release excess grit. Be careful that your fingers do not extend over the top surface, or they will leave eradicable prints. Allow to dry thoroughly, and repeat. Return leftover grit to its container.

Two coats are usually enough for medium and dark background colors; three may be required for lighter shades.

Transfer the pattern to the background when it is smooth and dry. You are

[5] Dressmaker's carbon and tailor's chalk can be purchased in fabric shops; conté crayon in art stores. Mason's powder is available in hardware stores. Do not use ordinary typing carbon for drypaintings.

now ready to build the design, working from dark to light colors.

Mix a solution of 4 parts glue and 1 part water. Using a pointed watercolor brush, #2 or #3 size, test the mixture on an area of the design that is to be filled in with a dark color. If it spreads, add more glue. If it piles up without flowing smoothly, add a few drops of water. Outline the area first, then fill in the center to make a thin, even pool. It should be about the thickness of a sheet of typing paper, and unless excess fluid is used, it will not flow beyond the wet outlines. If spreading does occur, blot up the solution with a paper towel and allow to dry before proceeding.

Sift on the grit, tap off excess, and blow away particles that may cling in the background crevices. Repeat until all sections of the same color are filled in, then allow to dry thoroughly.

Apply additional coats of glue and grit to obtain an effective three-dimensional quality. Not counting the background, four layers were used for the plaque in Figure 440. Three were used on the composite panel in Figure 442. The deeply sculptured design in Figure 441 required ten.

Dust the dried board thoroughly with a small bristle brush or a vacuum cleaner, and flick off any stray particles with a needle. Repeat the same steps to fill in the next color, saving the lightest shades until last.

When the design is finished, vacuum again and spray with several coats of clear matt varnish or plastic. This not only helps protect the painting, but it intensifies the colors. On black emery cloth it will also cause scratches and light dust to disappear like magic.

Fig. 422.

Figs. 422–424. Motifs from old pueblo pottery can be adapted for small drypaintings. Curving lines are easier to work with than precise geometrics.

Fig. 426. Tilt board on edge and shake off excess grit. Let dry, and repeat for two or three layers.

Figs. 425–430. MAKING A DRYPAINTING

Fig. 425. Paint a thin even coat of glue solution on the backing and immediately sprinkle with sand or other pulverized material.

Fig. 427. Transfer the design to very light or very dark finely textured backgrounds with dressmakers' carbon of an appropriate color.

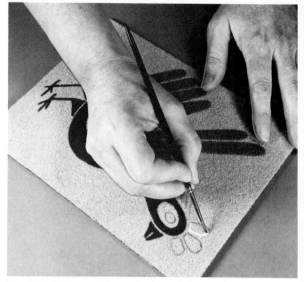

Fig. 428. Using a richer solution of glue and water, paint around outline of a color area, then fill in the center.

Fig. 429. Sift with sand and tap off excess. Repeat until all areas of one color are filled, then allow to dry before building up additional layers.

Fig. 430. When the finished painting is dry, dust it with bristle brush, vacuum off loose particles, and spray with clear matt varnish or plastic.

Fig. 431. DRYPAINTINGS ON EMERY CLOTH
BLOCKS
Often a very simple motif can become more interesting
and important if it is doubled, like a mirrored image.

This design was worked in white and yellow sands,
with colors reversed on opposite ends.

Fig. 432. Positive/negative design adapted from the Hopewell turtle shell comb in
Chapter 2.

Figs. 433–440. USING A PERFORATED PATTERN

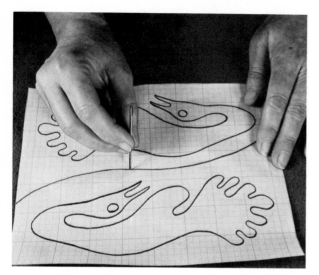

Fig. 433. Place drawing on a folded blanket or other soft surface and perforate lines with holes about 1/16″ apart.

Fig. 434. Turn pattern over and sand off raised burrs that could prevent a clean transfer.

Fig. 435. Tape pattern to a prepared board and scrub lines with tailors' chalk or conté crayon. Rub the chalk into the holes with a piece of felt or soft fabric wrapped around your finger.

Fig. 436. Inspect the transfer to make sure it is legible, then lift pattern straight up and blow off excess powder.

Fig. 437. Go over lines with pale acrylics. If the background is quite dark, undercoat areas of light colors with a wash of white. Medium fine emery cloth has an even texture that is easy to work on.

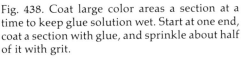

Fig. 438. Coat large color areas a section at a time to keep glue solution wet. Start at one end, coat a section with glue, and sprinkle about half of it with grit.

Fig. 439. Continue spreading glue from the wet edges into adjacent sections, sprinkling only part of it to avoid creating ridges between additions. The first coat is the hardest. Subsequent layers are easier since the grit particles will hold the solution.

Fig. 440. Continue building up the design in layers. Four layers of white builders' sand were used on the panel at the bottom. The pendant was cut from thin pressed board and painted dark brown. The design from a Hopi Kachina Sun mask was made with orange, green, turquoise, and white copper enamels.

Fig. 441. "Ocean Impressions" by Jan and Sharon Peterson, shows the shadow of a gull on a distant beach. It was made with ten layers of natural sands from California beaches.

290

Fig. 442. A standard sheet of black emery cloth is 9″ × 11″, but blocks can be combined to make very large pictures. This 24″ × 36″ panel was painted with white builders' sand, and brown sands made with mixtures of cement color and sand. It is not necessary to pretreat dark powdery grits when they are used on black, but each application should be vacuumed after it is dry. Faint films of dust that may cling to the background will disappear when the finished block is sprayed with matt varnish. *By Mary Lou Stribling.*

Fig. 443. Whole sheets of emery cloth were mounted on heavy mat board, then cut to size for the separate blocks. The finished blocks were arranged on a framed plywood panel, glued in place with pressure-sensitive cement, and weighted until they were dry. Undecorated spacers were cut from the scraps. Glue was brushed around framed edges, seams, and across adjacent spacers as indicated by dotted lines, then was sprinkled with brown sand.

CHRONOLOGICAL

HISTORICAL

NOTES

The prehistoric North American Indians had no written language, and what we know or theorize about their customs and arts has been pieced together from many sources. The following data are general in nature but will provide some understanding of the sequence of a few major events and developments.

10,000–20,000 B.C.	Stone Age peoples come to North America from Asia.
9000 B.C.	The land bridge between Asia and Alaska starts to disintegrate. Ice Age mammals are scattered over North America.
8000 B.C.	Earliest peoples of the Great Basin culture settle in caves in western Utah and Nevada regions. (Nets, and the world's oldest preserved basketry, have been found there.)
3500–2500 B.C.	The Small Tool culture appears in the Arctic. Oldest known American pottery is produced in regions of Colombia and Ecuador.
2000–1200 B.C.	Artisans in the pre-Incan cultures of Peru make fine pottery and woven textiles. Central America has an

established religion, calendar, and system of writing. Earliest North American pottery appears in Georgia, Florida, and South Carolina areas.

1000–500 B.C.

Olmec culture is established in Mexico. Crude pottery is produced in the Arctic. Agricultural economy covers most of the northern regions of South America, and spreads into the Caribbean area. Southeastern pottery is decorated with geometric impressions from carved wooden paddles, and in Adena culture is imprinted with fabric and basket textures. Their arts are dominated by animal forms. Burial Mound period starts in the Ohio Valley.

100 B.C.

The Anasazi culture in the Southwest is in the Basket Maker period. Agricultural and architectural proficiency increases.

A.D. 100

Cliff dwellings are occupied in the Southwest and true farming begins. The Mogollons make the first western pottery. Central prairie peoples farm along riverbanks, but remain primarily hunters in the arid western states. Eskimos carve fine figures from bone and ivory. The Mayan civilization flourishes in Central America.

A.D. 200–300

Hopewell culture in the Ohio Valley replaces the Adena culture. Burial mound building reaches its highest level. Hopewell Indians establish an elaborate system of trade routes throughout most of eastern America, and import obsidian, copper, and sheet mica for their mortuary arts.

A.D. 300–800

Hopewell culture declines in the Southeast. The Temple Mound Builders culture begins in the Mississippi Valley. Important arts are related to religious rituals and include stone effigies, decorated copper sheets, elaborate pottery, and engraved shells. "Basket Makers" in the Southwest develop pottery and weave rough textiles from yucca fibers. Seed gatherers of California and the High Plateau develop basketry. Influences of the arts of Central America spread northward into the

Southeastern area of North America. Pre-Incan peoples in Peru produce some of the finest textiles the world has ever known.

A.D. 700–1100

Other groups join the Southwestern Basket Makers in the Pueblo period of the Anasazi culture. Fine pottery is produced, and possibly some loom weaving. Mimbres and Sikyatki pottery is outstanding and represents the finest work of the prehistoric period.

A.D. 1000–1350

Northwest Coast Indians attain high levels of sophistication in basketry, textiles, stone, horn, bone, and wood carving. Basketry becomes a fine art among the California region tribes. Mortuary arts continue to dominate arts of the Southeastern Temple Mound Builders. Distinctive pottery is made from clay and crushed shells. Carved stone figures, embossed sheet copper plates, and engraved shells are specialties. Southwestern Hohokams etch shells with cactus acid, and model clay figures that reflect Central American influences. In the Southwestern Pueblo groups, architecture, pottery, cotton weaving, skin and stone work reach their greatest heights. Navajo raids destroy Cliff Dwellers culture in the Southwest. Eskimos migrate into eastern Canada. The Aztec civilization is established in Mexico.

A.D. 1400–1500

Columbus discovers the Bahama Islands. John Cabot explores parts of North America.

A.D. 1500–1600

Fine wood carvings and other ceremonial arts are produced in the Southeast at the peak of the Temple Mound culture. Cliff-dwelling survivors settle into pueblos in the Southwest and arts flourish. Spaniards bring sheep to the New World and loom weaving progresses. Pottery begins to decline. The Incan civilization in Peru and the Aztec civilization in Mexico are destroyed by Spanish armies. DeSoto explores the Southeast and discovers the Mississippi River. Ponce de León explores Florida. The Plymouth Colony is established in Massachusetts (1620).

A.D. 1700–1850

Spanish explorers and missionaries enter northern California. White settlers force most of the Atlantic and Gulf Coast Indians inland. Plains tribes defend their territories from white invaders. Silverwork is introduced. Pottery is revived in the Southwest. Weaving declines. Trade beads lead to the development of beadwork.

A.D. 1900

Many traditional arts begin to disappear except for the manufacture of goods for the tourist trade. The Indian Wars end. Surviving Indians are moved from their ancestral lands and confined on reservations.

SUPPLEMENTARY

REFERENCES

ALEXANDER, C. I. *An Introduction to Navajo Sand Paintings.* Santa Fe, N.M.: Museum of Navajo Ceremonial Art, Inc., 1967.

AMSDEN, CHARLES AVERY. *Prehistoric Southwesterners from Basketmakers to Pueblo.* Los Angeles: Southwest Museum, 1949.

AMSDEN, CHARLES AVERY. *Navajo Weaving: Its Technic and History.* Santa Ana, California: The Fine Arts Press, 1934. (Facsimile edition, Glorieta, N.M.: The Rio Grande Press, Inc., 1971.)

APPLETON, LEROY H. *American Indian Design and Decoration.* New York: Dover Publications, Inc., 1950.

BAHTI, TOM. *Southwestern Indian Arts and Crafts.* Flagstaff, Ariz.: KC Publications, 1966.

BAHTI, TOM. *Southwestern Indian Tribes.* Las Vegas, Nev.: KC Publications, 1968.

BOAS, FRANZ. *Primitive Art.* New York: Dover Publications, Inc., 1955.

BUNZEL, RUTH L. *The Pueblo Potter.* New York: Columbia University, *Contributions to Anthropology,* VII, 1929.

BURLAND, COTTIE. *North American Indian Mythology.* London–New York–Sydney–Toronto: The Hamlyn Publishing Group, Limited, 1965.

CAIN, H. THOMAS. *Pima Indian Basketry.* Phoenix, Ariz.: Heard Museum of Anthropology and Primitive Art, Project Number Two, 1962.

CHENEY, SHELDON. *A World History of Art.* New York: The Viking Press, 1939.

CHRISTENSEN, ERWIN O. *Primitive Art.* New York: The Viking Press, 1955.

COOKE, VIVA, AND SAMPLEY, JULIA. *Palmetto Braiding and Weaving.* Peoria, Ill.: The Manual Arts Press, 1947.

DENVER ART MUSEUM. Indian Art Leaflet Series.

DOCKSTADER, FREDERICK J. Indian Art in North America. Greenwich, Conn.: New York Graphic Society, 1961.

GALVIN, JOHN (ed.). The First Spanish Entry into San Francisco Bay, 1775. San Francisco: John Howell–Books, 1971.

GRANT, BRUCE. Leather Braiding. Cambridge, Md.: Cornell Maritime Press, Inc., 1961.

GRANT, CAMPBELL. Rock Art of the American Indian. New York: Thomas Y. Crowell, 1967.

HUNT, W. BEN. Indian Silversmithing. New York: The Bruce Publishing Company, 1960.

HUNT, W. BEN, AND BURSHEARS, J. F. "BUCK." American Indian Beadwork. New York: The Bruce Publishing Company; London: Collier–Macmillan, Limited, 1951.

INVERARITY, ROBERT BRUCE. Art of the Northwest Coast Indians. Berkeley, Calif.: University of California Press, 1934.

JAMES, GEORGE WHARTON. Indian Basketry and How to Make Indian and Other Baskets. New York: Henry Malkan, 1903. (Facsimile edition, Glorieta, N.M.: Rio Grande Press, 1970.)

KENT, KATE PECK. The Story of Navajo Weaving. Phoenix, Ariz.: The Heard Museum of Anthropology and Primitive Arts, 1961.

LA FARGE, OLIVER. A Pictorial History of the American Indian. New York: Crown Publishers, Inc., 1951.

LOWIE, R. H. Indians of the Plains. New York: McGraw-Hill (for the American Museum of Natural History), 1954.

LYFORD, CARRIE. Quill and Beadwork of the Western Sioux. Washington, D.C.: Office of Indian Affairs, 1940.

MARRIOTT, ALICE. Maria: The Potter of San Ildefonso. Norman, Okla.: University of Oklahoma Press, 1948.

MASON, OTIS TUFTON. Aboriginal American Basketry. Report of the United States National Museum, 1902. (Facsimile edition, Glorieta, N.M.: Rio Grande Press, 1970.)

MAXWELL, GILBERT S. Navajo Rugs—Past, Present and Future. Palm Desert, Calif.: Best West Publications, 1963.

MEILACH, DONA Z. A Modern Approach to Basketry. New York: Crown Publishers, Inc., 1974.

MILES, CHARLES. Indian and Eskimo Artifacts of North America. New York: Bonanza Books, n.d.

ORCHARD, WILLIAM C. The Technique of Porcupine Quill Decoration Among the Indians of North America. New York: The Museum of the American Indian, Heye Foundation, 1971.

ROSSBACH, ED. Baskets as Textile Art. New York: Van Nostrand Reinhold Company, 1973.

SIDES, DOROTHY. Decorative Art of the Southwest Indians. Santa Ana, Calif.: The Fine Arts Press, 1936.

STRIBLING, MARY LOU. *Art from Found Materials.* New York: Crown Publishers, Inc., 1970.

UNDERHILL, RUTH M. *Pueblo Crafts.* Washington, D.C.: Bureau of Indian Affairs, 1944.

WHITEFORD, ANDREW HUNTER. *North American Indian Arts.* New York: Golden Press, 1970.

WILSON, JEAN. *Weaving Is for Anyone.* New York: Van Nostrand Reinhold Company, 1967.

WORMINGTON, H. M., AND NEAL, ARMINTA. *The Story of Pueblo Pottery.* Denver, Colo.: Denver Museum of Natural History, 1951.

American Indian Crafts and Culture (monthly periodical)
Box 3538
Tulsa, Okla. 74152

SOURCES OF SUPPLIES

Sources for special materials are noted here for the reader's convenience, and do not represent endorsements or guarantees by the author. Some addresses are for mail order sources; others are of manufacturers who may be able to provide names of local dealers. Catalogues are available from many crafts supply companies, and all inquiries should be accompanied by a self-addressed stamped envelope. General and readily available materials, such as natural clay, copper enamels, white and epoxy glues, yarn, fabrics, and standard notions, are not included.

Acrylic Paints, Mediums, Gesso
LIQUITEX
Permanent Pigments
27000 Highland Ave.
Cincinnati, Ohio 45212

Adhesives
ELMER'S CONTACT CEMENT
Borden Chemical Company
277 Park Ave.
New York, N.Y. 10017

HOOKED RUG ADHESIVE
BACKING
Columbia Minerva
295 Fifth Avenue
New York, N.Y. 10016

SCOTCH PINLESS PATTERN
HOLDER
3M Company
3M Center
St. Paul, Minn. 55101

Basketry Supplies
CANE AND BASKET SUPPLY
COMPANY
1283 S. Cochran Ave.
Los Angeles, Calif. 90019

CREATIVE HANDWEAVERS
P.O. Box 26480
Los Angeles, Calif. 90026

DICK BLICK ART MATERIALS
P.O. Box 1267
Galesburg, Ill. 61401

NATURALCRAFT
2199 Bancroft Way
Berkeley, Calif. 94704

SAX ARTS AND CRAFTS
207 N. Milwaukee
Milwaukee, Wis. 53202

Beadworking Supplies
BEAD GAME
505 N. Fairfax Ave.
Los Angeles, Calif. 90036

BERGEN ARTS AND CRAFTS
P.O. Box 689
Salem, Mass. 01970

MANY FEATHERS TRADING
COMPANY
1855 E. 15th Street
Tulsa, Okla. 74101

NORTHEAST BEAD TRADING
COMPANY
12 Depot Street
Kennebunk, Maine 04043

WALCO PRODUCTS, INC.
(Looms-Beads)
1200 Zerega Ave.
Bronx, N.Y. 10462

WINONA TRADING POST
P.O. Box 324
Santa Fe, N.M. 87501
(Bead graph paper, Indian beads, tin
cones, hair pipes, abalone pendants,
dentalium shells, quills, etc.)

Cement Colors (dry)
TRUE TONE
Frank D. Davis Co.
South Plainfield, N.J. 07080
Los Angeles, Calif. 90023

Clay
FLORAL CLAY (nonhardening)
Beagle Manufacturing Co., Inc.
Pasadena, Calif. 91100

MEXICAN POTTERY CLAY
(self-hardening)
American Art Clay Company
Indianapolis, Ind. 46200

Decoupage Burnishers
SCOTCH BRITE NYLON PAD
(white)
3 M Co. (See adhesives)

Dressmaker's Carbon
DRITZ TRACING PAPER
Sewing Notions Div.
Scoville Manufacturing Co.
Spartanburg, S.C. 29301

Feathers
HOLLYWOOD FANCY FEATHER
COMPANY
512 S. Broadway
Los Angeles, Calif. 90013

PROGRESS FEATHER COMPANY
657 W. Lake St.
Chicago, Ill. 60606

Fusible Web
(IRON-ON) DETAIL PELOMITE®
Pellon Corp.
1120 Avenue of the Americas
New York, N.Y. 10036

Gourd Seeds
STOKES SEEDS, INC.
Box 548, Main P.O.
Buffalo, N.Y. 14240

W. ATLEE BURPEE COMPANY
P.O. Box 6929
Philadelphia, Pa. 19132

Indian Craft Supplies
GREY OWL INDIAN CRAFT MFG.
CO., INC.
150–02 Beaver Rd.
Jamaica, Queens, N.Y. 11433

PLUME TRADING AND SALES CO.,
INC.
P.O. Box 585
Monroe, N.Y. 10950

ROBERTS INDIAN CRAFTS AND
SUPPLIES
Dept. A1
211 West Broadway St.
P.O. Box 98
Anadarko, Okla. 73005

SUPERNAW'S OKLAHOMA
INDIAN SUPPLY
301 E. Rogers Blvd.
Skiatook, Okla. 74070

TREATY OAK TRADING POST
5241 Lexington Ave.
Jacksonville, Fla. 32210

WINONA TRADING POST
(See Beadworking Supplies)

**Jewelry Findings, General Craft
Supplies**
ALLCRAFT TOOL AND SUPPLY
CO.
215 Park Ave.
Hicksville, N.Y. 11801

AMERICAN HANDICRAFTS
(Check yellow pages of your
telephone book)

BERGEN ARTS AND CRAFTS
(See Beadworking)

CRAFTOOL
1421 West 240th St.
Harbor City, Calif. 90710

LEE WARDS
Dept. 5127
1200 St. Charles
Elgin, Ill. 60120

Leather and Leatherworking Tools
LEATHERCRAFTERS SUPPLY CO.
25 Great Jones St.
New York, N.Y. 10012

TANDY LEATHER CO.
(Check yellow pages of your
telephone book)

Needles
DE LUXE RUG NEEDLE
Columbia Minerva Corp.
(See Adhesives)

THE SINGER CO.
(curved and other special types)
30 Rockefeller Plaza
New York, N.Y. 10020

Needle Loom
WEAVE-IT LOOM
Scoville Mfg. Co.
Spartanburg, S.C. 29301

Pine Needles
ENSIGN'S HOBBY SHOP
6100 Seminole Blvd. (Alt. 19)
Seminole, Fla. 33540

Purse Frames and Handles
ROBIN AND RUSS,
HANDWEAVERS
533 N. Adams St.
McMinnville, Ore. 97128

Putty (wood)
DURHAM'S ROCK HARD WATER
PUTTY
Donald Durham Co.
Des Moines, Iowa 50300

Raffia (artificial)
LEJEUNE SWISSTRAW
Lejeune, Inc.
Sunnyvale, Calif. 94086

NATURAL RAFFIA
(See Basketry Supplies)

Self-Adhering Plastic
CON-TACT
Cohn-Hall-Marx
1407 Broadway
New York, N.Y. 10018

Stretcher Bars
THREE STAR MANUFACTURING
20665 W. Santa Clara St.
Saugus, Calif. 91350

Tapes
(double-stick carpet tape)
ARNO ADHESIVE TAPES, INC.
Tape Div.
Michigan City, Ind. 46360

(narrow drafting tapes, printed
circuit tape)
ALVIN GRAPH-A-PLAN
Windsor, Conn. 06095

FLAX
250 Sutter St.
San Francisco, Calif. 94108

ZIP-A-LINE
Para-tone, Inc.
512 W. Burlington
P.O. Box 136
La Grange, Ill. 60525

Tools
ALLCRAFT TOOL AND SUPPLY
CO.
(See Jewelry Findings)

(craft knives)

CRAFTOOL
(See Jewelry Findings)

X-ACTO PRECISION TOOLS, INC.
48–41 Van Dam St.
Long Island City, N.Y. 11101

Varnishes (decoupage)
DECOUPAGE VARNISH (spray)
Illinois Bronze Powder & Paint Co.
Lake Zurich, Ill. 60047

MOD PODGE (brush on)
Brocado, Inc.
2451 S. Ashland Ave.
Chicago, Ill. 60608

Varnishes (flat finishes)
BLAIR SPRAY VAR
Matt Damar Varnish
Blair Art Products, Inc.
Memphis, Tenn. 38110

KRYLON MATTE FINISH
277 Park Ave.
Borden Inc.
New York, N.Y. 10017

McCLOSKEY'S HEIRLOOM
VARNISHES
McCloskey's Varnishes
Philadelphia, Pa. 19136
Los Angeles, Calif. 90022

INDEX